MARKETING SCIENCE INSTITUTE
SERIES OF BOOKS

Published with Allyn & Bacon, Inc.:

Brand Policy Determination (1967)

Comparative Analysis for International Marketing (1967)

Experiments on the Value of Information in Simulated Marketing Environments (1967)

Industrial Buying and Creative Marketing (1967)

Personal Selling in a Modern Perspective (1967)

Promotional Decisions Using Mathematical Models (1967)

OTHER PUBLICATIONS:

Marketing Development in the European Economic Community (1964)

Promotional Decision Making: Practice and Theory (1964)

The Meaning and Sources of Marketing Theory (1965)

Marketing Education in the United States (1964)

Industrial Buying and Creative Marketing

MARKETING SCIENCE INSTITUTE
3401 Market Street
Philadelphia, Pa.   19104

THE MARKETING SCIENCE INSTITUTE was established in 1962 in Philadelphia for the purpose of conducting the kinds of basic research that would serve to advance the productivity and efficiency of marketing.   The Institute's research and educational activity is designed to (1) contribute to the emergence of a science of marketing, and (2) stimulate increased application of scientific techniques to the understanding and solving of marketing problems.

The Marketing Science Institute was established in 1962 in Philadelphia for the purpose of conducting the kinds of basic research that would serve to advance the productivity and efficiency of marketing.   The Institute's research and educational activity is designed to (1) contribute to the emergence of a science of marketing, and (2) stimulate increased application of scientific techniques to the understanding and solving of marketing problems.

Financial support for MSI is provided by leading business firms. In addition, the personnel of these firms contribute generously of their time and ability as members of MSI committees, study groups, and as advisors and consultants of MSI research projects and reports.

All research reports and findings of the Marketing Science Institute are made generally available through publication.   In compliance with MSI policy, publication of this report has been approved by a majority of the Board of Trustees.

MARKETING SCIENCE INSTITUTE
Philadelphia, Pa.

BOARD OF TRUSTEES*

INDUSTRIAL BUYING
AND
CREATIVE MARKETING

PATRICK J. ROBINSON
Director of Management Studies
Marketing Science Institute

and

CHARLES W. FARIS
Senior Associate
The Boston Consulting Group

With contributions by
YORAM WIND
Assistant Professor of Marketing
University of Pennsylvania

Allyn & Bacon, Inc.
Boston

Preface

THE PRESENT BOOK IS BASED upon a growing awareness of the need for a merging of the world of marketing theories and concepts with the world of empirical data. As the chief executive of a major company has said: "What I need is a frame of reference within which I can position and interrelate the many and diverse marketing decisions we have to make."

One of the uses of theory is to enable a manager to understand, explain, predict, and control relationships and their variables within a given framework. For example, the manager seeks to identify or classify the basic characteristics of a problem os that he will know how to proceed to solve it. Did it arise inside the company or outside? Does it involve a good customer, a potential customer, or a governmental regulatory agency?

Asking these kinds of questions represents an attempt to classify the significant variables; and an appropriate course of action will depend upon the answers. But the problem is not just to establish the usefulness of classification system. Instead, it is to develop and describe a specific classification system that will be useful in planning and executing an efficient industrial marketing effort.

The content of any classification system is dependent upon the level of decision-making responsibility as well as the particular circumstances surrounding a marketer. Three popular bases for classifying transactions are: market segments or *classes of trade reached; products or services* marketed; and *end-use applications*.

Classification according to *classes of trade characteristics* helps in analyzing the company or division buyers . . . according to *products or services marketed,* and according to *end-use applications* in developing technical specifications and preparing promotional materials.

Accordingly, a classification system aimed at the specifics of the selling task is needed; and such a system is presented in this book.

The development of an effective and efficient approach to the matching of buyer requirements and seller capacities is dependent on the marketer's understanding, and consequently his ability to classify or structure the decision-making process underlying industrial buying behavior. The *basic objective* is to try to develop and explain an operationally-useful classification system, focusing directly on the nature of individual customers, or potential customers' requirements and the resulting buying situations.

The present book is based on a growing awareness of the need for a merging of the world of theory or concepts and the world of empirical data. The book is divided into three parts each of which deals with a major objective:

Part One: Develop an *operational framework* for the analysis of industrial buyer behavior.

Part Two: Identify and analyze some of the *determinants* of industrial buyer behavior.

Part Three: Suggest *implications* of knowledge of industrial buying behavior for marketers.

Supplementary reference materials, keyed to these parts, is provided in the annotated bibliography which completes this book.

The BUYGRID framework, developed early in the book (in Chapter II), applies particularly to industrial buying behavior; but it may have utility also in analyzing consumer behavior. The BUYGRID analysis identifies and examines the procurement process in terms of eight distinguishable activities applicable to most purchasing situations, and three classes of buying situations. Complementary profiles of seller activities and influences may in turn be developed, on the basis of the BUYGRID framework and an understanding of buyers' decision making, to aid in the planning of industrial marketing efforts.

The analysis of these three subjects encompasses both the basic research, conducted by Charles W. Faris and myself and comprising the body of the present volume, and also a special study of industrial buying behavior, carried out by Yoram Wind, while at Stanford University, independently of our project and employing a different approach. Dr. Wind's findings, reported in Chapters VII and XI, supplement the analysis of the buying process and the determinants of buyer behavior respectively. These findings confirm and enrich the conclusions of the original MSI study. Hence, they were incorporated in Part III.

ACKNOWLEDGMENTS

Much of the credit for the success of the fieldwork in achieving these goals is attributable to the generous support of the management and key personnel of the participating companies. Their involvement provided the essential foundation on which to build and to test the BUYGRID analysis and to obtain evidence of the notion of creeping commitment. The detailed flow diagrams of the decision processes and the critical path analyses of buying situations were possible only because sufficient detail was obtained in the interviewing phases of the research.

Acknowledgments are also due a number of people who made significant contributions to our research.

Dr. Charles S. Goodman, Professor of Marketing at the University of Pennsylvania, has been a major contributor to the project *from its inception to its final writing and revision.*

Dr. Yoram Wind, Assistant Professor of Marketing at the University of Pennsylvania, helped develop the final organization of the study. He also wrote Chapters VII and XI, and collaborated in the writing of Part Three of this book.

Dr. Charles N. Davisson, Professor of Marketing at the University of Michigan, also served as a consultant and introduced a number of valuable concepts.

Sincere thanks are due Dr. Douglas M. Egan, Assistant Professor of Business Administration at the State University of New York at Buffalo, for his assistance in connection with the interviewing of companies Baker and Charlie.

Throughout the project Mr. James A. Singmaster, Jr., Assistant to the Vice President of Marketing of the Monsanto Company, provided guidance and encouragement from the point of view of an experienced industrial marketing executive.

Mr. G. Howard Ahl, Executive Director, National Association of Purchasing Agents, and Mr. Marshall Edwards, its Executive Secretary, made many helpful suggestions representing the purchasing viewpoint.

Both Professors Reavis Cox and Paul Green of the Wharton School of Commerce and Finance at the University of Pennsylvania also contributed valuable ideas and comments.

Encouragement and advice for refinement of the study was received from a number of interested industrial marketers from sponsor and member companies of MSI and from members of the American Marketing Association's Industrial Marketing Advisory Committee, in cooperation with the Industrial Section of the Philadelphia Chapter.

Professor Charles L. Hinkle of the University of Colorado deserves special thanks for his untiring efforts in assisting in the preparation and revision of the manuscript and the illustrations. Special thanks are also due my MSI associate, Bent Stidsen, who participated as a well-informed critic and able reviewer. Mrs. Patricia Coffey, another member of the Institute, is due thanks for her competent help. She was primarily responsible for preparation of the extensive annotated bibliography.

                              PATRICK J. ROBINSON
                              Director of Management Studies
                              Marketing Science Institute

October 1, 1967

Contents

Highlights
of This Book

THIS BOOK ON INDUSTRIAL BUYING identifies the critical variables affecting the procurement process—from the first identification of need to the final postpurchase evaluation.

Industrial purchasing can best be looked at as a *problem-solving
process*. From this view, three basic types of buying situations
are significant: the *new task*, the *straight rebuy,* and the *modified
rebuy*. Even though the end result may be the same, each of these
presents different purchasing problems.

The authors have "dissected" the buying process into eight different phases.

The *first* phase is the anticipation or recognition of a problem
of need. This phase entails both the realization that a problem
exists, and the awareness that a solution may be possible through
purchase.

Second is the determination of the quality and characteristics
of the needed item. This is usually done from within the firm, but
outside sources can be helpful. At this point the process of narrowing down the solution has begun.

Third, there is a specific description of the item needed. The
fourth phase is a search for potential sources for this needed item.
Fifth, these sources are examined, leading to a decision on how the
item is to be purchased.

In the *sixth* step, the supplier is selected. This is followed by
the *seventh* phase, where the order routine is established. Finally,
the *eighth* phase is an evaluation of performance feedback.

Depending on the particular buying situation, some of these
phases are more important than others. Generally, the more complex the buying situation, the earlier this critical phase occurs;
and an understanding of the particular buying situation will allow
the marketer to identify the critical phases.

(1) The *new task* purchase is one that comes from a need that
has not arisen before. The buyer has little or no relevant experience to draw upon. Even though the new task situation will occur

frequently, it is important to the marketer because it sets the pattern for the more routine purchases that will follow; and the new-task purchase can be anticipated and developed by creative marketing.

(2) The *straight rebuy* fills a reoccurring requirement, and is usually handled on a routine basis. The decision usually is made by the purchasing department; and formally or informally a "list" of acceptable suppliers exists. If a supplier is not on the list, he has little chance of being considered. Since buyers have had relevant experience, they consider that little new information is needed for the straight rebuy.

(3) The *modified rebuy* may develop from either a new-task situation or a modified-rebuy situation. Although the buying alternatives are known, the situation is changed. This might have come about internally, or from outside events, or have been caused by the marketer. For marketers who are not active suppliers, the attempt should be made to convert the customer's straight rebuys into modified rebuys.

With better understanding of the customer's decision processes, the industrial marketer can develop a profile of the customer's buying processes. Using this information for more effective marketing strategies requires, however, that the marketers also have some knowledge of the determinants of the buyers' decisions.

Environmental influences affecting the buying decision are identified and analyzed, including the internal organizational structure, roles of the functional areas of the buying company, and the external economic environment, as well as user-supplier interaction.

The basic premise of this book is that the creative marketer can benefit from a better understanding of the *entire* buying decision process.

A number of profitable opportunities for creative marketers are suggested, such as the consequences of "tailoring" the marketing effort to the various decision points.

The importance of identifying the buying situation is illustrated by the presentation of some of the alternatives open to the marketer in handling products, services, promotion, channels, and prices.

The main need is to understand buyer behavior, and thus to plan the course of events leading to increased market penetration, improved user-buyer relations, and a better matching of the buyers' needs with the supplier offerings.

STEUART H. BRITT
Editorial Director
Marketing Science Institute

PART ONE

The
Industrial Buying Process

I

Purpose, Scope,
and
Methodology of the Book

A PRELIMINARY SURVEY to define the major problem areas in industrial marketing revealed a need for investigation into industrial purchasing behavior. Of some 175 industrial marketing executives who responded to a mail survey, the majority expressed concern about recognizing potential customers, analyzing their needs and motivation, and understanding their behavior. Some of the more typical comments are listed below:

MAJOR PROBLEMS IN INDUSTRIAL MARKETING: A SAMPLING
    OF COMMENTS FROM IM EXECUTIVE SURVEY

. . .one of the many problems which concern us is the relative effectiveness of an "industry-oriented" versus a "product-oriented" marketing approach. --Vice President, chemical manufacturer.

The most critical problem in this division is to determine where to concentrate attention in marketing. . .Does influence (on product choice) filter back from the end user. . .or reside mainly with the manufacturer. . .? Not only must we determine who and where the customer is. . .but also how best to reach him. --Executive Vice President, malleable iron fittings company.

An especially difficult marketing problem is to select the most advantageous methods of product distribution in line with the requirements of our customers. --Manager of Product Planning, electronics manufacturer.

The most critical marketing problem is the determination of specific customer needs, both present and future, for individual market segments. --President, office equipment and supplies manufacturer.

. . .recently we have restructured our marketing division to include

a product planning department. . .in order to develop what our customers want and will buy rather than products which we develop
and hope they will buy. --Vice President of Marketing, machinery
manufacturer.

One of our greatest problems in determining with adequate lead time
the future requirements of our customers both with regard to product performance and service. . .it is necessary to establish and
maintain a concept of dynamic intelligence instead of static information. --Vice President of Marketing, diversified manufacturer.

. . .So long as the industrial sale is handled on a direct basis, we
have reasonable control and understanding of the sales situation. . . .
We have only a spotty idea of how effective our distributor sales effort is with respect to specific markets. What is needed is a better
understanding of our customers. . .how and why they buy. --Di-
rector of Marketing Research, manufacturer of automotive and ord-
nance parts.

Without end-use information, it is extremely difficult to broaden our
markets for similar applications. Our inability to determine end-
use starts with the customer's desire to keep this information proprietary. . .compounded by their purchasing department's general
disinterest in reporting the information to us. --Marketing Coordinator, specialty tubing manufacturer.

. . .the traditional patterns of industrial selling and distribution
may change. . . .More knowledge of the promotional aspects and
distribution processes. . .and a better understanding of the industrial customer's buying processes are needed. Of particular interest is how the 'marketing concept' can be implanted in this
changing environment. --Marketing Manager, electronic products
manufacturer.

. . .our primary problem is to know the need of the customer in a
particular purchasing situation, and to be able to focus our resources
toward satisfying the customer's requirement. --Vice President of
Market and Commercial Development, steel products manufacturer.

. . .the problem of determining what order we can anticipate, because of competition and because we do not know the customer's
continuing requirements due to technological advances and changes
in the customer's product content. --Vice President of Sales, electronic components manufacturer.

. . .to determine what forces prompt the buyer's decision, notwith-
standing the stated reasons for making a particular buying decision.
--Vice President, industrial minerals and chemicals manufacturer.

A major problem area is to better appraise the market potential. . .
especially because there is not a clear understanding of what motivates capital equipment expenditures. . .Tax investment credit? A
desire for increased production capacity? Availability of funds?
Anticipated improvement in costs?. . .What are the influences?
--Sales Manager, capital equipment manufacturer.

Supplementary interviews and seminars with key industrial marketers reflected the same apprehension concerning customer motivation and behavior and a rather widespread recognition of the inadequacy of the industrial marketer's grasp of his customers' decision processes.

PURPOSE AND ORGANIZATION OF THE STUDY

This research report, focusing on an area of prime concern to the industrial marketer, attempts to alleviate the foregoing deficiencies to some degree. It is divided into three parts. Part One (Chapters II–VI) is devoted to the understanding of the industrial buying process and presents a framework for analysis and findings of the MSI study. It examines in detail the decision process and behavior of the industrial buyer throughout eight differentiated phases of the procurement process. Fundamental differences among buying situations are discussed and their effects on procurement decision making described. This presentation is then validated and supplemented by the findings of Dr. Y. Wind's independent study on the buying process of industrial components (Chapter VII).

Part Two is concerned with the determinants of buyer behavior. Chapters VIII–XI identify certain of the interacting variables which influence the purchase decision. These findings are supplemented in Chapter XII by a theoretical framework for the analysis of industrial buyer behavior.

The framework serves as a guideline for a review of the relevant findings from the behavioral sciences, marketing, and purchasing literature concerned with the determinants of buyers' behavior, together with some of the findings of an empirical case study of the industrial buying process.

This report, seeking to heighten understanding on the part of the industrial marketer of the procurement process in general, suggests in Part Three specific areas and opportunities for improving marketing performance and effectiveness. The BUYGRID concept, which is introduced as an analytic tool in Chapter II, provides a frame of reference for further examination of procurement activity and together with the findings of MSI's and Dr. Wind's studies contributes toward developing a behavioral model of the industrial buying process.

THE SCOPE AND OPERATIONAL DEFINITION OF THE STUDIES

The purpose of the studies to be reported is to improve the understanding of the industrial buying decisions and their determinants

so as to provide industrial marketing managers with a better basis
for marketing decisions.

The term industrial marketing is used here to refer to the
marketing decisions aimed at the buyers of industrial goods.

For the purpose of this manuscript, the terms "purchasing,"
"buying," and "procuring" are used synonymously throughout the
report.   All of them refer to the purchase of industrial goods—
"goods which are destined to be sold primarily for use in producing
other goods or rendering services."   This definition excludes
buying for consumption by ultimate consumers or resale to them
(by retailers or any other intermediate marketing organization).
Likely, some of the models, findings, and conclusions of the studies
to be reported might be applicable to buying by retailers or whole-
salers.   The lack of any empirical evidence on the buying for resale situations indicates that this study may lead to some hypotheses
to be studied and tested empirically on the specific buying-for-
resale situation.

RESEARCH PROCEDURE

The basic approach of this study is to describe and analyze each
step involved in the procurement of goods in various types of buying situations, assess the possible determinants of the buying decisions, and suggest some implications for industrial marketing
decisions.

The MSI study was based on findings from three industrial concerns.   The three firms selected as subjects for the research (including a major division of a multi-division company) collectively
purchase a broad variety of goods and services.   In the two-year
period under examination, literally hundreds of vendors and thou-
sands of transactions were involved.

Each company is quite distinct from the rest with regard to
certain basic characteristics such as products manufactured, items
purchased, geographical location, markets served, and company
organization and philosophy, as well as with reference to the relative importance of various functional areas in the procurement
activities.   It was believed that using such diverse organizational
subjects would extend the representative character of the research
and render the subsequent classificatory scheme more generally
applicable to different types of manufacturing concerns.

A series of depth interviews was conducted in each company
with individuals involved in procurement activities to varying degrees and from diverse hierarchical levels and functional areas.
Included were members of top management, operating personnel
in purchasing, production, development and design engineering,
marketing, finance and accounting, and other specialized areas.   In
these initial exploratory interviews, general information was ob-

tained about each company its policies, procedures, and patterns of operation. With regard to purchasing, typical questions included the following:

What are the different types of purchases that can arise in a company?

How do they arise?

How are they handled after they are recognized?

Why are they handled the way they are?

Who are the people involved, and what role does each person play?

What kinds of information do the buying decision makers use, and where do they get it?

What differences and similarities may be observed among the different types of purchases?

What basic factors explain those differences and similarities?

After these exploratory interviews, a number of representative buying situations were selected for intensive study and analysis. They were chosen according to the following criteria: 1. Major purchase items, though numbering only 15-20 percent of total items purchased, typically account for 80 percent of the purchase dollars and should be accorded appropriate weight in the selection process; 2. Patterns of behavior should be examined for goods of varying type (*e.g.*, finished goods, raw materials) and monetary value (*e.g.*, capital equipment, repair and operation items); 3. Each of the differentiated basic categories of buying situations (see Chapter III) should be represented.

For each selected buying situation, independent investigations were conducted. Researchers observed at firsthand the buying decision process and procedures. They attended meetings of buying committees and other relevant groups and also reviewed copies of internal memoranda and pertinent correspondence.

Nonstructured, confidential interviews were conducted with each individual participant in the particular buying situation. Each participant was questioned about his own role and about those of other corporate personnel with whom he came in contact during the procurement process. This procedure helped to identify all of the buying influences in a given purchase situation and to verify the role of specific individuals. The number of participants varied with each buying situation, from relatively routine purchases involving only a handful of purchasing people to complex buying situations with some 30 to 40 participants.

Detailed memoranda were prepared after each interview. At the completion of each series of interviews, a detailed flow diagram or "decision network" was developed for the particular buying situation. This diagram graphically portrayed the "anatomy of the procurement"—the people involved, their roles, and the decisions made. Summary statements were developed, describing and analyzing each progressive phase in the procurement process for each particular product. The basic objective of this vertical analysis was to explain the purchasing procedure and the rationale behind it.

When interviews were completed for every selected buying situation, the summary statements were analyzed horizontally. Each individual phase of the procurement process was reviewed separately for all products in order to identify similarities and differences among purchasing situations.

Finally, the preliminary findings and tentatively drafted hypotheses were presented for comments and discussion to more than one hundred senior industrial marketing and purchasing executives in executive seminars and personal interviews across the country. These individuals helped immeasurably in refining the ideas and concepts presented in this volume.

Dr. Yoram Wind's study[2] was conducted independently of the MSI project utilizing a distinctly different research approach and different population. The study attempted to answer four important questions:

1. What is the behavioral process with which the decision to purchase industrial components takes place, and who are the major participants in this process?

2. What is the major set of determinants of the decision to purchase industrial components?

3. What are the specific organizational variables that affect the decision to purchase industrial components, and how do they affect it?

4. To what extent does source loyalty exist in the purchase of industrial components, and what are its major determinants?

To facilitate the collection and analysis of data in answering these four basic questions, the following research approach was designed and implemented.

1. An exploratory study of the buying process in general and the decision to purchase industrial components in particular was conducted. In this phase of the research project, data were gathered through unstructured interviews with, and by obtaining "protocols"[3] from "key" people concerned with the decision to purchase industrial components. These two methods, while generating a descriptive model of the industrial buying process, probably introduced a certain amount of bias into the study. They not only measured, but they also helped cre-

ate attitudes and decision rules, elicited "acceptable," and "rationalized" responses. These methods furthermore might have given undue emphasis to some aspects of the buying process.

2. The second research phase was aimed at refining the findings from the exploratory study, and specifically at reducing the inaccuracies resulting from the described research methods. In this phase too, the model generated in phase one was partially validated by repeating the interviews and protocols with other buyers. This validation process also served to minimize the (uncontrolled) individual determinants of the decision to purchase industrial components.

3. To supplement verbal responses about the relationship between variables and the actual buying decision, phase three attempted to incorporate some "objective" data about the buyers' overt behavior. Purchasing history cards and weekly cost saving reports provided such data, which were used in a multivariate statistical analysis.

4. Among the variables expected to affect the buyers' decisions were their attitudes toward the various sources. Hence the fourth research phase was devoted to a study of these attitudes by means of semantic differential scales. The results of this study were incorporated in the regression and discriminant models so as to examine the empirical relations between attitudes and actual behavior.

5. The last phase of the research was concerned with comparing buyers' behavior in two alternative organizational structures—one with a centralized purchasing department, the other with a decentralized department.

The data for the five research phases were generated within two advanced electronic firms located on the West Coast. The subjects studied were buyers, purchasing agents, and other organizational members concerned with decisions to purchase industrial components. In many respects, the organizations examined are typical of most companies buying industrial components.

NATURE OF COMPANIES STUDIED

Commodities around which the buying situations focus are not specifically identified in this report, nor are the organizations subjected to the research. Throughout the MSI study, participant firms are referred to as Company Able, Company Baker and Company Charlie. As background information, however, the following is provided about the companies, subjected to the MSI study, and their purchasing operations.

Company Able purchases more than 300,000 different items annually, although for only a few hundred of these do annual purchases exceed $1,000. The company has several thousand active suppliers, but fewer than 50 account for over half of the dollar purchases. A simple purchasing department serves Company Able, although it is subject to some advice and guidelines on policy matters for the staff purchasing activity at the headquarters of the diversified corporation which owns Company Able. Able competes in its markets largely on the basis of its superior design and development engineering. Production operations can be described as being in the job shop category.

Company Baker centralizes procurement policies including a policy of enlarging corporate-wide standardization and interchangeability. In addition, a centralized purchasing group purchases important items used in more than one plant and provides staff guidance to plant purchasing departments. Company Baker's purchases are more than double those of Able. Baker is essentially an assembler of a high-volume, consumer-type product. Its final product is comprised of several thousand separate items, less than twenty of which cost as much as five dollars. Competition in Baker's industry focuses on marketing; product development is thus a marketing rather than an engineering or manufacturing responsibility.

Company Charlie's purchases represent some 40 percent of its annual sales volume. Charlie produces a homogeneous, commodity-type product which is used in many different industries. It is manufactured in a continuous process operation. Of some 10,000 different items that are normally purchased, less than 100 account for more than two-thirds of total dollar purchases. The company has a strong central purchasing department and relatively weak purchasing departments at the plant level. Since Charlie produces a standardized product sold at standard prices, purchasing represents a major way of gaining an advantage over its competitors.

It should be recognized that these three organizations as well as the two organizations studied by Dr. Wind are ''large'' manufacturing concerns with very substantial sales volume, influence, and personnel forces. While ''big business'' accounts for an overwhelming portion of total purchase dollars spent, the smaller firms are more numerous and, clearly, may show different procurement patterns from those described here. Then, too, studies within the areas of commerce, the service industries, and the institutional market may reveal disparate, but perhaps even more valuable, insights regarding the procurement function. However, the method of analysis developed here should be applicable to buying organizations of all kinds and sizes.

II

The Procurement Process

UNDERSTANDING COMPLEX INDUSTRIAL BUYING PROCESSES requires a framework for the analysis of the major phases of the buying "decisioning process" (the continuous process of problem-solving and decision making) and of the various buying situations. One of the principal aims of this study was to develop and test the usefulness of such a marketing-oriented classification. Recently, the chief executive of a major company said:

> I'm not at all sure that I'm interested in marketing theory, but what I do need is a frame of reference within which I can position and interrelate the many and diverse marketing decisions we have to make.

One of the uses of theory is to enable a manager to understand, explain, predict, and control relationships and their variables in a given framework within which such variables may be identified and analyzed. For example, the manager seeks to identify or classify the basic characteristics of a problem so he will know how to proceed to solve it. Did it arise inside the company or outside? Does it involve a good customer, a potential customer, or a governmental regulatory agency? Asking these types of questions essentially constitutes an attempt to classify the significant variables of the situation he is facing. His course of action will depend upon the answers.

The question addressed here is not that of establishing the usefulness of classification systems in general; rather it is that of developing and describing a specific classification system of the industrial buying process which appears to be useful from the point of view of the planning and execution of an efficient industrial marketing effort.

The content or orientation of any given classification system is clearly dependent upon the level of decision making responsibility as well as the particular circumstances surrounding the individual marketer. Three popular bases for classifying transactions are as follows: market segment or class of trade reached, product or service marketed, and end-use application.

Classification according to class of trade characteristics helps to isolate the relevant company or division buyers. Classification according to product, service, or end-use can be helpful in developing technical specifications or preparing promotional material. While these approaches are helpful in formulating general marketing policy, they can be very usefully supplemented by a classification system aimed at the specifics of the selling task. Such a system is presented here.

The framework for the analysis of the procurement process, to be presented in the following five chapters, is based on three major premises:

1. *"Purchasing"* includes a sequence of activities of varying complexity. Buying can actually be described as a dynamic "decisioning" process involving diverse functional areas and hierarchical levels within an organization.

2. The central unit of analysis is a buying situation. It develops when some problem or need arises within an organization in the procurement of a good or service. Whenever an individual with some relevant authority recognizes the existence of a problem and that its resolution may require a purchase, a buying situation is created and the procurement decision process begins. There are essentially three types of buying situations, or *Buyclasses:* the New Task, the Modified Rebuy, and the Straight Rebuy. In Chapter III, distinguishing characteristics of these three situational types are discussed and analyzed.

3. The *procurement process* is the sequence of activities which must be performed in the resolution of a buying situation. Eight distinct activities, or Buyphases, are differentiated. Once a buying situation has developed, triggering the procurement process, these Buyphases will progress until the problem is resolved, either by means of a purchase or a decision to terminate or discontinue the process.

Chapter II presents the overall BUYGRID framework which analyzes the various activities of the procurement process and discusses some of the complexities included.

Chapter III presents an overall analysis of the three basic buying situations. Chapters IV, V, and VI examine some selected cases of the use of the BUYGRID framework under the three distinct buying situations. Chapter IV concerns the New Task Buying situation, Chapter V the Straight Rebuy, and Chapter VI the Modified Rebuy situation.

The MSI analysis of the buying process is then verified and supplemented by presenting in Chapter VII some of Dr. Wind's findings concerning the buying process of industrial components.

THE BUYGRID FRAMEWORK

The BUYGRID conceptual framework for the analysis of industrial buying situations incorporates three Buyclasses and eight Buyphases (see Table 1). It provides the frame of reference within which the procurement situations are designed to be general enough to apply to all procurements, yet specific enough to have operational relevance to the individual marketer.

It is hoped that the BUYGRID concept additionally can prove a useful analytical tool for the industrial marketer in examining buying behavior within his customer companies and in recognizing the critical decision points and information requirements. It may enable more effective adaptation of the sales effort to fit the critical pattern of buying decisions and to satisfy the needs of individuals whose influence is greatest in different purchase situations.

FUNDAMENTAL ACTIVITIES OF THE PROCUREMENT PROCESS (BUYPHASES)

A description follows of the eight fundamental activities or Buyphases which comprise the procurement process in an industrial concern. While some of these phases may occur simultaneously, they do tend to follow in sequence, as shown in Table 1.

Phase 1: Anticipation or Recognition of a Problem (Need)

The "triggering" device which sets in motion the procurement process may originate within the buying organization in the form of problem recognition, or it may come from a potential supplier who anticipates or precipitates a need for a product or service within the buying organization. Phase 1 consists of two parts: the recognition of a *problem* and the awareness that the *solution* may take the form of filling certain needs through a purchase.

Problem recognition may stem from several sources. Shelf inventory may run low. The firm's customers may want features which the present products do not offer, calling for a partial redesign of the item or for a completely new product. Equipment needs may arise due to unsatisfactory performance of present equipment, or a breakdown may spark an emergency need. Messages from a salesman or an advertisement may cause the user to

TABLE 1

The Buygrid Analytic Framework for Industrial Buying Situations

		BUYCLASSES		
		New Task	Modified Rebuy	Straight Rebuy
B U Y P H A S E S	1. Anticipation or Recognition of a problem (Need) and a General Solution			
	2. Determination of Characteristics and Quantity of Needed Item			
	3. Description of Characteristics and Quantity of Needed Item			
	4. Search for and Qualification of Potential Sources			
	5. Acquisition and Analysis of Proposals			
	6. Evaluation of Proposals and Selection of Supplier(s)			
	7. Selection of an Order Routine			
	8. Performance Feedback and Evaluation			

Notes:

1. The most complex buying situations occur in the upper left portion of the BUYGRID matrix, when the largest number of decision makers and buying influences are involved. Thus, a New Task in its initial phase of problem recognition generally represents the greatest difficulty for management.

2. Clearly, a New Task may entail policy questions and special studies, whereas a Modified Rebuy may be more routine, and a Straight Rebuy essentially automatic.

3. As Buyphases are completed, moving from phase 1 through phase 8, the process of "creeping commitment" occurs, and there is diminishing likelihood of new vendors gaining access to the buying situation.

doubt whether a product or service he is currently using is, in fact, the best method for performing an operation. Before the recognition of a problem can have any impact on procurement, the need must be made explicit within the buying organization. Someone with at least partial authority must do something to start the process. This may involve no more than "looking into" a situation to see if the prospective problem is in fact worth doing something about.

The second part of this phase is an awareness that the best solution to the problem is most likely to lie in a particular direction. For example, the general solution to a delivery problem may call for more trucks, or an electrical overload problem may suggest the need for new generating capacity.

Phase 2: Determination of the Characteristics and Quantity of the Needed Item

Decisions concerning the general problem solution are made largely within the using department or group. The decision makers involved at this point must determine, in a fairly specific way, how the problem is to be solved; *i.e.*, they must narrow down the problem and solution areas so that more precise analysis is possible. The buying influences seek answers to such questions as, "What application requirements must be met? What types of goods and services should be considered? In what quantites?"

For technical products, the using department may prepare performance specifications stating what the proposed product or service should do, or it may prepare a composite specification of ideal attributes, apart from cost and availability considerations. For less technical items, no more may be involved than ascertaining that an item now on the market could do the job and would solve the problem. The task of determining the need is thus internal to the using department, although people outside of the department may be consulted as information sources. In some cases this phase proceeds concurrently with later phases involving participation by other buying influences.

Phase 3: Description of the Characteristics and Quantity of the Needed Item

This phase begins as an extension of phase 2 and entails a translation of the need into a particular solution which can be readily communicated to others. Since this description becomes the basis for action by people inside and outside of the buying organization, it must be detailed and precise in order to facilitate later stages in the buying process, such as source selection, price validation, and inspection.

Phase 3 is often critical for the marketer, since it is here that specifying influences may enter the procurement process. At this point the marketer needs to know who prepares the specifications (or makes the selection from available specifications), what information sources the buying influences draw upon, and the roles of the various individuals in furnishing information, participating in the decision making process, and reviewing the decisions. In many situations, for example, potential suppliers are not aware that the buying company is in the market for an item until after phase 3 has been completed. In situations triggered by a marketer's anticipation of a need, however, the supplier may have been working closely with the specifiers in the buying organization on the solution to the particular problem.

Phase 4: Search for and Qualification of Potential Sources

The problem-solving organization shifts from its search for alternative ways of satisfying a requirement to the search for alternative sources of supply, which leads to the qualification of suppliers. The criteria for qualifying suppliers appear to vary not only with the buying organization and the specific buying situation, but also with the buying influences involved. Alternative sources are screened and evaluated. In simple cases, seeking out and qualifying sources may consist of no more than identifying a preferred source from a reference list. At the other extreme, qualification may require both extensive search to find appropriate suppliers and extended consideration of which suppliers are in fact qualified (*e.g.*, Value Analysis and Systems Engineering studies).

The emphasis on qualification may be directly related to the anticipated consequences of nonperformance. This factor is likely to play its greatest role where specifications can be only loosely defined (*e.g.*, Research and Development contracts), where the consequences of failure generally are serious, and where long lead times make late delivery a matter of concern to the buyer (*e.g.*, large forgings).

Regardless of how suppliers are qualified, the end result of phase 4 is that the buying decision makers have determined which suppliers out of the total universe will be considered as potential vendors.

Phase 5: Acquisition and Analysis of Proposals

After suppliers have been screened, the buying organization requests specific proposals. In the case of relatively routinized or standardized procurements, this may involve merely checking a catalog or telephoning a supplier to obtain information about prices or deliveries. In complex situations, the interactions may involve a series of counter-proposals and new offers, with activities extending over many months.

In many buying situations, phases 4 and 5 take place concurrently, becoming almost indistinguishable. It appears that these phases are separate and distinct when the buying organization has relatively little information, compared to what it feels it needs before a decision can be made. Thus, phases 4 and 5 tend to be treated as different activities in situations where the information needs are relatively high. On the other hand, where the information needed by the buying organization is minimal, phases 4 and 5 would be combined.

Phase 6: Evaluation of Proposals and Selection of Suppliers

Next, the various offers from potential vendors are weighed and analyzed. Perhaps a number of discussions and negotiations have been conducted with each prospective supplier, or perhaps the purchasing agent telephones a local distributor for cost data. During this phase, the supplier is selected when the buying organization approves one or more supplier's offers and rejects the others. After this screening has taken place, there may be further negotiations concerning prices, terms, deliveries, or other aspects of the supplier's proposal.

Phase 7: Selection of an Order Routine

This phase begins when an order is given to a vendor, but the procurement process is not completed until the item is actually delivered and accepted for use. The order routine that directs and monitors the remaining activities involves both *external* and *internal* aspects. The former include preparation of the purchase order for forwarding to the vendor, follow-up activities such as expediting, troubleshooting, securing status reports, receiving, inspection, and approval of invoices for payment. Internal activities of two types are involved in the order routine: status reporting to the using department, and inventory management, including the reordering of economic quantities at appropriate times.

It may appear that the activities undertaken in phase 7 are actually post-purchase activities of little value to an understanding of either purchase decisions or marketing. From the viewpoint of the using department, however, the purchase has not been completed and the problem has not been solved until acceptable material is on hand and ready for use. The effectiveness with which this is accomplished is, therefore, a matter of no small concern to the marketer. In addition, every procurement adds to the buyer's learning experience, and monitoring vendor performance provides important feedback for the qualification of suppliers in future procurements.

Phase 8:   Performance Feedback and Evaluation

While phase 7 includes some evaluation of the supplier's performance, a more fundamental evaluation occurs after the purchased
items are actually in use.   This review includes questions as to
how well the purchased product solved the problem and how well
the vendor himself performed.   Feedback of this information is
obviously necessary if future procurement problems are to be
handled more effectively.
    When feedback is not provided explicitly within the organiza-
tional network, it occurs informally as users appraise and report
on the utility of the products in use.   Formal feedback may be
limited to reports of what the product fails to do.   Or decisions
may be evaluated on an exception basis—unless the using group
complains, buying decision makers assume that the item and the
vendor have performed satisfactorily.   Whether purchasing is
viewed as a continuing set of relatively habitual relationships with
suppliers or as a series of independent events, feedback of performance information (whether explicitly provided for or not) is an integral part of the procurement process.

THE COMPLEXITY OF THE PROCUREMENT PROCESS

Relationships between Phases

The phases of the procurement process are closely interrelated.
While there is a sequential flow of phases or activities in a logical
sense, in practice two or more may take place concurrently.   This
is quite common in situations where both buyer and seller work together to develop a new item, a substantial modification of existing
items, or where new technologies or applications may be involved.
Similarly, the phases are not mutually exclusive.   For example,
some of the specific tasks which are normally performed in phase 3
may be performed in phase 2 in some procurements.   In practice,
it may be difficult—and is probably pointless—to determine precisely where one phase ends and another begins.
    The relative emphasis given to each phase is by no means equal,
either in the case of any given purchase or when comparing several
purchases.   Source qualification, for example, will be critical in
some cases, perfunctory in others, and in some computerized applications virtually automatic.
    As mentioned earlier, the fact that the procurement process has
begun is no guarantee that it will proceed, step by step, from the
recognition of a need to the acqusition of a good or service.   It may
be halted or aborted at any time by someone directly involved or
by veto from a higher organizational level.   A procurement may be

proceeding quite smoothly and predictably when suddenly a redefinition of the basic problem occurs, stalling or recycling the process
to some earlier phase.

The concept of a procurement process represents a dynamic,
ongoing, continually changing interaction of people and influences
focused on satisfying both new and recurring acquisition problems.
The concept holds import for the marketer, because it fosters some
insight into the problem-solving process within the customer company as buying decisions are being made. Although specific buying
influences are not identifiable in an absolute sense, the concept does
provide clues as to their identity and about the kind of information
required as inputs to the buying decision makers at different phases
of the procurement process.

The "Creeping Commitment"

Many writers and researchers tend to study the decision as a mechanistic moment-of-truth which can be analyzed apart from the
problem context and the environment which gave rise to it. More
realistically, however, it appears that the decision making *process*
rather than the *decision* should be the unit for study. In our concept of the procurement process, eight phases represent the critical decision points. From any given buying situation, the process
will evolve in more or less sequential order through these major
decision areas.

According to the concept of the "creeping commitment," decision making actually involves a sequence of incremental choices,
each of which eliminates certain alternative solutions from further
consideration. As each successive decision is made, the number
of possible alternatives is reduced. Eventually, the bulk of initial
alternatives has been eliminated and only a few alternate solutions
to the problem are yet feasible. The "decisioning" process continues until the final decision is made. The basic concern then is
really an independent choice between alternatives X, Y, and Z; the
question usually can be expressed, "As of now, to what extent are
we committed to alternatives X, Y, and Z?"

This creeping commitment notion seems particularly relevant to
the purchasing process under certain conditions. The likelihood that
it will accurately describe the problem-solving process increases
with the following:

1. the importance of the buying situation to the problem-solving
   company,

2. the number of people involved in the decision making process,

3. the reliance placed upon buying committees and similar arrangements for diffusing the buying responsibility.

The "Center of Gravity"

Dr. Charles N. Davisson, of The University of Michigan, has introduced the concept of the "center of gravity," which maintains that the relative importance within the procurement decision process of the eight phases or groups of activities will vary from purchase to purchase. In each purchase situation, a particular phase or combination of phases will be most significant with regard to the outcome of the situation. To this critical decision phase, or center of gravity, all other activities will tend to adapt themselves.

Certain patterns are evident with regard to the center of gravity concept. In complex buying situations in which the decision makers have little or no relevant experience, the critical stage would probably occur early perhaps phases 2-3 when they are seeking alternative ways of solving the problem. In this situation, the marketer has a capital opportunity to help the buyers actually formulate their requirements. In any case, the prospective supplier facing a nonroutine, complex buying situation should concentrate his efforts heavily in the initial stages of the problem-solving process. As the solution area narrows, in any direction, the marketer who has been working with the customer company will have a substantial advantage over competing marketers.

By contrast, in routine purchases the center of gravity will tend to occur later in the procurement process, perhaps between the period of acquiring vendor proposals and finally selecting a supplier (phases 5-6). In nonroutine purchases, where the buyers have some but not sufficient experience, the critical point might be when they are seeking and qualifying potential suppliers (phase 4). The specific center of gravity fluctuates, dependent upon the characteristics of each particular buying situation and upon the varying informational needs of the buying influences. In general, it is likely to occur earlier with more unique, nonroutine buying situations when the experience and immediate knowledge of the buying decision makers are less directly relevant.

CHANGES IN BUYING INFLUENCES

As the procurement decision process progresses, the importance of specific functional activities changes, as do the roles played and the relative importance of the various buying influences. In the early phases of a buying situation, during problem analysis and definition, corporate staff personnel may play key roles (*e.g.*, designers, product planners, finance and accounting people, materials standards people and others). As the requirements of the needed item become more explicit and detailed specifications are being drafted, purchasing or supervisory personnel in the using department may become key influences. Finally, as requisite characteristics are defined and vendor negotiations have begun, purchasing frequently takes a major role. Shipping, receiving, and inspection personnel play important parts after the order is placed, follow-up procedures have begun, and when the purchased item is delivered by the suppliers.

As any buying process unfolds, then, the significance of any individuals or functions involved in the process changes. While this is recognized implicitly by most industrial salesmen, the implications for a total marketing plan are somewhat more subtle. For example, in light of the decision making process within a particular company, for any given buying situation the marketer might want to recruit individuals of diverse background, levels of authority, areas of specialization or competency on his marketing team—each specifically responsible for dealings with a designated "counterpart" in the customer organization.

SUMMARY

This chapter introduces some basic purchasing definitions and key concepts used in the analysis. It then explains how a purchasing problem is handled when it arises in an organization, describing eight differentiated buying activities (Buyphases) which comprise the decisioning procurement process. Interaction and overlapping between Buyphases are discussed. Flexibility is introduced through the "center of gravity" concept, which acknowledges variations in the relative importance of the eight phases from purchase to purchase.

III

Characteristics of
Buying Situations

TOWARD STUDYING THE COUNTLESS TYPES AND COMPLEX-
ITIES of industrial buying situations, some original method of sys-
tematization is mandatory. The traditional product or market-
oriented classificatory schemes have been found by industrial
marketers to be inadequate for exploring or explaining buyer behavior. For any given buyer purchasing the same product, individual
purchasing patterns and the buying process itself have been found to
differ distinctly with subsequent purchases over time and in dealing
with different suppliers. This implicitly suggested that a buyer
might behave differently on an initial as opposed to subsequent purchases of an item and on initial as opposed to subsequent dealings
with a supplier. If this be the case, hypothetically then, buyer decision making might be categorized quite succinctly in one of four
circumstantial situations as presented in Table 2.

TABLE 2

Classification of Buying Situations
Based on Experience with Item and Supplier

		SUPPLIER	
		Tried	Untried
ITEM	Tried		
	Untried		

It was speculated that the types of information buyers would seek
and the relative importance they would attach to various criteria

would tend to differ in each of these four basic situations. Discussions with industrial marketing and purchasing executives, however, indicated a persisting conviction about the basic importance of the type of product to the buying situation. A lingering impression was evidenced to the effect that the buying situation and the procurement process itself must differ basically with the general broad categories of goods.

With this background, a classificatory scheme was developed which sought to recognize two separate dimensions in the buying situation: 1. the general category of product, and 2. the type of buying situation, i.e., the circumstances leading to consideration of a purchase. An initial classification differentiated products into three distinct types: 1. Capital Goods, 2. Parts and Materials, 3. Maintenance, Repair, and Operating Supplies (MRO). Within each product type, a number of distinct buying situations were distinguished. In all three product groupings, a total of 23 separate buying situations were discerned (see Table 3).

Using this frame of reference, field interviews began in Company Able. As the work progressed, it became increasingly apparent that the type of product was not clearly so important as the particular circumstances of the purchase in affecting patterns of procurement. The situation of the buyer with regard to information and experience was far more significant and consistent in explaining his buying behavior and the procedures he followed in the procurement process.

This led to a framework based strictly on the type of buying situation, implicitly incorporating something about the circumstances which occasion the consideration of a purchase. Withdrawing the product dimension from the classification scheme, twelve differentiated buying situations remained. As the work continued, common elements were recognized in certain of these situations, and the list was further refined. Eventually the present classificatory scheme had evolved. The total number of fundamentally distinct situations was reduced to three: the new task, the modified rebuy, and the straight rebuy. Any buying situation could be defined as belonging in one of these three categories and differentiated according to an equal number of primary characteristics.

PRIMARY CHARACTERISTICS OF BUYING SITUATIONS

Every buying situation, and each basic type of buying situation, can be characterized according to the following:

Newness of the problem to the buying influences and decision makers,

Information requirements of the buying influences and decision makers,

New alternatives given serious consideration by the buying decision makers.

TABLE 3

Initial Classification of Buying Situations

CAPITAL GOODS

First Buy	Start up
	New product or process
	Need established or "threshold" reached
Replacement	Physical destruction (old good inoperable)
	Economic destruction (old good uneconomic)
Addition	Add to output capacity

PARTS AND MATERIALS

First Buy	Start up
	New product or process
	Need established or "threshold" reached
Repeat	Rebuy
	Modified rebuy
Change	Change for superior performance attri-butes of the end product
	Change for manufacturing cost benefits
	Change for landed cost benefits
	Change for service benefits (all parts of the offer except price)

MAINTENANCE, REPAIR, AND OPERATING ITEMS

First Buy	Start up
	Need established or "threshold" reached
Repeat	Rebuy
	Modified rebuy
Change	Change for superior performance of MRO item
	Change for cost-to-use benefits of MRO item
	Change for service benefits of MRO item (all parts of the offer except price)

In any specific environmental context, these factors determine what the customers' needs from the marketing system will be.   The marketing efforts of suppliers, actual and potential, can be adjusted to the situation to some degree and to fulfill or attempt to modify the varying requirements.

These three characterizing features are here discussed as they relate to each basic type of buying situation, and as illustrated in Table 4.

TABLE 4

Distinguishing Characteristics of Buying Situations

TYPE OF BUYING SITUATION (Buyclass)	Newness of the Problem	Information Requirements	Consideration of New Alternatives
New Task	High	Maximum	Important
Modified Rebuy	Medium	Moderate	Limited
Straight Rebuy	Low	Minimal	None

Newness of the Problem

This characteristic alone is sufficient to differentiate among the three types of buying situations.   It refers to the extent to which the current requirement or problem is similar to others which have arisen in the past.   A major attribute of the new task is that the buying organization is confronted with a problem it has not dealt with previously.   Consequently, the buying decision makers have little if any relevant experience, and this factor will greatly influence the buying procedure.

In all rebuy situations, the problem-solving company has some relevant buying experience.   In straight rebuys, the problem arises on a regular or recurring basis, so that its solution is likely to be highly routinized.   Today's decision is largely a reflection of how current suppliers and products have performed in the past.   Since the buying influences in straight rebuy situations tend to place more weight on past experience than on the current statements of potential suppliers, it is often difficult for a new supplier to sell into straight rebuy situations.

In modified rebuy situations, the newness of the problem and the relevant experience of the decision makers is between those of the new task and straight rebuy situations. In general, the modified rebuy decision makers have relevant buying experience, but the experience factor is not complete because new alternative suppliers, items or marketing services are being considered.

If one visualizes a spectrum entitled newness of the problem, scaled from 0 (problem identical to previous one) to 100 (absolutely no relevant experience), the buying situations outlined above would be positioned as follows:

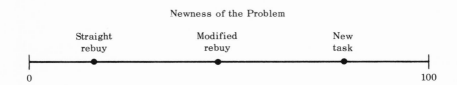

Newness of the Problem

Straight rebuy   Modified rebuy   New task

0   100

Information Requirements

This characteristic refers to the amount and type of information which the buying influences believe they must obtain before they can make their decisions with a reasonable degree of confidence. It is inversely related to the newness of the problem since, other things being equal, the less relevant experience the buying influences have, the more information they will require during the procurement process. This factor is expressed in terms of the information the buyers seek rather than the information they possess. From the marketing perspective, what the buying influences need to know is equally if not more significant than what they do know.

Differing awareness of important informational deficiencies causes buying situations to differ even when decision makers have equally relevant previous buying experience. It is also assured that the informational requirements and information-seeking patterns will vary within each developing phase of the procurement process. In plotting on a spectrum the amount of information sought by the buying influences, the different buying situations would be located as follows:

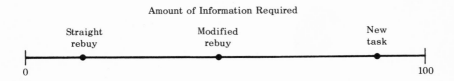

Amount of Information Required

Straight rebuy   Modified rebuy   New task

0   100

New Alternatives Considered

The third primary characteristic of buying situations is the number of new alternative solutions to the purchasing problem which the buying decision makers seriously consider. This characteristic is obviously related to the others—their previous relevant experience and informational requirements. It is most basically affected by their perception of the situation, however, on two counts: a) their awareness of available alternatives, and b) the distinction they make between the immediate problem and the last similar situation.

In the case of a straight rebuy, no new alternatives are considered. The need is continuing or recurring, the problem is recognized as routine, and serious consideration of new solutions is not required. The new task situation, constituting a new problem to the buying organization, involves all new alternatives in its decision making. The buying organization, with little, if any knowledge about solutions to the particular problem, will expend maximum effort in ferreting out new alternatives.

In the new task situation, the gains are thought to be large relative to the time, money, and effort involved in searching for more alternatives. This is less true of modified rebuys, where new alternatives are sought and considered on the basis of relevant experience and a large amount of pertinent information. In straight rebuys, the existing experience and information factors are great enough so that the decision makers believe that the time, money, and effort involved in seeking out new solutions to recurring problems are likely to be greater than the potential gains.

The distinction between types of buying situations with respect to the number of new alternatives which are seriously considered may be visualized as points on a continuum:

Consideration of New Alternatives

Straight rebuy	Modified rebuy	New task
0		100

THE THREE BASIC TYPES OF BUYING SITUATIONS (BUYCLASSES)

The three basic types of buying situations can be differentiated according to certain representative characteristics, including the three major determinants discussed above. Each type—new task, modified rebuy, and straight rebuy—is described below, with some of the more obvious marketing implications. Table 5 summarizes major differences between them.

TABLE 5

Types of Buying Situations
"Buyclasses"

I. NEW TASK

A requirement or problem that has not arisen before
Little or no relevant past buying experience to draw upon
A great deal of information is needed
Must seek out alternative ways of solving the problem and alternative
  suppliers
Occurs infrequently — but very important to marketers because it sets
  the pattern for the more routine purchases that will follow
May be anticipated and developed by creative marketing

II. STRAIGHT REBUY

Continuing or recurring requirement, handled on a routine basis
Usually the decision on each separate transaction is made in the pur-
  chasing department
Formally or informally, a "list" of acceptable suppliers exists
No supplier not on the "list" is considered
Buyers have much relevant buying experience, and hence little new
  information is needed
Appears to represent the bulk of the individual purchases within com-
  panies
Item purchased, price paid, delivery time, etc., may vary from trans-
  action to transaction, so long as these variations do not cause a new
  source of supply to be considered

III. MODIFIED REBUY

May develop from either new task or straight rebuy situations
The requirement is continuing or recurring or it may be expanded to
  a significantly larger level of operations
The buying alternatives are known, but they are CHANGED
Some additional information is needed before the decisions are made
May arise because of outside events, such as an emergency or by the
  actions of a marketer
May arise internally because of new buying influences, or for poten-
  tial cost reductions, potential quality improvements or potential
  service benefits
Marketers who are not active suppliers try to convert the customer's
  straight rebuys into modified rebuys

NEW TASK TO BE PERFORMED

In seeking a product or service to perform a new task, the problem from the perspective of the buying influence is new and different from any which have arisen in the past.

Either an internal stimulus or an environmental factor may "trigger" the recognition of a requirement. A decision to enter a new product line may require new types of equipment, parts, and materials; a casualty may induce the company to acquire new safety facilities; or a power failure may cause the organization to seek its own electrical generator capability.

This type of buying situation affords the marketer an opportunity to increase his probability of making the sale to the extent that he can precipitate a buying situation within the potential customer organization. Marketing objectives in new task situations aim to spotlight the problem situation and concurrently persuade the buying influences through the proper information that solutions suggested by the marketer represent the best possible alternatives to the problem. In such situations, the customer's requirement may be subsequently molded along lines beneficial to the marketer, substantially increasing his chances of becoming the supplier. The pioneer profits by anticipating and catering to a problem even before it has been explicitly recognized by the customer.

Straight Rebuy

The straight rebuy situation is the most common in industrial purchasing. Here the company considers only the same solutions that it considered the last time that the requirement arose. This differs from the new task because the company has faced this same problem in the past—most probably, many times. The problem is likely to be a continuing or recurring one, so the solution tends to become routinized.

In a straight rebuy, there may be variations from time to time in the quantity purchased, the physical or chemical properties (a different size desk, different weights or types of stationery, etc.), delivery time, method of shipment, or even the price paid, so long as these changes do not entail a reevaluation of the purchasing alternatives nor cause any changes in the procurement procedures and patterns. The purchase may even be made from a different supplier, so long as the selection is made from a previously approved or selected group.

Straight rebuys satisfy continuing or recurring needs in which, for all practical purposes, the basic specifications are closed. The various elements may change somewhat so long as they do not substantially alter the elements of the buying decisions. The alternatives are considered by the buying influences to be both *known* and *unchanged.*   No new evaluation of the alternative solutions is considered necessary.

When there is a high degree of relevant past buying experience, the buyers feel that the information that they possess or can obtain quickly, such as checking a catalog or telephoning a supplier, is sufficient to enable them to make a decision with a high degree of confidence.   The buyer may still believe that he could obtain a more favorable offering if he were to expend the effort to seek it out. But, he believes that the returns from devoting substantially more attention to the purchase would probably be small, relative to the time, effort, and money that would be expended in additional searching.

For items inventoried by buyers, straight rebuys arise when inventories are recognized as having reached reorder points.   For noninventoried items, the buying situation arises when the user identifies the recurrence of a need.

The marketing job required of the supplier depends on whether he is "in" as an accepted supplier.   If he is, the straight rebuy situation may require relatively little marketing effort for a relatively great return.   The supplier needs to provide good competitive service and to emphasize the need for maintaining strong, close user-supplier relationships.   The marketer's job may be to sustain the status quo, but at the same time he must remain alert to needs which may change.   He should anticipate the possibility that a straight rebuy may become a modified rebuy and make sure that his company is in a favorable position when (inevitably) a modified rebuy arises.

For a current nonsupplier, the prospects of becoming a regular source are dubious, unless or until a current supplier forfeits his position or the buyers foresee an advantage in changing or increasing the number of suppliers.   Continued cultivation of the accounts regularly serviced by a competitor may assure the nonsupplier of learning promptly when the potential customer becomes unhappy with his present vendor and may be ready to forsake the straight rebuy for a modified rebuy, thus changing the purchasing rules.   The nonsupplier's chances of becoming the new vendor are thereby enhanced to a considerable degree.

The opportunity for creative and imaginative marketing in such situations may be significant.   Indeed, if the potential vendor is competing with suppliers who are already "known quantities" to the customer, a premium is placed on creative marketing.   The potential supplier may be able to convince the buyer that a customary straight rebuy would be handled more appropriately as a modified rebuy.   If he can thus stimulate the buyer to reevaluate his requirements, the marketer who was instrumental in bringing about the reevaluation will probably be in a favored position for competing in the modified rebuy situation and in future straight rebuys.

Modified Rebuy

In both kinds of rebuy situations, the purchasing participants have at least some relevant buying experience. The differentiating characteristics lie in the customer's perception of the problem and approach to resolving it, specifically in whether or not serious consideration is given to new alternative solutions to the problem. In a straight rebuy, the decision makers neither seek nor seriously consider new alternative solutions. In the modified rebuy, a new evaluation is made of vendors' offerings. In the latter situation, decision makers speculate that gains to be derived from reevaluating alternatives may be significant relative to the effort involved.

The existence of a modify rebuy situation does not necessarily infer that the buyer will, in fact, change either the item purchased or its source. The result may be that he purchases exactly what has been purchased all along—even from the same source. The distinctive element is the reevaluation of alternatives—often the consideration of new ones—prompted by the conviction that it is worthwhile to seek additional information and alternatives before a decision is reached.

A modified rebuy may involve periodic variations among purchases normally handled as straight rebuys. These might be visualized as a series of smooth, routine straight rebuys, periodically interrupted by evaluations which constitute modified rebuys, as follows:

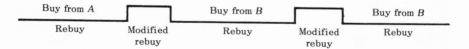

Buy from A		Buy from B		Buy from B
Rebuy	Modified rebuy	Rebuy	Modified rebuy	Rebuy

The illustration shows a small part of a long series of procurements, some of which considered new alternatives. In one instance a new source was selected (from A to B). In the other, the reevaluation led to the retention of the existing supplier (from B to B).

In some companies, such as those typified by mass-production and assembly line operations, buying situations usually may be handled as straight rebuys. In other types of companies, modified rebuys may be the normal rather than the exceptional case. This is likely to be the case when the buying organization operates on a job-shop basis. The manufacturer of oil well drilling rigs, for instance, may require an engine for each unit he produces. Yet each engine may be purchased as a modified rebuy, to take into account various sizes and power requirements, fuel types, customer preferences, and so forth.

Factors Occasioning a Modified Rebuy. An awareness of factors giving rise to a modified rebuy situation is important to the marketer toward fulfilling customer requirements and developing marketing opportunities. Though not always readily differentiable, one of four factors usually motivates the modified rebuy situation. The buying decision makers may anticipate, spontaneously or through persuasion, that a reevaluation of buying alternatives might yield significant cost savings, an improvement in an end product or production process, or improved service benefits from suppliers. The modified rebuy is particularly likely to occur under these circumstances when the buying organization is displeased or only partially satisfied with a current supplier. It can also be instigated by a marketer seeking differential advantage who offers a competitively significant improvement in price, quality, or service.

The fourth factor giving rise to a modified rebuy involves a change in the buying company's purchase requirement. It may reflect internal or environmental elements not even directly related to the buying situation but which nevertheless effectuate a change in purchase requirements. In contrast to the first three motivating factors, this final category is only marginally related to, or even affected by, marketing activities or efforts of the supplier. Examples of factors bringing about changes in the purchase requirements include: significant changes in the scale of buying, such as adding to output capacity; questions of timing in decisions as to when to replace capital equipment; considerations as to a forward buying position for inventoried items; the threat of shortages requiring the buying influences to place more emphasis on the assurance of supply; trade relations considerations; and so forth.

In each situation occasioning a modified rebuy, the buyer seeks more information before arriving at a buying decision and so begins an investigation into alternate suppliers, products, prices, or services. The items being sought are replacements, although not necessarily physically identical to the goods and services currently purchased. The nature of the buying requirements have changed; therefore, a relatively routine repurchase is moved out of the routine category for this particular buying situation. Finally, because the customer's needs have changed, the marketing effort must be transformed in response to the revised aspects of the customer's requirements.

Changes in the Type of Buying Situation

The first time a particular procurement problem arises in a company, it is likely to be handled as a new task situation. A very similar problem arising at a later time and involving basically the same alternatives might also be handled as a new task. This would occur if the buying decision makers perceived the requirement to be sufficiently different or because the buying influences were not aware that a similar problem had already been resolved by another group. A new task approach can also arise if buyers lack confidence that the previous solution was the best one or if the elapsed time is so great that the buying influences believe that the original solution may be out-of-date.

A problem handled as a new task will, as it recurs, tend to become more routinized. As a procurement problem recurs, it will tend to be handled as a straight or modified rebuy. However, there is no rigid, mechanistic sequence for predicting how a particular type of procurement problem will be handled on successive occasions, although new tasks that become part of normal routine do eventually become rebuys of one type or another. Moreover, given a certain need ("we need to drill certain types of holes"), for example, does not imply necessarily which of the three buying situations will prevail. Figures 1 and 1a illustrate the way in which a

FIGURE 1

Decision Network Diagram of the Buying Situations: Special Drill

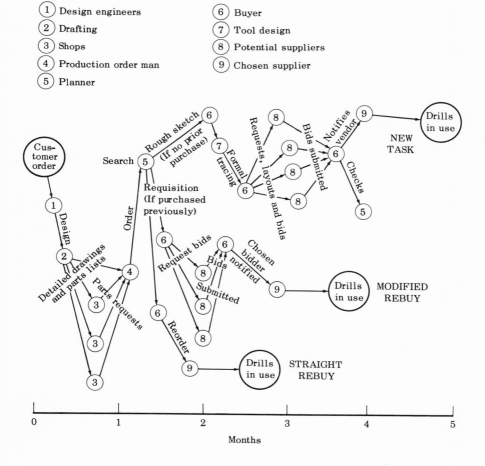

① Design engineers		⑥ Buyer	
② Drafting		⑦ Tool design	
③ Shops		⑧ Potential suppliers	
④ Production order man		⑨ Chosen supplier	
⑤ Planner			

FIGURE 1A
Outline of Buying Situations Involving Special Drill

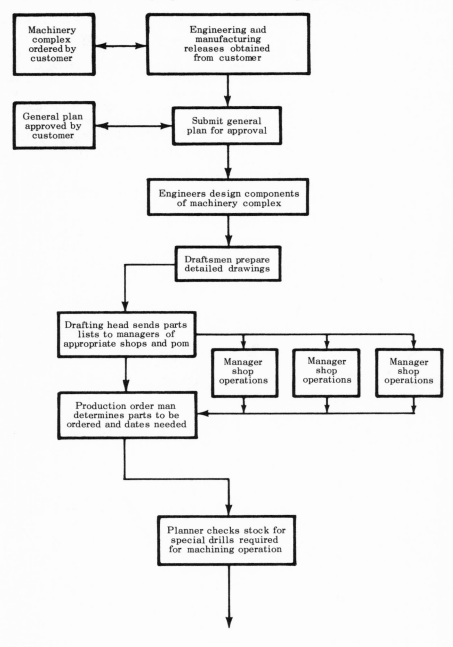

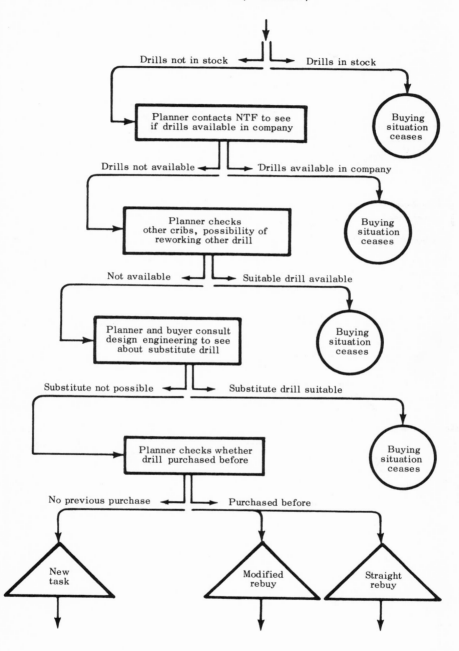

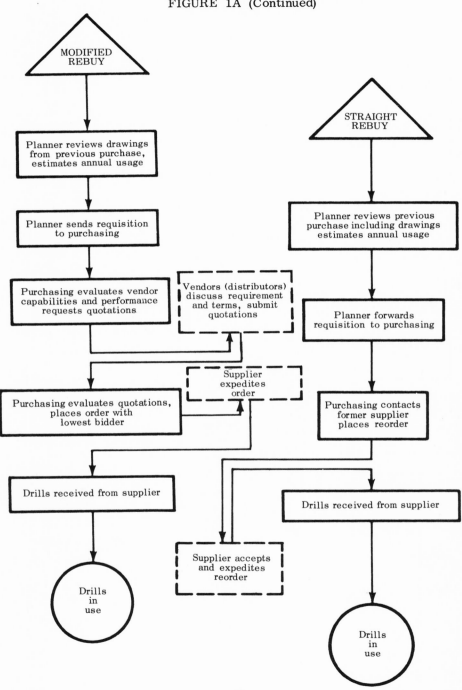

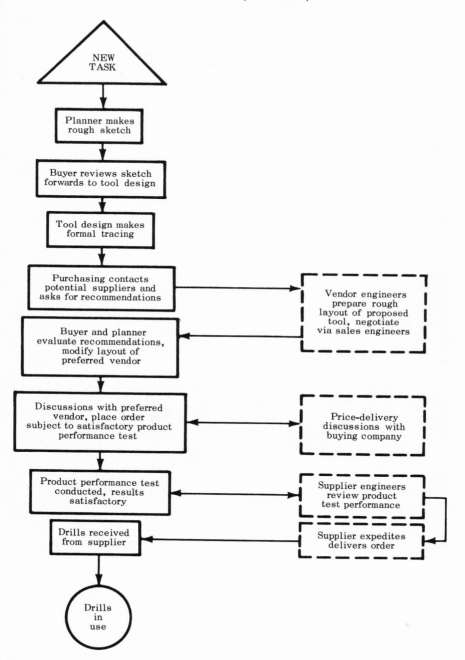

buying procedure can turn into either of the three buying situations and at the same time suggest the importance of the "creeping commitment" phenomenon. It presents the detailed buying procedures by the aid of a pert type decision network diagram (Figure 1) and a logical flow model (Figure 1a).

The distinction between a straight and modified rebuy or modified rebuy and new task can be made either as a conscious decision or develop as a learning function. When the decision maker determines that the cost of handling a problem as a modified rebuy exceeds the probable gain to be realized by the effort, he begins to handle subsequent transactions as straight rebuys. Similarly as users gain knowledge, their information needs and range of alternatives considered are reduced and new tasks develop into modified rebuys. At the same time, the chief purchasing officer should ensure that the system also works to reevaluate straight rebuys periodically to see if they could be better handled as modified rebuys, and similarly if modified rebuys could be better handled as new task situations.

SUMMARY

This chapter introduces the Buyclass framework, according to which all purchase situations may be categorized: the new task, the straight rebuy, and the modified rebuy. The buying situations are classified according to three primary, interrelated criteria: 1. the newness of the problem and the extent to which the decision makers have relevant past buying experience, 2. the amount and type of information demanded by the buying influences before they can make their decisions with confidence, and 3. the number of new alternatives given serious consideration by the buying decision makers in the course of solving the problem.

IV

Analyzing the New
Task-Buying Situation

THE NEXT THREE CHAPTERS are intended to indicate the applicability and utility of the BUYGRID framework for the analysis and understanding of industrial buying situations, and concurrently to demonstrate the dynamic, continuing process of solving acquisition problems which constitute buying. To accomplish this aim a set of selected examples is presented. The new task buying situation is examined in this chapter using three examples. Chapter V will present three illustrations of straight rebuys. Two modified rebuy situations will be analyzed in Chapter VI. The illustrative situations are necessarily disguised in order to protect the identity of the organizations and individuals involved. All the data incorporated in this and the following two chapters derive from direct observations of real buying situations and from interviews with the buying influences and actual decision makers.

Each situational example is first examined with regard to the eight phases of the procurement process. Information requirements peculiar to the particular buying situation are then revealed, and finally, significant characteristics of the procurement process are gleaned from the analysis.

EXAMPLE A—NONSTANDARD LATHE: COMPANY ABLE
(Figures 2 and 3)

The Fundamental Eight Activities of the Procurement Process

1. Anticipation or Recognition of a Problem (Need). Recognition of a need occurs when line production or production engineering people recognize that a forthcoming job cannot be performed with existing equipment or could be performed in a better way by different equipment. In the example of the nonstandard lathe, marketing had sold

a piece of heavy equipment which would require machined components substantially larger than present lathes could handle. The
manufacturing engineer determined that this particular job would
require a lathe with a capacity at least 40 percent greater than the
largest unit the company then had. The "need" is not so easily
defined, however, because Company Able, through its advanced
engineering group, believes that it should anticipate production, and
especially facilities, problems rather than wait for them to arise
and be reported by operating people.

*2. Determination of the Characteristics and Quantity of the Needed
Item.* In determining the characteristics of the lathe to be considered, the manufacturing engineer considered not only the attributes which would be required to undertake the job at hand—i.e.,
capacity and certain dimensional attributes—but also the probable
requirements of other work which might be required over the life
of the new equipment. On these matters he must consider the forecast of the engineering group as to future requirements. In this
case, the forecast and the manufacturing engineer's own expectations of future needs favored a size well beyond that called for by
the immediate need. In addition to the dangers of obsolescence
which buying ahead of current needs involves, overspecifying is
limited by a company policy calling for a payout period of not more
than four years on appropriations.

The characteristics set forth initially by the manufacturing engineer are not more than a general statement of the approximate
capacity, size, length, feed range, speed range, and so on. At this
point, the characteristics are outlined in a letter to the relevant
buyer with a request that appropriate vendors be called in to discuss requirements and to provide general ideas as to the relative
costs of different alternatives.

Since phase 2 requires information from outside the using department and outside of the company, it cannot be completed until
much of phases 3 and 4 has been undertaken. In the first round of
discussions with possible suppliers, basic concepts are refined
and estimates of the possibilities and the costs of alternatives examined. Vendor salesmen participate actively at this point.

Phase 2 also involves initiating procedures to secure internal
financial approval. The justification process is different for a machine tool bought on a capacity basis from that for one to be purchased for cost savings. In either case, various review echelons
appear. The critical one appears to be the corporate manufacturing
services group which must approve all capital appropriations. The
function of this group at this point is to raise questions such as: Is
this the best way to resolve the identified problem? Is solving this
problem worth the cost in terms of overall corporate objectives?

*3. Description of the Characteristics and Quantity of the Needed
Item.* Interchange of ideas with suppliers' salesmen has somewhat

narrowed down the range of choices as to how the problem should be solved. Further consultations with engineering personnel from supplier companies and with internal production and engineering people result in a further defining of what will be sought. With this somewhat refined statement of need, the manufacturing engineer again goes to purchasing, this time with some general specifications. Again suppliers are invited, although not necessarily the same group as before. This time the requirement is more clearly identified and suppliers are asked to outline their respective solutions to the problem. After further discussions, vendors are asked to submit formal proposals and quotations.

When the proposals are received, the manufacturing engineer makes a detailed comparative analysis of the offerings on spread sheets which list each basic unit and every feature which is being offered. The features are weighted as to their importance, priced, and each vendor is rated according to the technical merit of each feature. The manufacturing engineer describes the feature and includes his comments and opinions. The spread sheets are sent to the buyer, who reviews them and discusses them with the engineer to get his (buyer's) own opinion as to the relative desirability of each supplier and each feature.

The process of determining characteristics is thus a joint one involving both buyer and supplier personnel. At the time the spread sheets are prepared, the general solution to the problem has been outlined, but not the actual specifications. These are developed in connection with phase 5 and some, in point of time, actually occur much later.

4. Search for and Qualification of Potential Sources. The number of possible qualified suppliers is likely to be small and will be drawn from a known group constituting the supplying industry. In selecting vendors to invite to the first meetings, suggestions may come from the buyer, the manufacturing engineer, and from other internal personnel. The group is narrowed by lack of interest on the part of some suppliers who receive invitations and as a result of a screening process applied to those who are being considered.

The qualifying process is in two parts. In the first discussions, vendors' salesmen will be asked for basic concepts to solve the problem and about the capabilities of their equipment. Information is also sought on vendors' equipment now in use. These discussions with salesmen lead to the second part which consists of an examination by the manufacturing engineer of vendors' facilities and of discussions with vendor engineering personnel and with users of his equipment. These discussions serve to continue both the process of narrowing down possible suppliers and the process of narrowing down the specifications; they also provide information for the spread sheets.

In this lathe example, one of three suppliers who submitted acceptable designs was disqualified because the buyer and manufacturing engineer doubted their capability to perform. The vendor had never built a lathe of the type and size contemplated, and inspection of his machines in use suggested inadequate construction.

5. *Acquisition and Analysis of Proposals.* The development and analysis of proposals takes place over a period of time, much of it concurrently with the development of specifications. There is a substantial amount of interchange of ideas between the engineering personnel of prospective suppliers and the manufacturing engineer. These consultations involve both a narrowing down of the specification and a process of proposal evaluation and negotiation. The proposals emerging at this point are likely to be the result of discussions in terms of performance attributes rather than in terms of detailed construction specifications. Preliminary quotes are discussed and eventually quotations, expressed in terms of base price and extras, will be submitted. At this point it is not necessary that the proposal embody detail specifications, as the primary interest of the buyer is in what the lathe will do rather than what it looks like. The discussions must, however, provide the information needed for preparation of the spread sheets which the company will use to evaluate the alternatives in the next phase.

6. *Evaluation of Offers and Selection of Suppliers.* In this situation the evaluation of offers is fairly formal, with spread sheets being used to compare the offers of prospective suppliers with respect to the basic unit, the various features, and the terms of sale.

Qualitative ratings are assigned to each factor and the features are weighted as to their importance. A final numerical summary— *i.e.,* a subjective value analysis—is prepared. At this point the dominant role shifts from the manufacturing engineer to the buyer. The buyer brings into consideration a number of factors which are generally outside the concern of the manufacturing engineer, such as trade relations or buy-American considerations. Some of these matters involve the participation of the manufacturing manager or company president. In the particular case studied, the buyer preferred a foreign machine which he believed represented the better value, while the manufacturing engineer wanted an American machine because of known supplier capability as a result of recent work for the company, and because the auxiliaries regularly used with it were those of a well-known firm with which Company Able enjoyed fine relationships. The company president decided upon the domestic unit because of limited precedent for buying foreign machines. Company Able policy appears to discriminate against, but not to bar, foreign suppliers.

The buyer also undertakes negotiations with those suppliers still being considered. These negotiations embrace such matters as price, delivery terms, penalty clauses, payment terms, transportation, and special features.

7. Selection of an Order Routine. Using the detailed specifications
and design concepts which have been prepared by the manufacturing
engineer as a result of the extensive discussions with vendor's engineering staff, the buyer prepares an order for forwarding to the
vendor. Upon receipt, the vendor prepares a sales drawing which
sets the general outline for the lathe. This is not a detailed drawing.

Detailed drawings are prepared after the order has been placed
and over a period of months as the machine is being manufactured.
They are thus more in the nature of shop drawings prepared by the
vendor's design engineers and reviewed in each case by the customer's manufacturing engineer. The final specifications thus do
not really exist except as a set of approved shop drawings as the
machine nears completion. Working relationships are close and
continuous during this period, which may take several months.

Because of the close relationship between supplier's design
engineers and the manufacturing engineer during the production
process, expediting, trouble-shooting, and internal status reporting—usually buyer's functions—are taken over by the manufacturing
engineer. Inspection and testing at the point of production are also
the engineer's responsibility. To assure that the machine is capable of the jobs for which it is designed, samples of the work to be
done on it are sent to the vendor for use in testing.

8. Performance Feedback and Evaluation. Performance feedback
influences the manufacturing engineer's appraisal of the vendor's
capability for future jobs.

Information Requirements for Nonstandard Lathes

1. Information to *define the problem* in both technical and economic contexts. In this case, while the immediate problem
   is to provide the special lathe needed, a determination must
   be made as to other problems likely to arise over the expected
   life of the new equipment. Given that the present job cannot
   be accomplished on any of the existing equipment, is the particular job so unusual that the machining should be contracted
   out? Or is the requirement likely to be a continuing one, so
   that a lathe should be purchased? Information for such a decision comes from the ten-year forecasts of the advanced engineering group, supplemented by any further insurance
   margins which the manufacturing engineer might add.

2. Information on *ways to solve the problem* in a specific sense.
   It is largely technical in character and is provided through
   discussions with salesmen, and subsequently with the engineering design personnel of prospective suppliers.

3. Information on *vendor capability*. This is drawn from the
   experience of the manufacturing engineer, the buyer, and

FIGURE 2
Example of New Task Procurement Process
(Nonstandard Lathe)

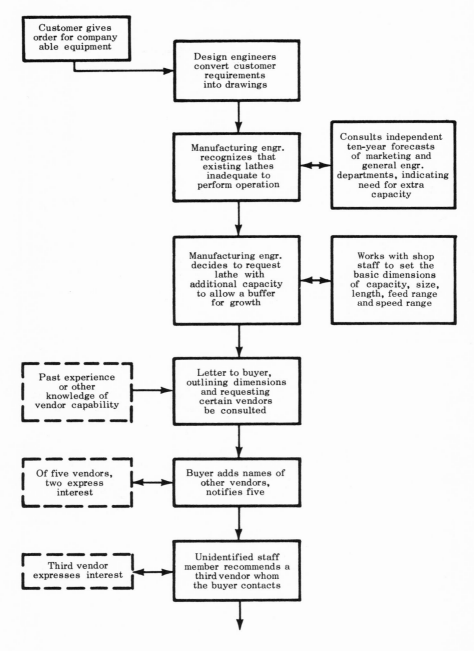

FIGURE 2 (Continued)

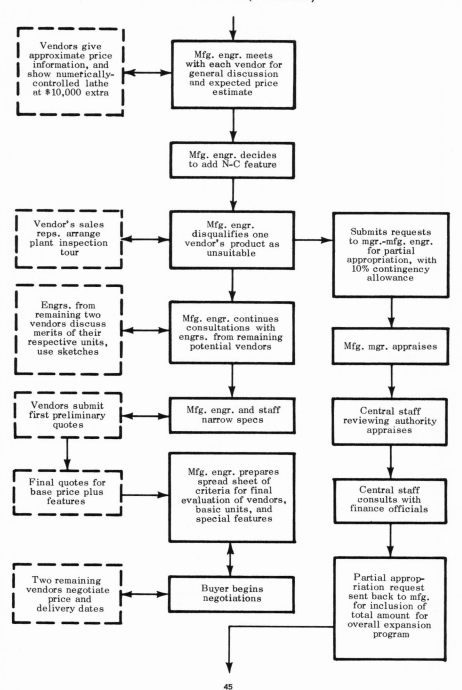

FIGURE 2 (Continued)

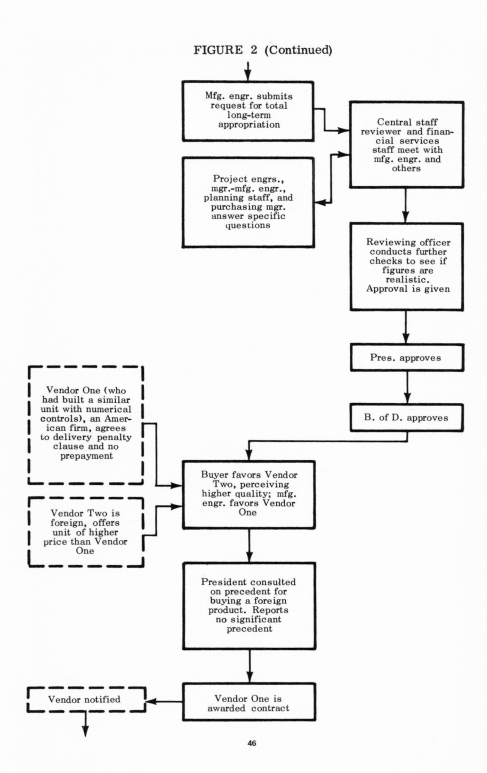

FIGURE 2 (Continued)

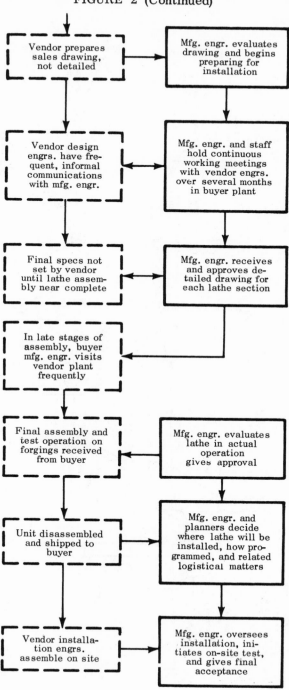

FIGURE 3

Decision Network Diagram of the New Task Procurement Process: Nonstandard Lathe

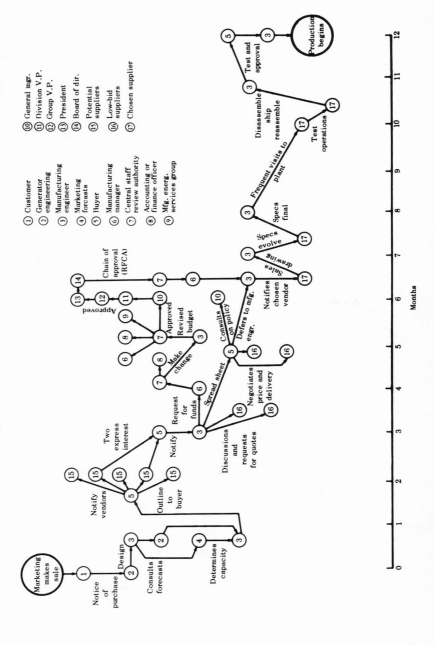

① Customer
② Generator engineering
③ Manufacturing engineer
④ Marketing forecasts
⑤ Buyer
⑥ Manufacturing manager
⑦ Central staff review authority
⑧ Accounting or finance officer
⑨ Mfg, energ, services group
⑩ General mgr.
⑪ Division V.P.
⑫ Group V.P.
⑬ President
⑭ Board of dir.
⑮ Potential suppliers
⑯ Low-bid suppliers
⑰ Chosen supplier

their associates. Plant visits and inspections of equipment in use are also used.

Significant Procurement Characteristics for Nonstandard Lathes

1. Buying a nonstandard machine tool may be viewed as a progressive narrowing of the "solution" to a problem. Supplier and user engineering personnel engage in this "defining" operation jointly.

2. Once the basic problem is solved, economic factors seem to influence features and optional extras.

3. Buying phases 2, 3, and 4 are closely interwoven. Source qualification may be concurrent with or precede determination of what is wanted.

4. Source qualification on "policy" basis (*e.g.*, trade relations) comes fairly late in the process after the major decisions as to the solution have been made.

5. Final specifications are not made until after the supplier has been selected.

6. This company considers future requirements formally, rather than wait for operating people to develop and bring in problems.

7. The buying influence's belief in the capability of a supplier to solve the problem is critical. An inferior solution (or one in which the buyers lack confidence) can be only partially offset by features, and probably not at all by price.

8. There are strong forces for conservatism on the part of specifiers.

EXAMPLE B—STANDARD MACHINE TOOL: COMPANY BAKER
(Figure 4)

The Fundamental Eight Activities of the Procurement Process

1. Anticipation or Recognition of a Problem (Need). Needs are recognized when engineering analyses at the factory level suggest that a new tool is economically justifiable. In the case of equipment needs for the production of new products, this may spring directly from the feasibility work of the project engineers in the production engineering group. Needs appear to arise as part of the process of examining the feasibility of making new products and parts rather

FIGURE 4

Decision Network Diagram of the New Task Procurement Process: Standard Machine Tool

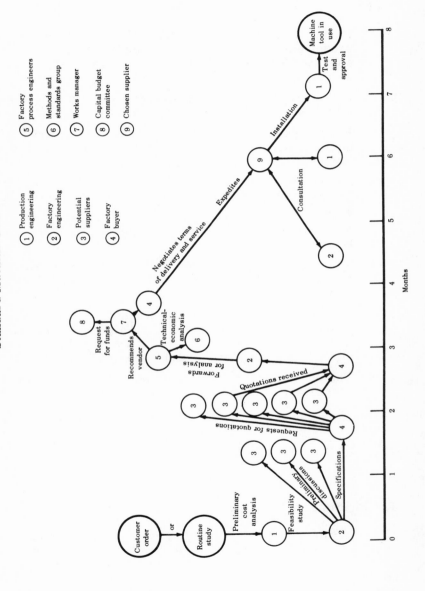

than as a result of any formal procedures of internal search for better methods.

2. Determination of the Characteristics and Quantity of the Needed Item. Production engineering determines what is needed.

3. Description of the Characteristics and Quantity of the Needed Item. Factory engineering, having identified the requirement, formulates specifications and furnishes them to the factory buyer in the form of a request for quotation. In the process of formulating the specifications the factory engineering group will have held preliminary discussions with one or more prospective suppliers. Purchasing officials do not participate in these discussions.

4. Search for and Qualification of Potential Sources. The initial selection is made by the factory engineers in their selection of vendors with whom to discuss their problems. Factory purchasing personnel suggest additional possible suppliers to bring the total number within the company policy of considering three to five sources wherever possible. Even where the engineering group suggests three possible vendors, the buyer is likely to add one or two more, thus serving to broaden the range of alternatives. The policy of considering at least three suppliers is not followed where machine tools are needed for special or nonstandard applications. This suggests that on such applications, the choices made by the engineering group become, in fact, final unless the purchase itself is disapproved at a higher level.

5. Acquisition and Analysis of Proposals. The buyer invites quotations from the sources suggested in phase 4. Quotations are analyzed by a factory process engineer who evaluates each proposal on both technical and economic grounds. He obtains assistance from the methods and standards group.

6. Evaluation of Proposals and Selection of Suppliers. The factory process engineer completes his analysis (phase 5) and selects the supplier. This recommendation is forwarded through the works manager up the line for approval on capital planning and financial grounds.

If approved, the factory then sends a requisition to the buyer directing him to place the order with the designated supplier and to negotiate terms of delivery and service.

7. Selection of an Order Routine. The factory buyer prepares and forwards the purchase order and undertakes expediting and other follow-up activities, including the forwarding and negotiation of change orders.

8. Performance Feedback and Evaluation. If there is any system of performance feedback, it is informal and largely confined to the production and production engineering group within the plant.

Information Requirements for Machine Tools

1. Information to *define the problem.* In Company Baker, this appears to come entirely from internal analyses of the feasibility of performing operations, chiefly in connection with new product proposals.

2. Information on ways of *solving the problem.* Solutions are formulated by factory engineering personnel who determine the ways in which the problem will be solved. There seems to be little drawing upon outside sources. Where such sources are used, factory engineering personnel call upon preferred suppliers for aid.

3. Information on *vendor capability.* Impressions of vendor capability derive from the judgments of the factory engineers who are the key influence in the selection of sources, although factory purchasing may suggest leads.

Significant Procurement Characteristics for Machine Tools

1. The key decisions, both in problem recognition and in the specific purchase, are made by operating engineering personnel subject to the constraints imposed by corporate level capital planning.

2. Factory purchasing personnel serve largely an information function in suggesting alternative sources and providing for the order routine. Corporate level procurement officials may suggest alternatives and act in a reviewing capacity to assure that appropriate consideration of alternatives has taken place.

EXAMPLE C—PACKAGING FOR NEW FABRICATED METAL INDUSTRIAL PRODUCT: COMPANY CHARLIE

The Fundamental Eight Activities of the Procurement Process

1. Anticipation or Recognition of a Problem (Need). The project engineer in the division planning a new product advises the purchasing manager of the general categories of packaging which will be required. In this case four types of materials were required: (a) wrapping paper, (b) polyethylene bagging or tubing, (c) corrugated material, and (d) wire-bound material.

2. Determination of the Characteristics and Quantity of the Needed Item. Preliminary requirements are developed by the project engineer and a potential supplier who has been selected for this purpose (phase 4, below).

3. Description of the Characteristics and Quantity of the Needed Item After the development reaches the stage of fairly firm details, the project engineer asks the purchasing manager to request tests of the proposed materials.

4. Search for and Qualification of Potential Sources. A potential supplier is selected for each item by the purchasing manager to aid project personnel in the development of specifications. Prudent choices here are important because they provide inside tracks for the selected firms and, more importantly, because the selected firm may be expected to have a substantial influence on the specifications. Additional vendors are contacted when it is time to obtain proposals.

5. Acquisition and Analysis of Proposals. When tentative specifications have been reached, the purchasing manager requests three to six suppliers to quote. These quotations are received by the purchasing manager and forwarded to the project engineer, sometimes with the purchasing manager's preferences indicated.

As soon as the specifications have ben set, the project engineer will ask the purchasing manager to request tests. These tests will be performed by the supplier. Where two or more suppliers are being considered, an independent testing agency may be used. Evaluation of the reported test results is undertaken by the project engineer.

6. Evaluation of Proposals and Selection of Suppliers. If test results are satisfactory, a purchase order for sample quantities will be issued. If these samples prove satisfactory, the conditions exist for final negotiation of prices and services with prospective suppliers. In addition to price, such factors as the contribution of the supplier to the development effort, the location of plants which will use the material, a desire for one or more alternate sources for all items, and a preference for existing suppliers will be considered.

7. Selection of an Order Routine. One year blanket contracts are signed with the selected suppliers.

8. Performance Feedback and Evaluation. No formal performance feedback exists, but prior experience with suppliers is the principal criterion in inviting them to participate.

Information Requirements for Packaging for New Product

1. Information to *define the problem*. This is largely a by-product of product development and is provided by the division needing the package.

2. Information on ways of *fulfilling the requirements*. Potential suppliers are called in by the purchasing manager to work with the using departments in developing specifications.

3. Information on the *qualifications of prospective suppliers*. The purchasing manager's prior experience is the principal source.

Significant Procurement Characteristics for Packaging for New Product

1. The purchasing manager's prior experience is the major factor in the selection of suppliers to call in.

2. Because of their active participating in specification writing, invited vendors are likely to become the final suppliers.

3. Because buyers are seeking problem solutions, sellers are likely to have a better opportunity to secure business by proposing solutions to problems than by selling products.

THE PROCUREMENT PROCESS IN NEW TASK SITUATIONS

The goods or services being purchased, the use to which they will be put, as well as a number of environmental influences, will determine the nature and outcome of specific new task situations. Nevertheless, from the foregoing and other procurements traced in the fieldwork, some generalizations can be made about new task procurements.

1. New task buying may be viewed as a progressive narrowing of the solution area for a problem. In some cases, such as the purchase of capital equipment or technically complex or advanced items, user and supplier technical people may work together closely throughout the procurement process. In other instances, such as the purchase of fairly standardized or simple items, there is likely to be much less participation by sellers.

2. The narrowing down process (phases 2 and 3) and the qualification of sources (phase 4) are closely interwoven. In more

involved instances source selection may proceed with, or even precede, the determination of what is needed.

3. Final specifications are likely to follow, rather than precede, the selection of the supplier, especially in more complex situations.

4. Economic considerations and evaluations enter the picture only *after* the basic problem has been solved.

5. Specifiers and buying decision makers are subject to strong pressures which cause them to act cautiously and conservatively. A new item not only involves risk to the buying company, but also involves personal risks for the decision makers. The buyers feel more secure if they use the accepted products and suppliers. They are vulnerable if they try new products or suppliers. Hence, a guarantee, to be an effective marketing aid, must remove or reduce the personal risks of error failures for the buyer.

6. Purchasing personnel are involved in new task situations primarily as information switchers. They are primarily responsible for source discovery and the generation of information about alternatives. They play a limited role in the selection of suppliers.

7. Competition among sellers tends to be qualitative and based on reputation for capability rather than based on comparative costs. The order goes to the supplier, previously screened, who offers the best solution. Therefore, the marketer's best opportunity seems to lie in formulating improved solutions to customers' problems, even when selling a standardized product.

8. Because commitment to a course of action tends to "creep" as the specifications become narrowed, early entry by the supplier into the procurement decision making process is essential.

SUMMARY

The examples described here of the new task procurement process give some indication of the complexity of buying when few or no precedents are available to the decision makers. Application of the BUYGRID framework not only helps to structure this complex decisioning process from an observational point of view, but also helps define a number of decision points at which the marketer (who is aware of precedents in other companies) can assist the buying company in its information acquisition process. This assistance to the buying company can significantly influence the trend of its decision making process in a direction favorable to the selling company.

Perhaps the most significant lesson to be derived from these examples pertains to the considerable amount of communicative interaction occurring between buying company personnel and selling company representatives. It is abundantly evident here that the least part of the salesman's task is that of order taking. He is the communication arm of the selling company, constantly mediating between representatives from the two companies, and it is evident that his ability to ferret out critical decision making points and to provide the kind of data which is meaningful to any given decision maker (be he an engineer or a purchasing agent) has the potentiality of making a substantial difference in the final outcome of the procurement process.

The critical path analyses shown in Figures 3 and 4 give some indication of the long-term nature of new task buying situations. They further stress the role of industrial marketing, and more specifically the salesman, as one of developing and maintaining long-term, dynamic communicative relationships with actual and potential buyers.

V

Analyzing the Straight Rebuy Situation

IT IS THE PURPOSE OF THIS CHAPTER to examine in detail a few examples of the straight rebuy, or routine buying situation. Since the great majority of buying situations, both in quantity and dollar value, fall into this category, it is particularly important to recognize some basic patterns in the accompanying procurement processes, including the critical decision points and information requirements of buying organizations.

EXAMPLE A—FORGINGS: COMPANY ABLE (Figures 5 and 6)

The Fundamental Eight Activities of the Procurement Process

1. Anticipation or Recognition of a Problem (Need). Recognition of the need for a heavy forging follows automatically from receipt of an order for the end item in which it is to be used.

2. Determination of the Characteristics and Quantity of the Needed Item. The sale of the end product has set in motion procedures that are relatively routine (see Figure 5), even though the items to be purchased may be very nonroutine. Phase 2 comes down to the question: What things are we going to have to get if we are to assemble the end product; and, in general, what rough characteristics must these items have? It should be noted that, at this point, no thought has been given to the forging or to what it must look like.

The Company Able salesman and the requisitions engineer (who, in effect, provides the salesman with technical backup) have previously taken the customer's requirements as to what the machinery must do—provided by the customer's engineering staff—and translated them into the requisition summary sheet. This describes in general what the customer is buying. It is sent to the customer for approval.

The approved summary sheet is sent to the product engineering manager.   He then assigns a design engineer to translate these customer requirements into a product specification.   The designer's information comes from his own experience designing similar units, backed up by the engineering manuals that furnish the "boundaries" within which he works.   The overall design of the machinery is circulated to a number of engineering groups charged with designing particular sections of it, and to the requisitions engineer and the drafting group.   These people are concerned with the question: Can you design your part of the machinery to meet the customer's requirements and do so within this overall design?   One or more meetings will be held by this group, and revisions will be made in the overall design until all agree that they can work with it.   Even up to this point, no specific thought has been given to specific forgings.

3. *Description of the Characteristics and Quantity of the Needed Item.*   The more detailed part of the specifying process begins when the overall design has been approved and is given to the drafting group to prepare the one-quarter scale layout.   This is a detailed cross section of the completed machinery complex, showing all items that go into it.   It is at this point that the draftsman first must determine the configuration of the particular forging studied here. These one-quarter scale layouts are critically reviewed by those attending the design meetings, and necessary modifications are made.   Sooner or later the one-quarter scale layout is approved, and the final design is frozen.

The draftsmen obtain information on the general characteristics of the forgings from the appropriate design engineer.   In addition, the draftsmen use various company and general engineering handbooks to resolve questions which may arise concerning the basic capabilities, limitations, or design characteristics of the items they are drawing.   The drawings are consolidated and reviewed and sent to the manager of drafting administration.

Detailed parts lists are prepared from the drawings.   These parts lists contain a listing of every item that goes into the machinery.   These items are listed by drawing number, so the company and its suppliers can see exactly what the item's dimensions must be and what functions it must perform.

Responsibility for ordering and manufacturing is in the hands of the production people—the manager of shop operations and his deputy, the production order man.   Their authority to procure a forging is in the form of a manufacturing instruction issued by the manager of drafting.   It will be followed by that portion of the parts lists under the cognizance of the manager of shop operations.   The manager of shop operations' group is generally responsible for transforming that portion of the parts list pertaining to the manager of shop operations' product area into order cards for specific products.   Distinctions are made between items never ordered before, ordered before and not stocked (the situation pertaining here), and ordered before and stocked. Order cards specifying a particular item by drawing number (so its exact dimensions and characteristics are known) are sent to purchasing.

To this point the participants have been primarily technicians in the using departments and those of the customer. Except as these people have drawn on handbooks, the influence of sellers of forgings would appear to be nil.

4. Search for and Qualification of Potential Sources. When the buyer receives the order card from the production people and sees that it calls for a heavy forging, he knows that there are only three approved suppliers for forgings of this size. Since the buyer has forgings on order with all three suppliers, he is in contact with each supplier at least once a week. Hence, he has very good information as to each supplier's work load, ability, and interest in bidding on the new equipment.

5. Acquisition and Analysis of Proposals. With the order card from production and a copy of the relevant drawing, the buyer sends a copy of the drawing to each prospective vendor, inviting proposals containing prices and delivery dates. In about two weeks, the three replies will have been received. The buyer takes no action, nor does he contact any of the potential suppliers, until he has heard from all of them.

6. Evaluation of Proposals and Selection of Suppliers. When all three bids have been received, the buyer determines who will get the order. Principal considerations are price, delivery, and the need to keep all three suppliers interested. The order is usually given to the lowest bidder. However, the prices quoted are typically quite close, so the buyer is concerned with delivery dates and with dividing his heavy forging business as nearly as possible into three equal parts. There may be several telephone calls between the buyer and the suppliers. "Joe is two cents lower than you are, but your delivery is better. Can you come down two cents to get the order?" The vendor will usually do so, so Company Able usually gets whatever supplier it selects at the lowest price quoted by any vendor. "As low a price" may be the result rather than the actual cause of getting the order.

Delivery is crucial: Early delivery inflates inventory and causes storage problems; late delivery holds up assembly operations. The timing problem is complicated by two factors. As lead times are long and the forging manufactured to order, the dates given by vendors are merely estimates as they see things at the time. In addition, various steps are performed to make a forging, and it may be completely ruined in the last stages of its production. Hence, absolute reliability of delivery cannot be assured. It takes several months to get another forging if one is ruined.

7. Selection of an Order Routine. The order is usually given over the telephone by the buyer and is followed up with an official purchase order.

Expediting and trouble-shooting activities are among the buyer's major concerns. As mentioned, the delivery dates quoted by the supplier are only estimates and are constantly changing, almost always being pushed back rather than brought forward. The buyer secures status information weekly by telephone on every forging on order—and there are many at any given time. He maintains a complete file of this information.

The vendor performs various inspections and tests as the forging is made, and the buyer is aware of the results through his weekly telephone status check. When the forging has been completed, the vendor subjects it to a series of tests. He then furnishes a certificate to the buyer that the tests have been performed, and gives the results.

Upon receipt of the forging, it is subjected to a similar battery of tests by the manufacturing people before the invoice is passed for payment.

Since the buyer has an intimate knowledge of how long it takes to perform each step in making a forging, he has a good idea of when he can expect delivery of any particular one. He reports the status of all forgings weekly to the production order man. This information is passed upstream within the manufacturing division. The complete status of every machine on order is reviewed at weekly meetings, and production and shipping schedules are adjusted as necessary.

8. Performance Feedback and Evaluation. Feedback on performance is limited to that secured through operation of the exception principle. Unless there is a complaint, the product is assumed to have been satisfactory.

Information Requirements for Forgings

1. Information on *specific needs*. Requirements are highly technical. The data is secured from standard manuals and from engineering personnel with design responsibilities. These engineers have a primary information-gathering responsibility to keep abreast of new developments in the design of the types of machinery sold by Company Able through reading, participation in professional groups, and attendance at trade shows. They write the manuals used by the designers. For products of this type, supplier influence must generally be aimed primarily at this level—at the advance engineering groups who establish the permissible characteristics rather than the design engineers themselves. It is the advance engineering group which also suggests problem areas to suppliers.

FIGURE 5
Example of a Straight Rebuy Procurement Process
(Forgings)

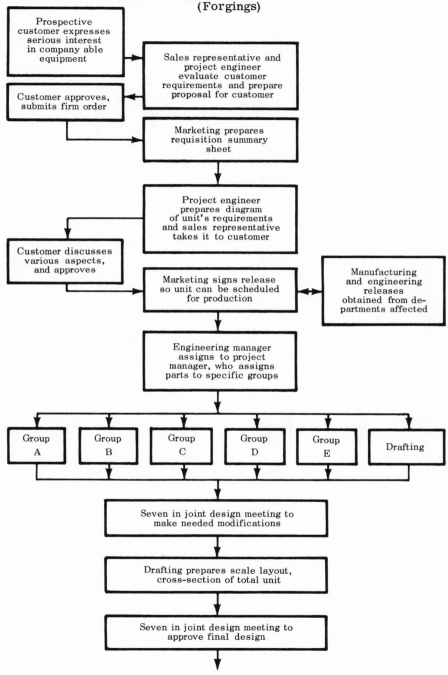

FIGURE 5 (Continued)

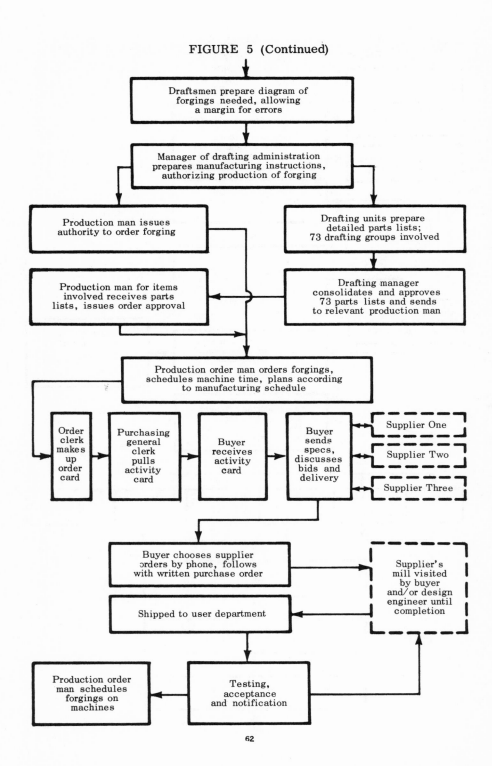

FIGURE 6

Decision Network Diagram of the Straight Rebuy Procurement Process: Forgings

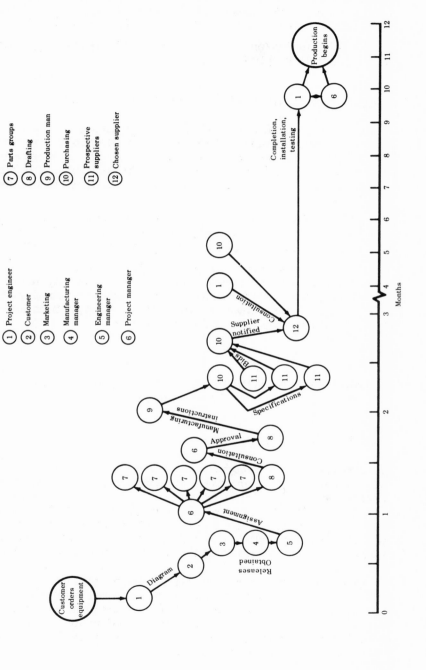

2. Information on *supplier capability*. The list of eligible suppliers is small and established. Information pertaining to vendors' work loads, their ability to meet schedules, and interest in bidding is obtained by the purchasing functionary.

3. Information on *prices*. The buyer invites proposals from eligible suppliers.

Significant Procurement Characteristics for Forgings

1. Since the general technology of building the end product is fairly well established, important elements of routinization appear in the procurement of forgings. A large amount of technical information must be utilized, but this is largely if not entirely within the internal capabilities of the designing staff.

2. Previous experience with suppliers and their small number leads to close working relationships, primarily in terms of scheduling and delivery rather than technical matters.

3. Given the small number of eligible suppliers and explicit predetermined specifications, the purchasing man has full responsibility for selecting the vendor and subsequent dealings. Note, however, that he has no specification or pre-specification role in this instance.

EXAMPLE B—NONDURABLE TOOLS (DRILLS): COMPANY ABLE (Figure 7)

The Fundamental Eight Activities of the Procurement Process

1. Anticipation or Recognition of a Problem (Need). Recognition of need for a drill or other nondurable tool which has been purchased before can arise in two ways. In the case of tools which are inventoried, the need will be recognized automatically when the inventory reaches a pre-determined reorder point. For items which are not carried in inventory, the need is recognized in the same way as for similar items being purchased for the first time.

2. Determination of the Characteristics and Quantity of the Needed Item. For noninventoried items, the general determination of the need is the same as described for first-time procurements. Information is obtained on how the recognized problem can be solved and, if purchase is indicated, a determination is made whether the tool has been previously purchased.

If the tool has been previously purchased, it will be listed in the catalog of tools which have been purchased by the company. The drawings are obtained from the vault and the planner estimates yearly usage. (Phase 2 does not apply to stock replenishments.)

3. Description of the Characteristics and Quantity of the Needed Item. For a noninventoried item, the planner's estimate of yearly usage will provide the basis for a decision by the relevant buyer as to the quantity to be ordered on this procurement.

On inventoried items which have reached their reorder points, the quantities to be ordered are determined by the application of an economic order quantity formula.

4. Search for and Qualification of Potential Sources. Where the need has originated because of the demands of a particular job rather than because of inventory depletion to a reorder point, the buyer selects those vendors from an eligible group of six to eight who are deemed most capable of providing the particular tool—the same procedure as for an initial procurement. Although the vendor who first provided an item involving design work by the supplier is sometimes given the opportunity to bid on a noncompetitive basis for one order beyond the first, the general practice is to request quotes from four to seven vendors on all rebuys. For the most part, these vendors will be distributors rather than manufacturers. When appropriate, competitive performance runs are made.

Similar practice governs the selection of vendors from whom to seek quotes on nonstandard tools needed because of inventory depletion. In the latter case all of the vendors will be distributors. Standard drills carried as inventory items are purchased on an annual requirements contract with a local distributor.

5. Acquisition and Analysis of Proposals. Except in the case of standard tools ordered because of inventory status, the purchasing department requests proposals for specific tools from appropriate vendors. Bids are received in two to four weeks.

Since standard inventoried items are purchased under annual requirements contracts, when reorder points are reached the appropriate quantity is determined from an economic order quantity formula and ordered from the distributor holding the contract for the current year. Most such tools are obtained under Company Able's distributor stock program. Under this program, Company Able agrees to buy all items covered by the contract which is awarded on a price basis. The distributor in turn agrees to carry a minimum stock of at least three times Company Able's own inventory of the item and more than twice the inventory which Company Able would need to carry if the distributor did not stock the item. Because of the stocking obligation, Company Able feels that it pays perhaps 10 percent higher prices under the program. For this, it saves the inventorying burden.

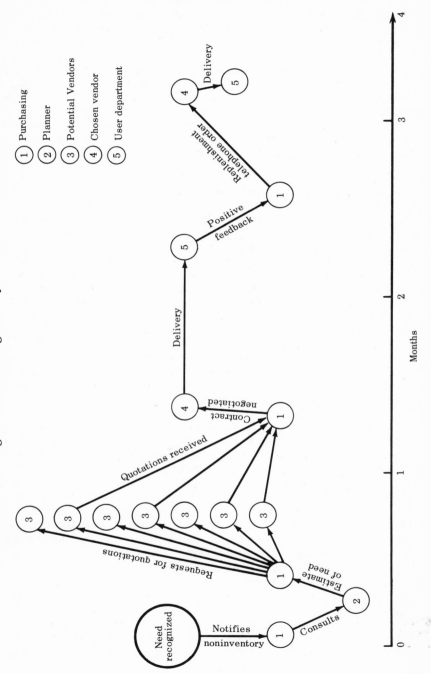

FIGURE 7

Decision Network Diagram of the Straight Rebuy Procurement Process: Drills

1 Purchasing
2 Planner
3 Potential Vendors
4 Chosen vendor
5 User department

66

Annual contracts are also signed with distributors for items not covered by the distributor stocking program, but these are open contracts involving neither commitment for business nor obligation to stock.

6. Evaluation of Proposals and Selection of Suppliers. For standard stocked drills the evaluation takes place at the time of annual contracting. Thereafter, selection is routine and, in the case of distributor stocking program items, obligatory.

For all nonstandard drills, awards are made to the lowest bidder.

7. Selection of an Order Routine. Standard stocked items under distributor stock program contracts are ordered by phone for same-day or next-day delivery by the single-source, distributor-supplier. Regular purchase orders are sent in other cases.

8. Performance Feedback and Evaluation. There may be none, except as secured through the exception principle. Unless there is a complaint, the drills are assumed to perform satisfactorily.

Information Requirements for Nondurable Tools (Drills)

1. Information on *specific needs*. Except for purchases derived from inventory management routines, the need is developed by the planner who determines how a particular machining operation is to be performed and the tools needed to do the job. Internal sources are then used to determine if the drill is stocked or, if not stocked, if drawings for it are on hand as a result of a prior purchase. If a purchase is required, estimates of usage are made by the planner to assist in determining the quantity to buy.

2. Information on *supplier capability*. Only limited data is needed. For items under distributor stocking programs, the supplier has previously been selected. For other items, all that is required is inquiry of approved distributors as to their ability to provide the specific item.

3. Information on *prices*. Bids are requested from approved vendors, in the less complex cases by telephone.

Significant Procurement Characteristics for Nondurable Tools

1. Rebuys tend to be routinized. Search, and thus the opportunity for "out" suppliers, tends to be limited.

2. At least in Company Able, buyers are willing to pay higher prices if vendors will assume inventorying responsibilities.

EXAMPLE C—COMPONENTS, PARTS, AND MATERIALS FOR CURRENT PRODUCT: COMPANY BAKER

The Fundamental Eight Activities of the Procurement Process

1. Anticipation or Recognition of a Problem (Need). Need recognition on rebuys follows directly from production scheduling. Blanket orders are used and production scheduling determines when goods are desired. For some parts and components, IBM-controlled inventories are maintained.

2. Determination of the Characteristics and Quantity of the Needed Item.

3. Description of the Characteristics and Quantity of the Needed Item. In the "rebuy" buying situation, recognition of need embraces determination of what and how much is required.

4. Search for and Qualification of Potential Sources. As blanket orders are in force, the supplier is known; phases 4 through 6 do not apply unless consideration is given to alternative suppliers. Resourcing may be considered: 1. when a nonsupplier makes an attractive proposal, 2. when the supplier advises of a significant increase in price, say five percent, 3. when a supplier has proven not fully satisfactory in product or service, or 4. as a result of the annual price review process attendant to the company's setting the standard costs for the year. In these cases a modified rebuy situation has developed.

5. Acquisition and Analysis of Proposals. The use of blanket orders does away with the need to obtain quotations on routine replenishments, although some negotiation may be involved when suppliers advise of a price change or in connection with the annual price review process. Nonsuppliers may submit proposals as noted above in their efforts to obtain some or all of the business.

6. Evaluation of Proposals and Selection of Suppliers. An item may be resourced as a result of a change in the make/buy decision or because an attractive offer suggests changing suppliers. Economic considerations are often tempered by the desire to maintain stable relationships with vendors.

In the more routine situation, blanket orders eliminate the need to consider sources.

7. Selection of an Order Routine. Order routines are tied to production scheduling. In the case of IBM-controlled inventoried items, authorizations are issued under the blanket orders advising suppliers as to quantities to ship, quantities to fabricate, and even amounts of raw materials to buy in anticipation of forthcoming requirements.

8. Performance Feedback and Evaluation. Plant quality control and materials handling departments appraise vendor's service and quality of product on the initial selection of each vendor but not on a continuing basis. The coordinator in the process engineering group makes continuous reevaluations of performance during production. The production control department has two means by which to feed back the results: asking purchasing for remedial action and objecting to a proposed vendor on the basis of prior experience.

Information Requirements on Components, Parts and Materials for Current Product

1. Information on *specific needs*. Obtained from production schedules and automated inventory management routines.
2. Information on *supplier capability*. Not needed, except as performance may be unsatisfactory.
3. Information on *prices*. Provided by supplier. Reviewed annually in connection with establishment of cost standards.

Significant Procurement Characteristics of Components, Parts and Materials for Current Product

1. Operations are highly routinized. Rebuys are tied closely to production planning and inventory management routines.
2. Pressures to consider new alternatives are relatively weak. Thus, existing suppliers have a measure of security until some event (*e.g.*, large price increase) occurs which calls for review. Nonsuppliers have full burden of converting to modified rebuy if they wish to participate.

THE PROCUREMENT PROCESS IN STRAIGHT REBUY SITUATIONS

There are many different types of straight rebuys. Some involve the purchase of identical products on an almost automatic reorder basis, while others may involve the repurchase of items which differ in dimensions, cost, quality, and the supplier from whom they are purchased. All straight rebuys, however, are characterized by the fact that the problem to be solved is not a new one, and no really new alternatives are considered. A few tentative generalizations about straight rebuys are suggested here:

1. The role of the purchasing department in need recognition and in supplier selection is stronger than the roles of any other buying influences. Frequently, the purchasing agent is the only significant buying influence. The purchasing department tends to play a stronger role in straight rebuys than it does in either modified rebuys or new tasks.

2. While the buyers seek creative problem solutions in new tasks, in straight rebuys they seek assurance of supply. They must be assured that the supplier's delivery and general marketing performance are completely reliable.

3. In straight rebuys, the center of gravity or the critical phases in the procurement process tend to occur in the later stages—when obtaining and analyzing proposals evaluating offers, or selecting sources.

4. Straight rebuys are by no means confined to the procurement of low value items. In Company Able, for example, an important component which is purchased in relatively high quantities, and costs from $10,000 to $20,000 each, is handled as a straight rebuy.

5. In order to minimize effort and expenditure, purchasing departments attempt to routinize straight rebuys as much as possible. Even when the item itself is nonstandard (*e.g.,* where dimensional tailoring is required) attribute decisions are made by the using department and the purchasing operation may still be routinized.

6. Pressure for technological and quality improvements does exist in straight rebuys and is usually generated inside the buying company. Suppliers are not normally expected to become involved in this upgrading, nor to suggest new solutions. The job of the non-supplier who wants to become a supplier may be considered to be that of getting the procurement changed from a straight to a modified rebuy.

SUMMARY

Although information on specific ways of solving problems is sometimes required in straight rebuys, most of the information gathered in the more routine cases is concerned with supplier capability, performance, and prices. Since the needs are repetitive, the technical information requirements can be obtained from internal manuals, drawings, parts lists, and so forth. Some supplier participation may be involved when the product is complex and made to order, but usually the major technical issues are resolved during earlier buying situations involving the particular item. The information needed is likely to be limited to less complex design questions, such as dimensions or required strengths.

The flow of information is generally from internal technical to purchasing personnel, although some information flows from purchasing to designer-specifiers on such matters as sizes and grades available and limits of vendor capability.

An important task of purchasing is the identification and selection of suppliers. As continuity of supply is often important to buyers in their efforts to routinize procurements, purchasing personnel may be judged on how well they develop and maintain working relationships with suppliers. Information on supplier availability and capability, especially capability to meet scheduled needs, is important in straight rebuys. Information on past supplier performance comes from records of the buyer and, in some cases, the using department. Information on prices is gathered by buyers but is probably less important in straight rebuys than where new alternatives are being considered, *i.e.*, modified rebuys.

A significant ingredient in the straight rebuy situation is buyer commitment whether economic, legal, or psychological. Economic and legal commitments are generally organizational and involve financing, credit policies, and various contractual relationships. Psychological commitment, on the other hand, involves individual buyers and sales representatives and is far more subtle and complex than is often realized.

From the supplier's, or the marketer's, point of view, psychological commitments can clearly be both favorable and unfavorable. That is, a significant decision influence in the buying company can be committed to a given seller because he perceives certain benefits peculiar to him in the relationship. He can also be committed against a given seller for purely personal reasons. Although the present study did not reveal sufficient data on this point to allow for generalizations, there are at least indications that such personal commitments are significant variables in the buyer-seller relationship.

The key factor in the straight rebuy situation, however, derives from this concept of commitment and pertains to the information requirements of the buying influences. The more a buyer ''knows'' about a given component, the less he needs to rely on the seller's guarantee or reputation for quality. Consequently, an aspiring supplier is faced not only with possible commitments between a potential buyer and a competitor but also with the fact that the buyer is convinced that he ''knows'' everything he needs to know about the product in question.

Clearly, many straight rebuy situations eventually become modified rebuys or even new tasks by virtue of environmental changes such as market requirements. This does not dispute the contention, however, that the basic problem facing the seller, attempting to capture an account which is already routinely attached to a competitor, is essentially *educational*. Even a product which is substantially better than the competitor's may be unable to gain access to the buying organization on its own for the simple reason that the buyer already ''knows'' everything significant to him about that particular product and has turned his attention to other, more pressing, problems. Few salesmen are capable of achieving change in the face of routine purchasing procedures, primarily because they are deliberately trained to behave in a decidedly routinized manner themselves. The communication problem involved here is particularly emphasized in the straight rebuy situation where the buyer is not deliberately searching for information; consequently, he has little reason to consider the salesman anything but a nuisance.

VI

Analyzing the Modified
Rebuy Situation

THE MODIFIED REBUY CATEGORY ENCOMPASSES buying situations which are neither entirely structured, since the buyer does not possess all the information required to complete the procurement process, nor entirely open-ended, for the buyer does have some relevant information. Modified rebuy situations develop as new task situations gradually become routinized, or from a customary straight rebuy situation which has been opened to question. As discussed in Chapter III, factors which most frequently give rise to a modified rebuy situation include the following:

1. A change in the required *specifications* of the buyer's end product,

2. Efforts on the part of the buyer and supplier, to *improve* a given end product or production prices,

3. Efforts, on the part of the buyer, to explore opportunities for *cost savings*,

4. Efforts, on the part of the buyer, to obtain improved *service* from suppliers, or efforts on the part of suppliers to offer and implement an improved service package.

The conditions which cause the modified rebuy situation to develop obviously influence the buying company's orientation and standards for evaluating suppliers. This chapter presents, as examples, two representative modified rebuy situations from a selection studied in the fieldwork.

EXAMPLE A—HYDRAULIC PUMP: COMPANY BAKER
(Figures 8 and 9)

The Fundamental Eight Activities of the Procurement Process

1. Anticipation or Recognition of a Problem (Need).   In this case, hydraulic pumps were in use as components and purchased as routine rebuys when a nonsupplier brought about a reconsideration of sources by offering a substantially lower price. In this company source reevaluation might have resulted as well from a price increase by the regular supplier or through the continuous reevaluation program of production engineering toward cost savings.   (See Figure 8 for a graphical outline of the procurement process.)

2. Determination of the Characteristics and Quantity of the Needed Item.   No new determination involved.

3. Description of the Characteristics and Quantity of the Needed Item.   The determination of the needed item and its description were not separate, identifiable phases.   These decisions had been made, in effect, much earlier, during the initial new task decision process which determined the specifications of the hydraulic pump to be used in the particular end product.   In most modified rebuys these phases are virtually automatic, as a result of earlier new task situations and their outcomes.

4. Search for and Qualification of Potential Sources.   The initiative came from the aspiring supplier's salesman who approached and convinced the purchasing agent at Company Baker of his company's qualifications to provide the pumps.

5. Acquisition and Analysis of Proposals.   There was no search for proposals by Company Baker.   The proposals originated with the would-be supplier.   Although the purchasing agent has the responsibility for seeking out alternative sources of supply on his own initiative, pressures to do so are usually lacking.   As a result, purchasing agents originate action only infrequently.   Company Baker's preferences for single sourcing and for maintaining established relationships tend to discourage later new supplier development activities by the purchasing agents.   In this regard, the dominance of engineering and marketing in the original new task supplier selection also should be noted.

6. Evaluation of Proposals and Selection of Supplier.   Two issues are involved in evaluating an offer from a nonsupplier.   First, does the price advantage warrant departure from the company's policy of single sourcing and maintaining strong relationships with suppliers?   The single sourcing policy is supported by simplification of repair parts, work and inventories, and by the desire to routinize recurring purchases to the fullest extent.   In this example, the purchasing agent believed that the addition of a second and lower-priced supplier would cause the primary supplier to reduce his own prices.

FIGURE 8
Example of Modified Procurement Process:
Hydraulic Pump

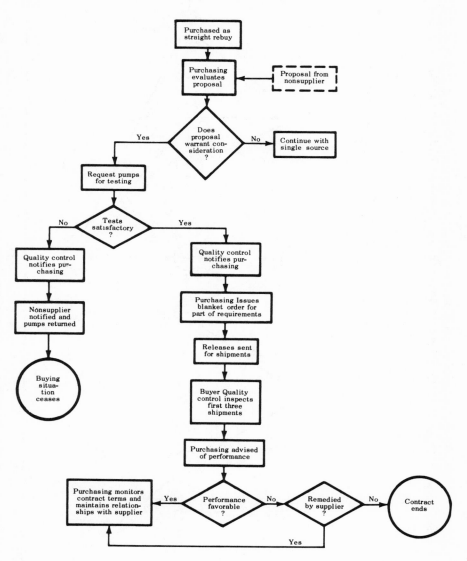

FIGURE 9

Decision Network Diagram of the Modified Procurement Process: Hydraulic Pump

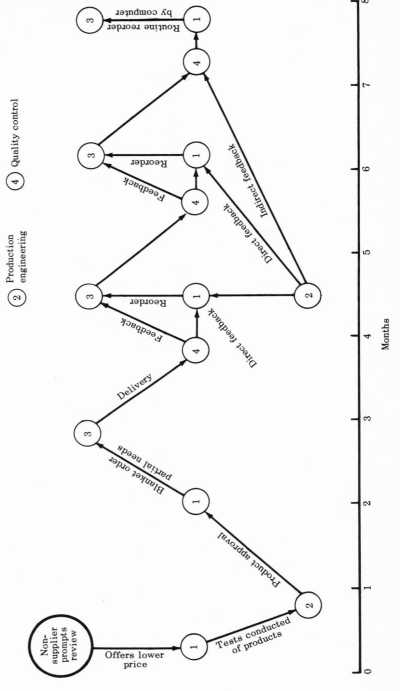

76

Subsequent developments proved the purchasing agent's assessment to be correct. Second, extended tests are run to determine if the product of the proposed supplier will perform satisfactorily. The direct costs of these tests are borne by the prospective supplier if his product fails to pass the test, but are absorbed by Company Baker if the product is acceptable. In this example, the new hydraulic pumps passed all tests satisfactorily.

Because of Company Baker's commitment to a philosophy of stable relationships with suppliers, the new supplier was only considered as a secondary source, to receive some 20 percent of Company Baker's pump requirements. In spite of the substantial price differential, no thought was given to replacing the existing pump supplier.

7. Selection of an Order Routine. Blanket orders are issued. Inventory management is computerized and provides for issuance of releases to vendors, indicating the number of pumps to ship. The normal lead time for pumps is four weeks. In addition, the release system indicates future requirements so that suppliers can schedule fabrication and materials procurement. The purchasing department's role under blanket orders is limited to monitoring contractual terms and maintaining relationships with vendors.

A quality control group inspects incoming products, at least of the first three deliveries from a new supplier. In the event of problems, quality control may make suggestions for remedial action directly to suppliers or may refer difficulties to the purchasing department.

8. Performance Feedback and Evaluation. Performance feedback is primarily limited to possible objections raised by engineering personnel to the acquisition of parts or components from a given supplier in future procurements.

Information Requirements for Hydraulic Pumps

1. The *problem is defined* when the prospective vendor's proposal is analyzed and potential cost savings are recognized.

2. *Resolution of the problem* requires information about the prospective supplier's qualification to meet quality and service standards and whether estimated cost savings will actually materialize through resourcing.

3. *Vendor qualifications* are determined by extensive product testing; in some cases by quality control inspections of vendor facilities.

Significant Procurement Characteristics for Hydraulic Pumps

1. This procurement was shifted from a straight rebuy to a modified rebuy as a result of action by a nonsupplier and not as a result of a search for benefits by the buying organization;

2. Simplification in stocking and servicing repair parts is supported by policies of single sourcing and long-term relationships with suppliers. The attractiveness of such policies is further reinforced by tendencies to program or automate production planning and inventory management operations.

EXAMPLE B—PIPING ELBOWS: COMPANY ABLE (Figure 10)

The Fundamental Eight Activities of the Procurement Process

1. Anticipation or Recognition of a Problem (Need). The need for a procurement is recognized when the production order man, who initiates orders against the blanket procurement, notes that the quantity of large diameter piping elbows provided for in the current blanket contract is practically exhausted. He notifies the appropriate design engineer who reviews the manufacturing schedule for the next 18 months and determines the number of assemblies that will be needed, their specifications, and components, including elbows. In this case, a redefinition of performance requirements for the ultimate product, a machinery complex, had transpired since the last blanket order contract for piping elbows was made. A one percent increase in machine performance had been guaranteed by the sales department, and this put pressure on the designers to find ways to increase efficiency. They recognized that an increment in efficiency could be realized by shifting from the more economical lobsterback (mitred) construction to an elbow of smooth construction.

2. Determination of the Characteristics and Quantity of the Needed Item. Since belows are relatively standard products, determination of characteristics required is largely a matter of calculating the different sizes and types which will be needed for the blanket order. In this situation, the information came from examining the designs of machinery on order from Company Able. If a new application were involved the material engineering group would be consulted on setting materials specifications.

3. Description of the Characteristics and Quantity of the Needed Item. The machinery designs are forwarded to the drafting department, where they are converted to detail drawings and parts lists. These are sent to the production order man. Order cards are then prepared for use by purchasing.

4. Search for and Qualification of Potential Sources. Eligible suppliers for this item have previously been determined, the materials engineering group having approved three suppliers. Generally the policy on fairly standardized items of this type is to have at least three potential vendors in order to insure competition and not more than five vendors so that the company's business is important enough to the supplier to provide the basis for good supplier-user relationships.

5. Acquisition and Analysis of Proposals. Requests for quotations are sent to the qualified suppliers. If, as is usually the case, the suppliers have queries on technical matters, the buyer puts the vendor in touch with the design engineer. If phone conversations indicate to a vendor that he can do the job, meetings between the vendor's salesman and the design engineer are arranged to resolve further questions.

Suppliers then quote on the entire blanket order. These quotations may become the basis of negotiations.

6. Evaluation of Proposals and Selection of Suppliers. Decision is made on the basis of price and the desire to maintain multiple suppliers. In the case example studied, the order was split, giving each of two suppliers the type of elbows lying within their especial capability. This was done to bring in a new supplier who might become an important source for one type.

7. Selection of an Order Routine. Detailed blanket purchase orders are forwarded to the vendors; in addition, both the vendor (manufacturer) and his local distributor are advised by phone.

As particular elbows are required against the blanket order, the production order man will advise the buyer. He will in turn place an order by phone, followed by written confirmation, with the local distributor. Any special machining or shipping instructions are sent by the buyer directly to the manufacturer at this time.

The production order man retains status responsibility. Whether on initial order or on a routine order against the blanket contract, he has the responsibility for assuring the availability of parts required for assembly. A group of assistants act as expediters to keep track of the status of all items to be brought together.

8. Performance Feedback and Evaluation. On parts, performance feedback is necessarily of the exception type. If they should fail in use, it is unlikely that they will be used again unless the occurrence is infrequent and their supplier moves rapidly to remedy the situation without cost to Company Able or to its customer.

Information Requirements for Large Diameter Piping Elbows

1. Because the item is fairly standardized and its nature and function accepted, information requirements are rather limited. Information *to define the problem* comes from the production order man's recognition of the status of existing blanket orders and the design engineer's examination of manufacturing commitments. The material's engineer draws on other in-house technical personnel for more detailed definition of the problem when required.

2. Information requirements on *alternative solutions* to the problem are limited because this is basically a reorder situation. However, the design engineer can call on the materials engineering group for information on possible substitute materials or processes. He calls on this group for guidance when a new application is involved.

3. *Information to qualify vendors* comes from the design engineer's experience which is passed on to the buyer via the engineering release letter approving a proposed supplier.

   Vendors without previous experience with Company Able can become qualified vendors by taking the initiative and inducing the buyers to ask for an evaluation. For example, a prospective supplier of castings sent quotes to Company Able which were well below prices being paid. When this situation persisted, the buyer initiated an evaluation. This involved review of the vendor's credit ratings and an inspection of the vendor's facilities by the buyer, a design engineer, and a metallurgist. The inspection team was concerned with such questions as: What applications could this vendor fill? How good is his quality control? How meaningfully do his personnel respond to questions about hypothetical situations? Trial orders followed and when performance was good, the vendor was added to the qualified list.

Significant Procurement Characteristics for Large Diameter Piping Elbows

1. The buyer is more a broker in this situation than those in which more searching for sources is required.

2. There is functionalization of responsibilities on both sides. The buyer acts as a broker but refers technical questions and answers directly to the design engineers. The latter may not discuss price or delivery unless the buyer is present. On the vendor side, the salesman who makes the first call on the Company Able engineer is concerned with formulating the problem. He is followed by a problem-solving team.

FIGURE 10

Decision Network Diagram of the Modified Rebuy Procurement Process: Piping Elbows

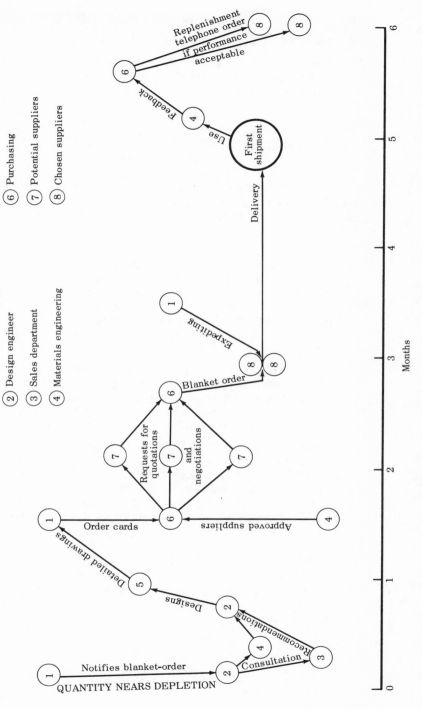

① Production order man   ⑤ Drafting
② Design engineer   ⑥ Purchasing
③ Sales department   ⑦ Potential suppliers
④ Materials engineering   ⑧ Chosen suppliers

81

3. The buyer has an interest in broadening the supply base.

4. The role of the distributor is unclear.

5. The need for modifying the solution—*i.e.*, considering a different type of elbow—was triggered by customer interest in improved performance.

THE PROCUREMENT PROCESS IN MODIFIED REBUY SITUATIONS

Because modified rebuys may develop in so many different ways, generalizations about them are more difficult than is the case for either new tasks or straight rebuys. However, a few observations may be made:

1. In a new task situation, the purchasing agent is frequently in the role of a junior partner in the procurement decision making process. In a straight rebuy, he tends to be the dominant—and frequently the only—buying decision maker. In a modified rebuy, the purchasing agent may be characterized as one of a number of participants in the procurement process.

2. Modifications of straight rebuy situations may be triggered by the actions of using departments, buyers, or sellers. Marketers could benefit through greater initiative and creativity in providing solid bases for buyers to convert straight rebuys to modified rebuys.

3. Timing is likely to be critical in modified rebuys. In some types of modifications *(e.g.,* changed requirement), the seller's only real chance for entry is at this time. Chances of success are enhanced if contact is made when the buyer reconsiders his position. Yet, as the hydraulic pump example illustrates, the door may be open at other times if cost or service benefits are apparent.

4. Automating the procurement routine tends to favor single sourcing and discourages modifying arrangements.

5. Buyers may be interested in broadening the supply base to supplement their sources of information about the supplying industry.

6. Assurance of supply is an important factor in patronage decisions, especially for major materials.

7. Awards may be made with regard to their effect on future supplier attitudes.

8. Short lead times, superior packaging, or other forms of marketing services may provide entry for an "out" supplier if he can demonstrate relevance to the buyer.

9. "Understandings" rather than formal contracts may be useful bases of continuing relationships, providing stability without a rigid commitment.

SUMMARY

The original definition of the problem which occasioned the modified rebuy situation has a basic effect on the orientation of the buying company decision makers regarding the resultant procurement process.

In the first type of modified rebuy—a changed specification of the end product—designing personnel realize that existing suppliers or supply arrangements might not be suitable for meeting the new requirement and that new sources or modifications be examined when the product is due to be redesigned.

Where the modified rebuy arises as part of a search for improvement of the buying company's products, the need is likely to be identified by engineering design personnel, although it could conceivably originate with marketing personnel involved in developing performance specifications for a new or changed product.

In the third type of modified rebuy situation—a search for cost savings—the role of purchasing personnel is likely to be greater. In the cases examined, buying personnel, either on their own or at the suggestion of "out" vendors, acted to convert a routine straight rebuy into a modified rebuy by opening up new alternatives for consideration. The triggering cues may vary: In one of the cases studied, a new purchasing manager called for a review of items involving large dollar expenditures, while in another, the forthcoming expiration of a requirements contract led the buyer to begin an intensive review of possible alternatives to renewal. In a third case, an "out" vendor made an offer which was sufficiently attractive to induce reconsideration of the arrangements with the existing supplier. Value analysis groups may be used to offset engineers' tendencies to conservatism and overspecification as well as to bring in broader solutions to existing needs. The work of such groups may well convert straight rebuys to modified rebuys.

Since service mix improvements may be of so many types, it is not surprising that need recognition in this area may arise from a number of sources. Prospective suppliers may suggest new inventorying, delivery, financing, or packaging arrangements which offer advantages to the buying company. Using or purchasing personnel may learn that others, perhaps competitors, are benefiting from arrangements more favorable than those being enjoyed. Sometimes production schedulers find that existing suppliers fail to meet delivery or service needs or seem to be unable to meet future requirements.   Finally, internal capacity, operating problems, or labor situations may make a reconsideration of make-or-buy decisions desirable in the hope of obtaining more reliable deliveries or those more attuned to scheduled needs.

In comparison with the complex and often lengthy procedures involved in new tasks, the determination of what is generally required in most modified rebuy situations is simple and straightforward.   Where the goal of modification is cost savings or service improvements, the general character and even the specific product descriptions may be unchanged.   In other cases, such as where a modified product is needed to meet a changed need or to improve the buyer's product, engineering design personnel are likely to indicate what is required, possibly in terms of performance specifications.   Where service mix advantages are being sought, those directly concerned with the benefit may be expected to participate in the decisions, such as a handling or using department where an improvement in incoming packaging is involved, or an inventory manager or production scheduler where improved timing of receipts is desired.

Whatever factor has precipitated the modified rebuy, cost information is very important, since an improved solution is generally being sought and costs represent a key aspect of the decision. This may merely involve obtaining quotations on a comparable basis from a number of prospective suppliers for the purpose of selecting the best buy or of determining if resourcing will afford savings.   On the other hand, it may require a formulation of detailed estimates for the complexity of factors involved in a "make" alternative. Generally, cost information is of primary importance when the problem and solution sought by the buying organization are clearly defined.

In the selection of potential sources, purchasing personnel are likely to play a much greater role in this buying situation than in new task buying situations.   For technical products, there may already be a list of approved vendors for the item in question.   For all products, there will be one or more existing suppliers of the same or a related item.   Lists of known suppliers may be supplemented by asking the using departments for additional leads.

Where there are a number of existing suppliers and a service-mix improvement is being sought, the existing supplier group may constitute at least a starting point in seeking out vendors interested in providing the desired service.   In other cases, "out" vendors may take the initiative by contacting the using company.

The information sought in the modified rebuy situation about prospective vendors' qualifications usually gives less emphasis to their problem-solving capacity than to capabilities with regard to delivery and conformance to specification.   Policy matters may enter at this stage, such as the desire to have enough suppliers to reduce dependence, yet few enough so that the business is important to the supplier and of not patronizing firms which compete with the buyer in product markets.

All qualified vendors are asked to quote. In some cases, vendor personnel may have many questions about what is wanted, which prompts discussions with the buying company's technical personnel. In such cases, the buyer fills the role of contact man. More commonly, the items wanted have been determined by this stage, and all that remains is to obtain offers.

Offers may be analyzed in a number of ways. The products of various suppliers may be subjected to performance tests. Informal discussions may be held with prospective vendors to determine their qualifications and interest. The cost of the item must be compared with the additional costs to the buying company of making the required changes, if any. The exact criteria vary from situation to situation.

VII

A Case Study of the Purchase
of Industrial Components*

PURSUING MSI's ANALYSIS of the procurement process, the following questions are likely to be raised by marketing and purchasing
practitioners and students.

1. How valid is the description of the procurement process pre-
    sented in Chapters II-VI?

2. Is the classification of the buying situations into a New Task,
    Modified and Straight Rebuy sufficient as a guide for market-
    ing decisions, or is it necessary to superimpose on the anal-
    ysis additional dimensions such as product type?

3. Is it realistic and/or useful to describe the industrial buying
    process in terms of the eight Buyphases?

4. How does the fact that the buying process is carried out by a
    number of people affect the MSI analysis of the buying
    process?

5. Can the industrial buying decisions be considered as part of
    a broader class of decisions, the knowledge of which might
    help understand the purchase decisions?

Although complete answers cannot be given, it is the purpose of
this chapter to shed some light on these issues. Specific buying
processes of industrial components are analyzed. Differing from
the MSI project both in the data base and research approach, a reasonably objective evaluation of the MSI findings is possible as well
as the answering of some of form. Obviously, not every purchase
decision is a result of the whole process to be presented; shortcuts
due to personality differences, time pressure, environmental conditions, etc., are often utilized. For example, a repeat purchase
requisition for parts used in the production process is initiated by

* By Yoram Wind

production control, not by an R & D engineer. The actual buying process is not nearly as smooth and clear-cut as depicted here in these pages. The degree of complexity, importance, and time of each of the buying phases varies widely. Despite this, the model as presented here is believed to represent accurately, although in a simplified form, the major steps and flows of a buying decision process for industrial components.

The buying process, for expository convenience, is divided into ten stages. The first three are concerned with the R & D stages in which the major decision making unit is the R & D engineer. Stage 1 represents the process from its inception, when the engineer perceives some stimulus for a new product, to the formulation of the goals for the given product. Although this stage might not seem to be connected with the decision to purchase industrial components, a seller of components can start his marketing penetration at this stage by providing the engineer with some looked-for support which might affect the engineer's attitude and future behavior toward this source. At the early stages, especially during the formulation and development of an idea, the R & D engineer is eager for any information that might help him in developing the idea or in "selling" it to his organization. Hence, information and support from a potential supplier might be highly appreciated (and rewarded!).

Stage 2 deals with the R & D design process. Throughout this process, the engineer needs, looks for, and uses components; thus, there are real advantages in selling a component at this early stage ("back door selling") rather than waiting until the production stage. Moreover, from the evidence gathered, it was concluded that many promotional activities should take place at this stage and be directed at the R & D engineer. For example, the use of free samples was found to increase the probability of including the specific brand in the system being designed. Similarly, providing information and technical advice when sought by the R & D engineer improves chances for a supplier's products being considered and accepted.

The third stage is concerned with the testing of the design. Each new product goes through several tests, the results of which can lead to changes in the components used or to their substitution. Consequently, a certain component, even if rejected for the original design, can be reevaluated as a result of these tests. It is important, then, that "rejected suppliers" be on the alert and ready to provide any information, advice, or parts when needed. This suggests also to the "accepted suppliers" that, even if their part has been accepted, the job remains to provide necessary assistance to the users.

Stage 4 takes up the transfer of the product from the R & D stage to production. In this subprocess, R & D engineers collaborate with manufacturing engineers in deciding on final specifications for each part; production control decides on the quantity needed and delivery schedule. This information, which sets some of the constraints on the buyer's discretionary power, is gathered and transferred to purchasing in the form of a purchase requisition.

The last six stages of the buying process are carried out by the buyers. They represent the ways in which the buying decisions are being made. The buyer's decision process starts with the gathering of information and the implicit setting of the goals for the given purchase (Stage 5). The specific decision process, although following the major elements of any problem solving behavior, differs when a part is bought for the first time (the new task situation) as compared to a repeat purchase, and when the purchase is of a standard (off the shelf) variety rather than a specially fabricated one. Differentiating between these two elements—the nature of the part and the newness of its purchase—provides a framework for presenting the buyer's decision processes as presented in Table 6:

TABLE 6

Clarification of Buying Processes Based on the Nature of the Product and the Newness of the Tool

	Standard Parts	Fabricated Parts
Repeat Purchase	Repeat Purchase of Standard Part (See Stage VIII in Figure 11)	Repeat Purchase of Fab. Part (See Stage X in Figure 11)
First Purchase (New Task Situation)	First Purchase of Standard Part (See Stage VII in Figure 11)	First Purchase of Fab. Part (See Stage VI in Figure 11)

A further distinction—dollar volume of the order—provides another distinct path of the buying process for standard parts. This can be explained by the fact that large orders make possible direct ordering from the manufacturer, involving a somewhat different buying process than when the choice is limited to buying from distributors or other middlemen. Fabricated parts are usually purchased directly from the manufacturer. Most of the first orders of standard parts are for small quantities. Hence the above distinction is useful only for repurchase of standard parts.

These ten stages are presented next in schematic flow charts.

The four decision makers whose decisions comprise the essence of the industrial buying processes, as described above, are not the only participants in the buying process. Their superiors and other

FIGURE 11
A Flow Model of the Purchase Process of Components for Electronic Systems
Stage I

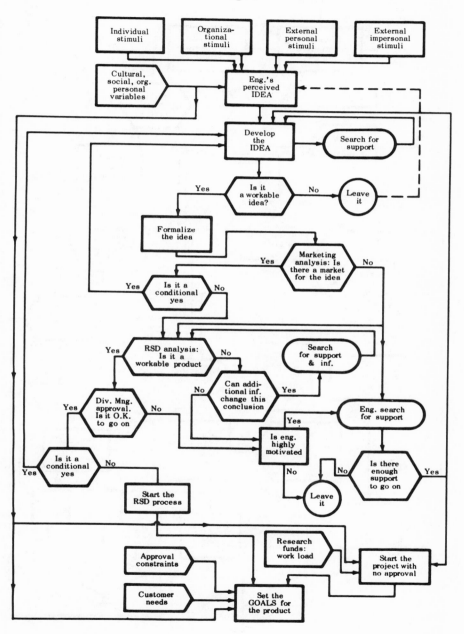

FIGURE 11 (Continued) Stage II

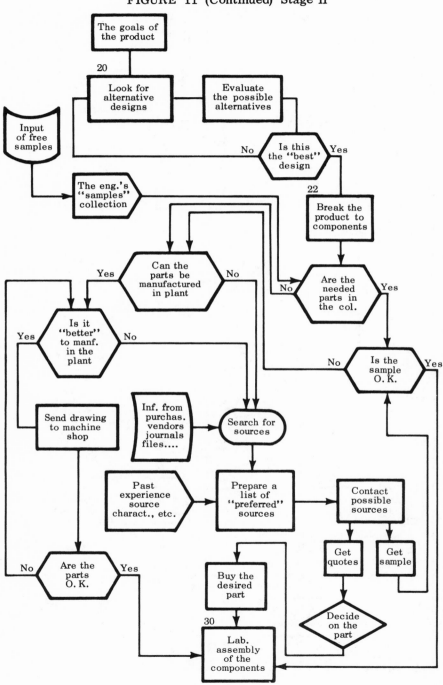

FIGURE 11 (Continued) Stage III

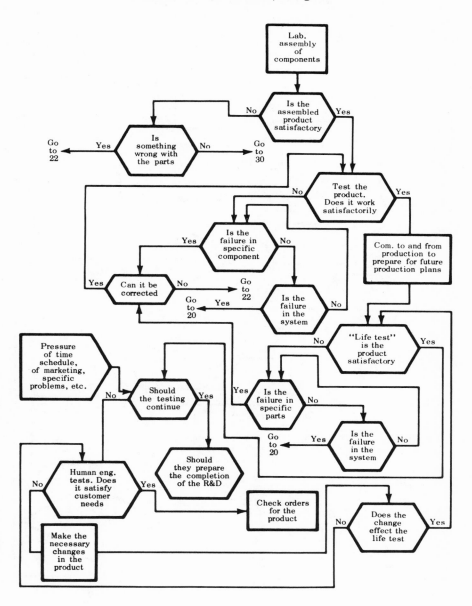

FIGURE 11 (Continued) Stage IV

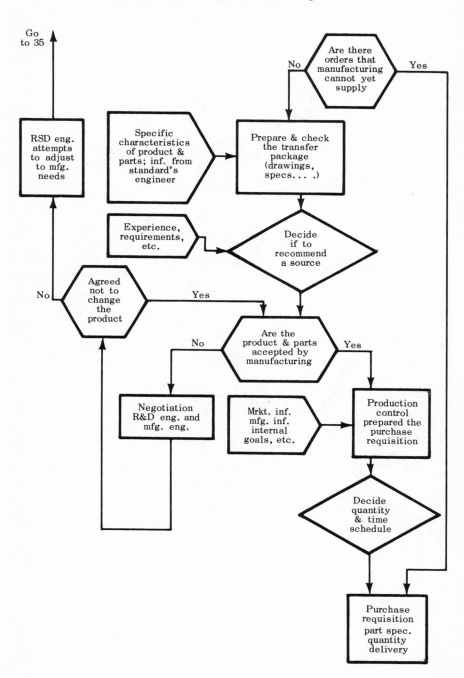

FIGURE 11 (Continued) Stage V

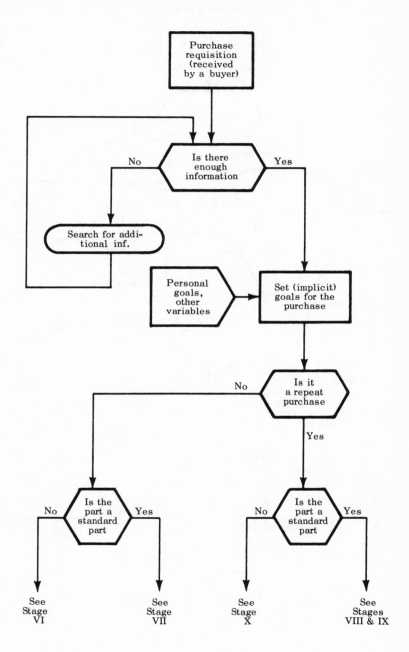

FIGURE 11 (Continued) Stage VI

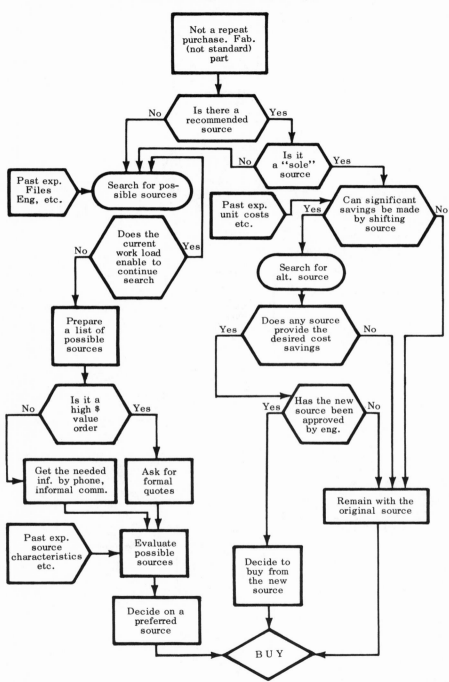

FIGURE 11 (Continued) Stage VII

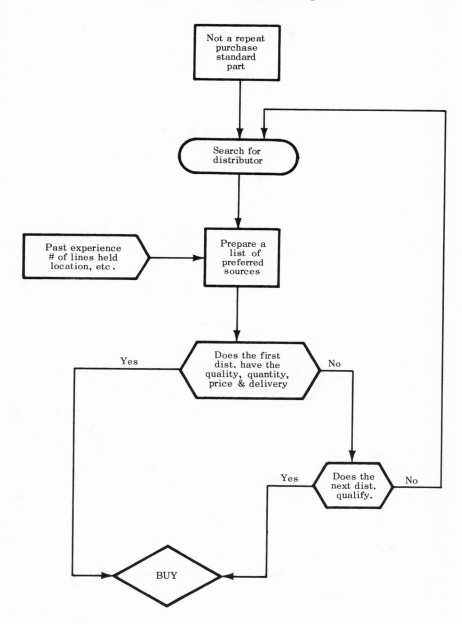

FIGURE 11 (Continued) Stage VIII

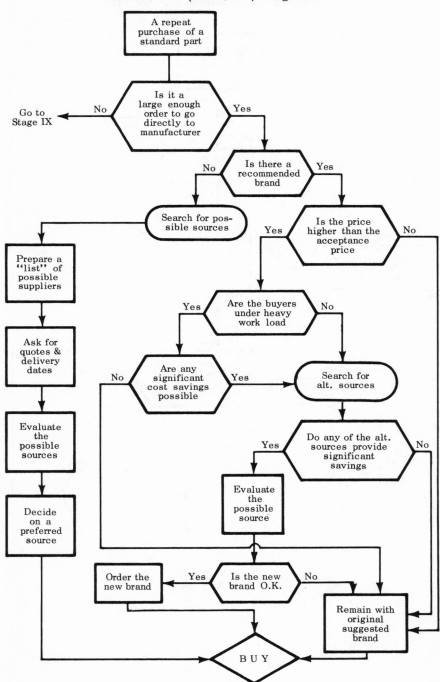

FIGURE 11 (Continued) Stage IX

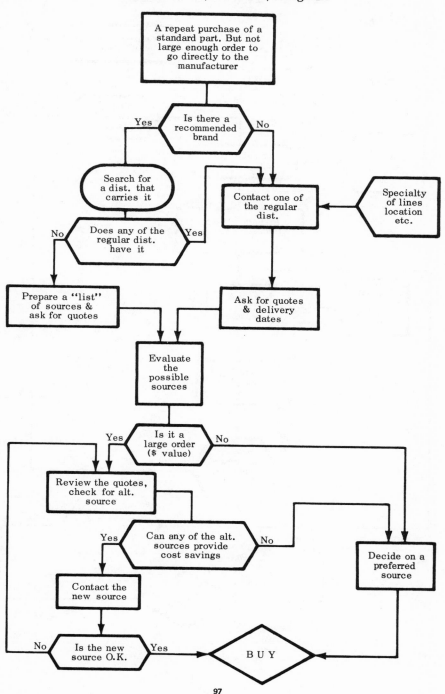

FIGURE 11 (Continued) Stage X

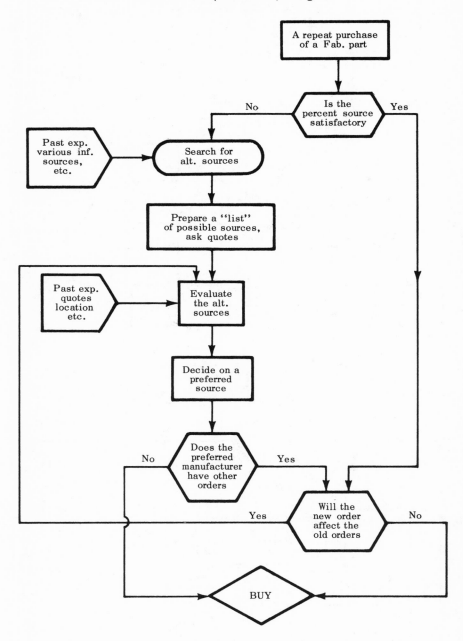

organization members as well have considerable indirect effect on the buying decisions of these DMU's through two processes:

1. Required approval for certain decisions. In Stage 1 of the buying process, for example, the R & D engineer must secure the approval of the manager of R & D and the division manager for each new project. A buyer has to obtain approval from specific organization officials for certain purchases, usually above a certain dollar volume. The identity of this official varies with the organizational structure. It might be the purchasing manager in a centralized purchasing department, the divisional production control manager in a decentralized department, etc.

2. Setting constraints on the buyer's discretionary decision power. The buyer's behavior is affected, however, not by the actual specific constraints, but by perceived constraints. Thus those organization members who are perceived by the buyers as the constraint setters should also be considered in the buying process. The study revealed that buyers in a centralized purchasing department perceive the purchasing manager as the major constraint setter, whereas buyers in a decentralized department added the division manager and the production manager.

VALIDATING THE MSI STUDY

One of the advantages of, and reasons for, including this appendix is that the findings described herein of an independently conducted study on industrial buyers' behavior make it possible to better establish the validity of the MSI report. A critical comparison of MSI's findings with those of this independent study indicated the following conclusions.

1. It is clearly evident that the description of the procurement process as presented in Chapters II through VI is applicable in the case of industrial components.

The distinction may be overemphasized, however, between a modified rebuy and a new task situation on the one hand, and a straight versus a modified rebuy situation on the other. Inasmuch as buyers' behavior reflects among other things their perception of the newness of the task, an operational distinction is not always possible among the three buying situational types. If changes in purchase requirements are slight (below the buyer's perceptual threshold), a distinction between modified and straight rebuy will not indicate any changes in buying behavior. Similarly, if the perceived changes are perceived to be significant, a modified rebuy can be regarded as a new task. Nevertheless, the classification of buying situations into three distinguishable types is extremely useful in analyzing industrial buyers' behavior. This classification scheme enables the development of measures that will provide clear-cut criteria to differentiate various degrees of "newness" of the task, which in turn determines the information requirements (page 33) and the new alternatives to be considered (page 34).

2. Whereas this independent study confirmed that basic differences between buying processes are attributable to the newness of the task, it also indicated clearly that better insights into the buying process are possible through the addition of other dimensions such as product type to the analysis.

The generalized model of the buying process of industrial components illustrates this point by differentiating between the buying processes for fabricated and standard parts. Another factor, dollar value of the order, was found to affect significantly the purchase of standard (off the shelf) components.

It is possible that the explanatory power of these added dimensions is limited only to the case of components. If additional dimensions, however, can add to the understanding of the industrial buying process in general, any classification of buying situations into new, modified, and straight rebuy should be viewed only as a preliminary step to be subjected to further modifications and subclassifications.

3. Each of the buying situations is characterized in the MSI study by eight Buyphases. Applying these phases to the data on the buying process of industrial components indicate that the buying process can be described by these phases.

As suggested in the text, not all buying situations follow the suggested path from phase I to phase VIII. Similarly, not all the decision makers that are involved in the purchase decision follow these processes explicitly. It is clearly evident that there is a strong interaction and interdependency among the various phases. Despite these considerations, it was found that the division of the buying process into eight distinct Buyphases does improve our understanding of the industrial buying process. Moreover, by examining the buying process within a formal decision making framework, the way is paved for developing a normative (prescriptive as opposed to merely descriptive) model of industrial buying behavior.

4. Buying by industrial firms is characterized by the participation of several individuals. Despite this, the buying process can be described and analyzed as one (although complex) process carried out by a number of individuals according to some (implicit or explicit) flexible division of labor.

The individuals who are related directly to the purchasing process, whether users, buying influences, decision makers, or actual purchasers are members of what can be termed a "buying center." Within the buying center, at least in the purchase of industrial components, there is a reasonably flexible division of labor. Decision making, for example, might depend on various individuals, affected by the nature of interpersonal relationships within the buying center, specific decisions to be made, environmental conditions, etc. Some decisions are made jointly by a number of DMU's. Specifications of the components, for example, often are prepared together by the R & D and production engineers. Sources of supply may be decided by either the R & D engineer or the buyer. This flexible division of labor within a buying center makes it particularly important to analyze the industrial buying process in terms of functions performed (the eight Buyphases) rather than by identifying individual DMU's. While identification of DMU's associated with the various functions is valuable, this should supplement the functional analysis.

Generally, the fact that industrial buying decisions are carried out within a buying center indicates the complexity of the process, and therefore a formal analytical approach, such as the one proposed by the MSI study, is useful in understanding industrial buying behavior.

Despite necessary simplifications in the MSI presentation of the industrial buying process, it can be concluded that the framework proposed is useful in the analysis of buying situations beyond those considered in the MSI studies. Furthermore, if the data on purchase of industrial components are as representative as one would like to believe, it is deemed that the MSI findings are a valid, general framework for the analysis of industrial components. Additional insight into the understanding of industrial buyer behavior may be gained, however, by slight modification of the MSI framework as illustrated by these supplemental findings.

INDUSTRIAL BUYING DECISIONS AS A SPECIAL CASE OF THE BEHAVIORAL THEORY OF THE FIRM

Industrial buying decisions being made by organizational members in the course of performing their tasks can be viewed as a specific case of the decision process hypothesized by the behavioral theory of the firm. Whereas the analogy to existing managerial decision theories applies to all types of buying decisions, this section focuses only on the buyer's source selection decision. Only casual references are made concerning the applicability of the framework proposed by the behavioral theory of the firm to buying decisions made by other members of the buying center.

The behavioral theory of the firm as developed by Cyert and

March (1963) suggests four relational concepts that represent the core of the behavioral theory of business decision making. Each of these propositions is summarized and followed by the relevant empirical findings on the industrial buyer's decision process. Throughout the analysis it is assumed that the propositions regarding a business organization in general are also valid for one unit of the organization—the buying center. Thus for convenience of presentation the word "organization," as used in the behavioral theory of the firm, is replaced in the following analysis by the term "buying center."

PROPOSITION 1: QUASI-RESOLUTION OF CONFLICT[1]

A buying center is a coalition of members with differing goals. These goals are a series of independent aspiration-level constraints that may include nonessential, sporadic, and nonoperational demands as well as essential, continuous, and operative goals imposed on the buying center by its members. The conflict of goals with which the organization "lives" most of the time is assumed to be resolved by using local rationality, *i.e.*, delegation and specialization in decisions and goals reduce the buying situation involving a complex set of interrelated problems and conflicting goals to a number of simplified problems. The effectiveness of this system of "resolving" conflicts depends on whether the decisions generated by the system are consistent with each other and with the demands of the external environment. Two characteristics of the decision process which promote consistency are: acceptable level decision rules rather than optimization rules and sequential attention to goals, *i.e.*, the conflict is resolved, in part, by attending to different goals at different times.

Empirical Findings

The findings of the empirical study conform to the above proposition. More specifically, it was found that each subgroup of the buying center has different goals, in addition, of course, to unavoidable personal differences in goals. The differing goals of these subunits can be presented as the following stereotypes. The R & D engineers are basically concerned with the performance and quality of the products which they design and develop. The buyers, on the other hand, are concerned with the maximization of cost savings subject to the satisfactory performance of their jobs. The production manager's subgoal as related to the buying process is the delivery on schedule of all needed parts.[2] Given this conflict of goals, the buying center reduces it, to a degree, by using local rationality, *i.e.*, some of the buying decisions are distributed among various members of the buying center. Despite the use of local rationality, the buyer's decisions are still subject to conflicting goals. This is resolved by applying sequential attention to goals, *i.e.*, the buyer attempts to satisfy the goals of an R & D engineer in a certain buying decision, the goals of the manufacturing engineer in a different buying decision, etc. In all buying decisions, buyers are inclined to use an acceptable level decision rule.

PROPOSITION 2: UNCERTAINTY AVOIDANCE[3]

The members of a buying center attempt to avoid uncertainty in making buying decisions. This avoidance of uncertainty is achieved by using decision rules that emphasize short-run reaction to short-run "feedback" and by arranging a negotiated environment.

Empirical Findings

As the decision to buy industrial components is, by its very nature, a short-run decision dominated by a day-to-day "feedback" and information inputs, it is hard to infer the tendency to avoid uncertainty. The second way of avoiding uncertainty by a negotiated environment is evident, however, in the industrial buying process. Buyers tend to arrange a negotiated environment both within the firm and with other firms. As an example, in making any unplanned changes in the decision to purchase components, the buyer attempts to get the user's approval prior to making the decision. As to the buyer's efforts to have a negotiated external environment, persuasive evidence derived from depth interviews with buyers indicates that, whenever possible, he avoids making decisions which involve a high degree of uncertainty. This propensity can also be inferred by the use of behavioral measurements. It can be assumed that an engineer tends to specify higher tolerances than actually needed so as to reduce uncertainty. A buyer, if motivated to avoid or, what is more frequently the case, to reduce the uncertainty, can be expected to make the following decisions:

1. To split every order between two or more sources;
2. To be loyal to reliable sources and
3. To avoid using new sources unless no risk is involved.

The findings from a study on buyers' behavior in three divisions indicate an overwhelming subscription to these decisions with the exception of the split order decision. The reason for the exception is that, in several cases, the R & D engineer specifies a sole source, and the buyer tends, in the majority of cases, to comply with this recommendation, which reduces the uncertainty involved in the engineer's reaction. As to the specific findings, a study of about 500 fabricated parts indicated that:

1. Sixty-three percent of all fabricated parts had single sources. In 83 percent of these cases, the source to be used was specified by the R & D engineer or by both the buyer and the R & D engineer together. Of the remaining 17 percent of cases, the buyer thought in 11 percent of them that only one source was "acceptable." The other six percent of the cases were described as involving the use of only very small quantities of relatively cheap and noncritical parts which gave no specific incentive to change the source.

2. Twenty-four percent of all fabricated parts had two sources, and only 13 percent had three sources. About one-half of the cases were split about equally, and the other half had one dominant source.

3. Ninety-seven percent of the companies actually bought from were members of what can be termed "the feasible set of suppliers," *i.e.*, those companies that the buyers perceived as most reliable (least amount of uncertainty) in terms of quality and delivery. A supplier was included in this set if the buyers were aware of its existence as a possible source. This measurement was supplemented by objective data as to whether the company was asked to submit quotes or not. There was an almost complete overlap between the findings of the two measurements.[4] Using the ranking of awareness, it was found that 76 percent of all purchases were made from companies that were ranked as the first three possible suppliers for a given part.

The "uncertainty avoidance" proposition is confirmed even more definitely when applied to the standard (off-the-shelf) parts. When dealing with this component category, buyers tend to have several possible suppliers at all times. Even where the buyer has a special preferential agreement with some source, he will keep a number of alternatives open by giving them a few orders from time to time.

PROPOSITION 3: PROBLEMISTIC SEARCH[5]

Any search carried out by the members of a buying center is stimulated by a problem and is directed toward finding a solution to that problem. Every search has three assumed characteristics:

1. The search is motivated. Variations in search activity (and

search productivity) primarily reflect the extent to which motivation for search exists.

2. The search follows the simplest route. It is based on the following rules:

   a. Search in the neighborhood of the problem symptom.

   b. Search in the neighborhood of the current alternative.

When the above two rules do not result in an immediately successful search, two additional rules are introduced.

   c. Apply a more complex ("distant") search.

   d. Search in organizationally vulnerable areas.

3. Search is biased. There are three different kinds of search bias:

   a. Bias reflecting special training or experience.

   b. Bias reflecting the interaction of hopes and expectations.

   c. Communication biases reflecting unresolved conflict within the organization.

Empirical Findings

Throughout the industrial buying process, DMU's engage in search activities. The empirical study confirmed the importance of the motivation for search and provided some additional insight into the forces that encourage and discourage search. Buyers are usually subject to two conflicting forces: on the one hand, the work-load time pressure which they are under tends to minimize search activities and, whenever needed, tends to restrict the search to the immediate neighborhood so as to minimize the effort and time involved. On the other hand, many of the buyer's positive rewards come only after making decisions that involve extensive search activities. Given these two forces, it was hypothesized that the buyer would engage in search activities whenever the rewards expected from the search outweighed the cost of the search and measured subjectively as to time, effort and money.

The second characteristic of search is implied by the buyer's tendency to minimize the cost of the search. It was found that buyers, whenever engaged in search activities, start in their immediate neighborhood and initiate a search that is perceived to be the least expensive in terms of time and cost. Only if this search does not produce the desired outcome, do they engage in a more "distant" and expensive search process.

Following is an example of a buyer's search process when faced with a purchase requisition for a new uncommon fabricated part. This example is drawn from interviews with 17 buyers and is presented schematically in Figure 12.

All respondents completely agree that search process 3 was more costly (subjectively) than 2, and that 2, in turn, was more costly than 1. The buyers were split, however, as to the order of stages 4 and 5; nine of the respondents answered that they would use search process 4 first and, only then, 5. On the other hand, eight respondents indicated that they would call on the R & D engineers (stage 5) first. This difference can be explained by studying the nature of the relations between the buyers and R & D engineers. Of the eight buyers who indicated a prior search with the R & D engineer, seven ranked the R & D engineer among the top two groups of people with whom they liked to have contact, as compared with the nine buyers, who searched first with outsiders, among whom only two ranked the R & D engineer in the top two groups of favorite contact people. It thus can be seen that the direction of the search activity is closely related to the social relations of the buyers. This example clearly illustrates the third characteristic of a search process—that search is biased.

PROPOSITION 4: ORGANIZATIONAL LEARNING[6]

A buying center exhibits adaptive behavior over time with its members as the instruments of carrying out the adaptive behavior. The buying center is assumed to change its goals, to shift its attention (from some parts of its comparative environment to others, etc.), and to revise its procedures for search as a function of its experience.

Empirical Findings

The empirical study of buyers' behavior suggests that Cyert and March's discussion of organizational learning was underweighed in their theory. Learning in the form of "past experience" was found to be the *only* variable that entered *all* of the buying decisions. This is a finding that was based not only on answers to direct questions but was also inferred from the analysis of the "protocols" and the reports of the "depth" interviews with the buyers. In view of this evidence, it can be said that each step in the buyer's decision process is directed, to some extent, by the buyer's past experience, *i.e.*, his learning. The important place of learning in determining the buying process is clearly evident, for example, from the analysis of the search process. The behavioral theory of the firm states that:

FIGURE 12
The Process of a Buyer's Search for a Source of Supply

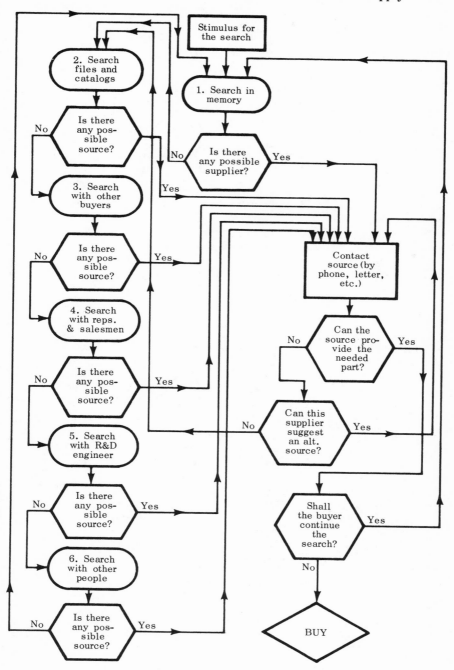

FIGURE   13
A Buyer's Search Process When Learning Is Involved

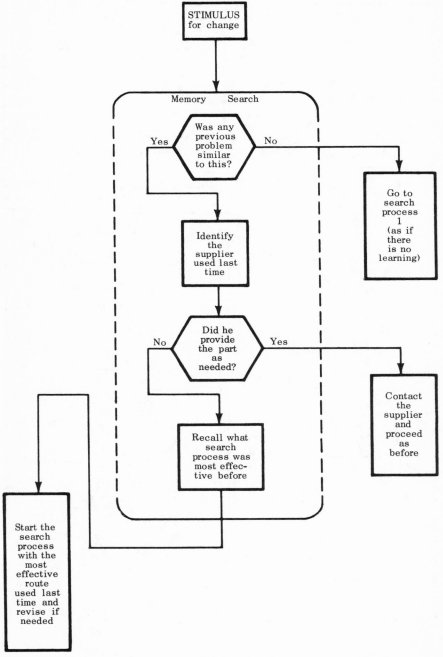

When an organization discovers a solution to a problem by searching in a particular way, it will be more likely to search in that way
in future problems of the same type. ... Thus, the order in which
various alternative solutions to a problem are considered will change
as the organization experiences success or failure with alternatives.

The empirical study of the 17 buyers overwhelmingly supported
the above proposition. These buyers were asked the following question:

You have just received a purchase requisition from an R & D engineer for a new part. You have never bought this part before, but
in its general description it resembles a part you bought a few
months ago.

Please describe, in detail, how would you go about finding and selecting a supplier for this part?

All 17 of them stressed that the exact search procedures which they
had presented before[8] would be changed in accordance with their
previous experience. Schematically, this learning affect is presented in Figure 13.

SUMMARY

It is hence evident from the empirical findings on the industrial
buyer's decision process that the propositions proposed by the behavioral theory of the firm do apply to the specific case of industrial buyers' behavior. Consequently, one should take account of
this knowledge in analyzing and planning opportunities for industrial marketing.

PART TWO

The Determinants of
Industrial Buyer Behavior

VIII

Environmental Influences
Upon Buying Situations

THE NECESSITY FOR UNDERSTANDING buyers' behavior and its
determinants in order to achieve successful planning and implementation of marketing strategies has been widely recognized and
accepted by many marketing practitioners and by scholars who are
concerned with the marketing of consumer goods. Experts in industrial marketing have, nevertheless, rarely given evidence of having
realized the full implications of this interdependence. Alexander,
Cross, and Cunningham, however, provide a notable exception,
e.g.:

> Any attempt to understand the managerial problems of marketing a
> product or group of products must include, at or near its beginning,
> a study of the persons or the establishments that buy or can buy
> those products. Without a knowledge of his market, *the buying units*
> *that comprise it, and the working conditions of and the objectives*
> *sought by the purchasers in their operations,* the marketing mana-
> ger finds himself forced to make decisions and formulate plans and
> programs in a sort of informational twilight of assumed facts and
> conditions that can only result in useless error and loss.[1]

Part One provided the necessary background and understanding
of the buying process under a variety of buying situations. The
study of buyers' behavior has to answer, however, a major question—
what are the determinants of the buyers' decisions?

It is clear from the previous analysis that the direction and outcome of the industrial procurement process is determined by a
large number of factors. It is the purpose of this part to identify
these factors and analyze their effect on buyers' behavior. The
present chapter is concerned with the environmental influences,
both internal and external, which affect the procurement process.
Chapter IX is concerned with the roles of the various buying influences. Chapter X concentrates on one specific determinant of
the buying process—the user-supplier relationships. Chapter XI

is a presentation of Dr. Wind's conceptual scheme for the analysis of buyer behavior and the determinants of his decisions. It then uses this framework for the presentation of existing findings and concepts from the literature and tests the applicability and usefulness of this framework for the analysis of buyers' source loyalty behavior.

It is hoped that this part will improve the reader's understanding of the determinants of industrial buyers' behavior and in turn provide the necessary background for Part Three of this study.

ENVIRONMENTAL INFLUENCES

The present chapter is devoted to an examination of some of the more significant environmental influences and their effect upon buying situations and the ways they are handled. It is these environmental dimensions which explain why individual buying situations of a given type are not always handled the same way.

While the variety and complexity of relevant factors can only be suggested here, a basic distinction is generally made between the internal and external environment. In essence, internal variables reflect the personal characteristics of individual buying influences within the organization and certain organizational characteristics, such as the goals, policies, and patterns of operation of the particular firm—even its bases of competition within its industry. Significant external influences, in contrast, are not within the jurisdiction of the buying organization, although a certain amount of inter-action and interrelationship exist. External variables usually relate to the supplying industries of the buying firm, the socioeconomic and political environment, or to specific, significant events.

INTERNAL ENVIRONMENTAL INFLUENCES

The Human Element

Effective salesmen recognize intuitively that the buying decision makers are human and are therefore subject to worries, fears, frustrations, conservatism, and inertia. The astute salesman also knows that a buying decision may be rationalized or justified after the fact and that the reasons given for a choice may not be the actual ones. With any personal interaction between representatives of using and supplying companies, each naturally reacts and adjusts according to his interpretations of the personality and psychological makeup of the other. Salesmen who can develop empathy with buyers are likely to be more effective than those who cannot or do not identify with, and *understand*, the customer's viewpoints and problems.

Organization of the Buying Company

The organization, philosophy, policies, and practices of the problem-solving firm are important determinants of the outcome of a particular buying situation. For example, the type of purchasing department that the firm has will be an important determinant. Is buying authority centralized or decentralized? What is the relationship of corporate purchasing to buying at the plant level? What authority limits, in terms of dollar expenditures or other criteria, are imposed upon each buyer? Is the item under consideration to be capitalized or expensed? Is trade relations a factor? Do "buy American" or other policies constrain the selection of alternatives?

How important are this buying situation and this supplier to the buying company? "Importance" may be defined in terms of the dollars per transaction, the dollars per year, the criticalness of a failure to the total product offering, the technical specifications and the tolerances required, or other criteria. The more important the problem, in whatever sense of the word, the more time and attention will tend to be devoted to the buying situation.

One of the significant factors in the setting of a buying situation concerns the extent to which the buying organization is its own potential supplier. That is, to what extent can the company make all or part of the needed item? The buying company itself may be viewed as an alternative source of supply. The degrees of make-or-buy range from a single-source position with a particular vendor to an organization that is vertically integrated and manufactures many of its own requirements. Because of the complexity and the importance of the various degrees of make-or-buy, the subject is discussed more fully in Chapter X.

Variations in purchasing philosophy may be illustrated by a scale ranging from "soft" to "hard." A company whose purchasing is typified as soft would tend to place great emphasis on maintaining strong relationships with its suppliers over time, would stress "being a good customer," feel loyal toward its suppliers, and take a long-run view of the prices it paid. The cost-price economic aspects of the supplier's offer would tend to get somewhat less emphasis.

At the opposite end of the scale, a "hard" purchasing orientation would take a shorter-range view of the situation. Greater emphasis would be placed on obtaining the best possible cost-price terms, and the other aspects of the supplier's offer would be relatively less important, assuming that certain minimum conditions such as performance specifications, delivery dates, or terms of sales were

met. The hard buying company will tend to place less emphasis on
its relationships with its suppliers and with suppliers' opinions of
the buying company. Hard purchasing companies will not necessarily change suppliers more frequently than do soft purchasing
companies, but their *willingness* to change is greater and they feel
less committed to remaining loyal to existing suppliers.

It appears from the fieldwork that the purchasing patterns of an
organization will reflect its position with respect to a hard or a
soft outlook. This, in turn is partially related to the basic goals of
the organization. The buying patterns of a firm whose executives
are under pressure for "profit now" may be expected to differ
from those of a similar firm whose goal was to make the best
product on the market or those of a third firm concerned with efforts to "skim the cream" off a market segment.

Bases of Competition in the Buying Company's Industry

The relative position or "niche" of the buying organization in its
own industry or business needs to be considered. The bases upon
which the firm competes will strongly influence its buying activities
and patterns. In a company which stresses its technical excel-
lence and engineering skills; for example, the engineers and technical specialists will tend to be the dominant buying influences. By
contrast, the marketing people may play major roles in companies
where marketing bears a major responsibility for the introduction
of new products. In companies producing a standard, undifferen-
tiated product, purchasing and accounting people are likely to play
major buying roles. If the company is a major purchaser of expensive capital equipment, finance people will tend to be important
buying influences.

The general buying outlook of some of the major functional
specializations is analyzed in Chapter VIII. Here it is sufficient to
note that design and development, manufacturing, marketing, purchasing, and other functionally specialized individuals will tend to
place different emphasis on the various aspects of the supplier's
total offering of goods and services. The functional areas that are
most important in the buying company's own sales activities will
tend to have a strong influence on the company's buying activities.

Type of Operation of the Buying Company

The output of different organizations varies greatly. The nature of
the end product of automobile factories, railroads, universities,
food processors, and janitorial services firms will naturally have
some impact on the buying patterns of the various organizations.
Only manufacturing operations have been studied on this project,
but it seems logical to expect that their general purchasing pro-

cedures would differ in significant aspects from those of service firms and non-business institutions.

Even within the manufacturing sector, the fieldwork uncovered three basic patterns of operations: job shop, assembly operation, and continuous process operations. In a *job shop* operation, a number of variations are offered on one or more basic models. Products may be produced and inventoried, or may be built to order. The value of direct labor as a percentage of total costs is likely to be high. Some purchased components or parts are assembled into the final product, and many of the purchased materials lose their identity in the final product.

In such companies purchasing tends to be quite complex and, because of variations in size and features from product to product, large inventories may be required. It is, however, relatively easy to phase out a particular part, component, or product and to phase in a replacement. Except for commodity-type items, the buying company tends to select suppliers because of their technical capability, delivery, testing, and "emergency" services. Supplier performance tends to be considerably more important than price in selecting vendors. The final product itself tends to be expensive, and purchased items probably account for some 25-40 percent of the final cost to the customer. In general, producers of such job shop products appear to be quite responsive to the technical and other services aspects of the marketer's offering.

Assembly operations are characterized by the fact that many of the suppliers products retain their identify in the buying company's final product. Automobile bumpers, picture tubes for television sets, and electrical motors in room air conditioners are examples of products used in assembly-type operations. In many instances, the final customer may be able to identify the original supplier. His forklift truck may have Goodyear tires, for example. In other cases, the final customer may not be able to identify the original supplier—but the buying company can. This might be the case with the electrical motors used in washing machines, for example.

For assembly operations, the production process consists primarily of purchasing a variety of parts, components, and sub-assemblies which are combined into the final product. The buying organization may do little forming or shaping of items but may concentrate on assembling items made by others. In such operations, the cost of purchased parts tends to represent a high proportion of the final cost of the end product. In the assembly-type company studied for this project, for example, purchased parts and components accounted for some 60 percent of the final cost of the product to the company.

Since many suppliers' products retain their identity, buyers can quickly pinpoint the responsibility for failure in most instances. Perhaps the best recommendation a supplier can have is for the buyers to say, "We have very few problems with his stuff—and when a problem does arise, he gets out here fast and straightens out the situation." Marketers need a good reputation for quality and reliability, both with the buying organization and with its customers. In general, buyers of assembly-type items which retain their identity appear to be most susceptible to the marketing efforts of suppliers aimed at the buying company's own customers. Especially in companies where marketing people may be significant buying influences, procurement may be used to enhance the market acceptance of the buying company's product. For example, assume that X sells wheels to Y which are incorporated into an item sold to Z. X aims advertising and other forms of marketing effort at convincing Z of the superiority of X wheels. This effort, designed to create final customer "pull" for the wheels, is likely to make it easier for X to sell wheels to Y.

Continuous process operations are typified by the chemical and petroleum industries. The production output tends to be a steady flow, rather than separate products. Purchased items not only lose their identity, but typically are transformed into a state or material different from that originally sold to the buyer. Since the end products, such as paint, sulfuric acid, or paperboard, tend to be standardized and homogeneous, the purchased materials are usually treated as commodities, and the importance of price tends to increase.

Since the final product sold by the buying company is, itself, likely to be highly price sensitive, the buyer places more emphasis on the price aspect of the marketer's offer than would be the case in job shop or assembly-type operations. Also, purchased ingredients tend to make up the largest part of the final cost to the buying company. This is not to imply that this type of marketing is characterized entirely by price selling. However, price tends to establish a "floor" under the marketer's efforts. With competing suppliers selling "at the going rate" or market price, a given supplier has as much latitude as he can afford in developing creative and imaginative ways of differentiating his offer. Even in price sensitive industries, long-term buyer-seller relationships develop. Continuous process operations tend to be differentiated, however, because the normal relationships and buying patterns can be quite volatile. A price reduction by one supplier can cause chaos in the market and instability in user-supplier relationships.

In negotiations between buyers and sellers, both parties often seek to reduce the uncertainty and instability inherent in such price sensitive markets. Sellers may use special price concessions as a negotiating device. Buyers tend to use volume or a specified share of the business in return. Since purchasing skills represent a major means of obtaining an advantage over one's competitors and since announced price reductions tend to create confusion in the market, many such special price arrangements are known only to the parties involved.

In practice, the purchasing patterns for a given manufacturing company tend to be a composite of job shop, assembly, and continuous process operations. Other types of operations also may exist. While no organization is likely to be entirely consistent with regard to any categorization, buying philosophy, attitudes, and policies of a company are likely to reflect certain of these patterns.

EXTERNAL ENVIRONMENTAL INFLUENCES

The external environmental influences are those factors whose control is largely outside of the individual buying organization. Although the buying company's actions obviously will have some impact on the external environment, in the short run, at least, these external variables are beyond the control of the individual firm.

Characteristics of the Supplying Industry

The most obvious way in which potential suppliers influence the buying situation is with regard to their individual salesman's behavior. The content and quality of his presentation will have either a positive or negative effect on the buying influences contacted by him.

The number of potential suppliers definitely affect the customer's perception of the situation. All organizations seek to assure themselves of dependable sources of supply. This is a major consideration in multiple sourcing decisions, even when it would cost less to buy from a single supplier. The fieldwork further revealed that the number of qualified suppliers had an impact upon the criteria for supplier selection. In industries with relatively few suppliers, buyers are naturally more concerned with user-supplier relations. The development and maintenance of these relationships become an important aspect of the purchasing job. Orders are sometimes given to suppliers who are higher in price to assure the buying organization of dependable, continuing sources of supply. In industries where the number of suppliers is small, the customer may be almost as concerned with providing suppliers with business as the suppliers are in securing that business.

At the other end of the scale are industries characterized by many suppliers. In this situation two different patterns emerge. For many items, the buying company may have a relatively small number of regular suppliers. This may be formally recognized by an approved list of vendors or may be an informal ''list'' that exists only in the buyer's mind. The user–supplier relationships appear to be quite similar to those which develop when buying from suppliers in industries where there are only a few companies. There is a major difference, however, in that the availability of many alternate sources makes the buying company less likely to think of itself as being "in the same boat" with the supplier. Rather, the buying influences are more likely to feel themselves "on the other side of the desk" from the supplier and see their own interests as being different from those of suppliers.

When a number of different sources of supply are available, the buying organization may continually seek out new alternatives. In some instances, additions and deletions are made to the vendor list. In other instances, the searching activity is undertaken primarily to "keep current suppliers on their toes."

A second pattern may be observed when there are many suppliers to choose from. The buying organization may take a short-run view of the user-supplier relationships. The buyers may assume that they do not need to be concerned with running out of suppliers and attempt to resolve each transaction or contract in their own favor without regard to the interests or viewpoint of the seller. In this case, buyers and sellers may approach the matter as a zero sum game: One party may gain only at the expense of the other. In buying situations where this pattern is observed, buyers may think that their interests are in opposition to the supplier's interest, and their buying behavior is likely to reflect that attitude.

The type of competition within the supplying industry also appears to exert a strong influence on the ways in which buying situations arise in customer organizations. Where suppliers compete on a price basis, it is more difficult to establish close, long-run buyer-seller relationships—primarily because buyers tend to be evaluated in their own organizations according to how much they spend and so concentrate on minimizing the price paid for a particular transaction.

When suppliers stress nonprice competition, the buying influences may give more consideration to the longer-term user-supplier relationships and to the other aspects of the suppliers' offers. Price may still be one of the major considerations, though not the dominant one, and it often enters the buying decision making process much later than many industrial marketers appear to believe.

The threat of material or parts shortages, whether real or imagined, will have an impact on purchasing. Fears of shortages typically lead to forward buying and stockpiling. Larger customers may seek their own captive sources of supply. Buyers may tend to concentrate their purchases and rely upon long-term supplier relationships to assure that their requirements will be met if and when shortages do occur.

The traditional ways of doing business and the methods of operation in the supply industry will also have an impact on customers' procurement decisions. The terms of sale, types of discounts, minimum order sizes, maximum quantity discounts allowed, product perishability and obsolescence, seasonality of production and sales, new product introduction procedures and timing, method and speed of delivery, and so on will be reflected in the buying patterns of customers.

Socio-politico-economic Conditions

The general socio-politico-economic environment within which the buying company operates has an impact on purchasing as well as other activities of the business organization. If the economy is growing and the mood expansive, buyers may feel sufficiently confident to make substantial forward commitments. Similarly, if prices are expected to rise, buying companies may feel encouraged to build up inventories and to seek long-term, fixed price contracts. During recessions, buyers may take a short-range view of their activities and order only on an "as needed basis."

Significant Events

A significant impact on purchasing can be exerted by any number of events not even directly related to the procurement process. For example, a technological breakthrough, congressional investigation of the industry, major fire or fatal accident—any of these can stimulate the development of numerous buying situations, as well as changes in buying policies and patterns.

Such unpredictable events generally occur in only one or few companies at any given time. They may become known to the marketer only if a salesman calls on the account periodically or if the marketer has other reliable information sources. Certain events, such as the East Coast power failure in the fall of 1965, are the subject of widespread publicity and automatically create many marketing opportunities for aggressive firms.

SUMMARY

This chapter has discussed various environmental influences, internal and external which affected the procurement process. Internal variables include personal attributes of individuals involved in the buying situation, the organization of the buying company, the bases of competition in the buying company's industry, and its patterns of operation. External variables include characteristics of the supplying industries, socioeconomic and political conditions, and significant events. Each buying situation occurs, is modified, and is resolved within a unique combination of environmental factors. It now remains to examine in more depth the environmental dimension which is most generally open to the activities of the marketer: the various buying influences and the roles they play.

IX

The Roles of
the Buying Influences

THE DIRECTION AND OUTCOME of the procurement process is subject to influence by a number of individuals in diverse corporate roles. The objective of this chapter is to evaluate the perspective of various categories of buying influences most likely to become enmeshed in industrial buying situations. Where production men are involved, for example, how are their particular backgrounds and points of view likely to influence the buying decisions? With an understanding of those different outlooks, the industrial marketer might better tailor his marketing efforts to meet the needs of a specific buying situation. A related objective of this chapter is to examine the role of the purchasing department and the scope of its activities.

THE BUYING INFLUENCES

A buying influence is anyone who becomes involved, directly or indirectly, in the problem-solving or decision making activities which constitute the procurement process. They are numerous types and levels of buying influences, and they vary to the extremes in significance. One of the purposes of the BUYGRID framework developed earlier is to enable the industrial marketer to become familiar with his customer's buying processes to such an extent that he can predict the more significant influences in any given situation with a high degree of accuracy.

People appear to become involved in buying situations for one of two reasons. Organizational position can give them a formal stake in the outcome of the buying decision by virtue of either responsibility or authority. Otherwise, an individual can become a buying influence if he is a source of information critical to the decision making process. For example, metallurgists from the advanced engineering department may become major buying influences when the company is considering a change to a new type of steel, even though persons at their hierarchical level within the organization would not normally become involved.

FUNCTIONAL CLASSIFICATION OF BUYING INFLUENCES

User-supplier relationships and communications between buyers and sellers usually revolve around the job activities of the buying influences. Since organization charts, too, are constructed largely along functional lines, this approach seems to be the most useful way of distinguishing between different types of buying influences. In the following discussion, the types of involvement and the general perspective of "typical" buying influences from each of the following functional areas within an organization are examined: marketing, manufacturing, product engineering, finance and accounting, research and development, and general management. An analysis of the purchasing agent function completes the chapter.

It should be noted that the activities which represent important buying influences vary considerably from company to company. Even within a given company, there may be shifts in the types of jobs held by the buying influences over time. This is particularly true in industries sustaining rapid technological change and new product innovation and in companies undergoing expansion through mergers or acquisitions.

Marketing

In general, marketing men tend to view the procurement process in their own companies as a means of enhancing the salability of the goods and services marketed by the company. Marketers recognize that the procurement of both direct and indirect parts and materials affects the acceptability of the final product by intermediate and final customers. In many instances, the procurement of indirect items may influence the marketability of a product. For example, a new numerically controlled machine tool may help to increase the quality of the final item.

As a natural extension of this basic viewpoint, the marketers may consider the use of trade relations as another procurement variable to enhance the salability of the offering. The marketer may view trade relations as one of a number of ways of differentiating his offer from those of competitors. Trade relations are discussed more fully in Chapter X. Here it is sufficient to note that in many types of businesses, the marketer may look upon trade relations as leverage—using his company's purchasing power to help sell his company's goods and services. Each of the companies studied is buying some products because the producers have created a strong demand for these so-called proprietary items among the customers of Companies Able, Baker, and Charlie. More precisely, the marketing people in the subject companies believe, and probably correctly, that the suppliers have built up a strong proprietary position with intermediate and final customers.

The marketing group may actually select the supplier in the case of proprietary items, when the inclusion of a particular brand product is believed likely to increase customer acceptance of the supplier's own product. In determining the characteristics and features of a new model, marketing also influences the procurement process because its decisions necessarily eliminate a large number of suppliers who would otherwise be qualified as potential vendors.

The greatest number of proprietary items are purchased at Company Baker, which incorporates them into its final product, a consumer durable. In fact, proprietary items account for some two-thirds of the dollar value of the direct items which go into Company Baker's final product. Company Able purchases fewer proprietary items than Company Baker for incorporation into its high-priced capital equipment. Company Able's proprietary items are typically relatively inexpensive components, but of a highly critical nature. A failure of one of these items, such as the failure of a small switch in a missile firing, can have serious consequences far out of proportion to the value of the item itself. Fewer examples of the purchase of proprietary items were observed at Company Charlie, which markets basic materials to general industry standards. However, executives reported that proprietary items are purchased for resale through the channels of distribution.

Proprietary items are typically made by large, well-known manufacturers. Many buyers appear to equate these items with technical, product, or service superiority. For many items, the determination of the specifications may be made by buying influences who specify by name or number the item to be purchased. Purchasing people, on the other hand, may see these items as overpriced and overengineered. As one buyer said, "They don't meet the specifications, they exceed them, and we pay dearly for that excess." It is not surprising, therefore, that proprietary items are selected less frequently in those situations where purchasing people are the major buying influences.

In Company Baker, proprietary items account for well over one-half of direct parts and materials purchases. Marketing personnel are strong buying influences, since the general characteristics and performance specifications are determined by marketing working with engineering. The decisions are constrained by a predetermined final retail price and upon the appraisal of current and anticipated competition. Marketing sets the ground rules which govern the buying decisions of engineering and purchasing. At Company Baker, suppliers may be vetoed or blackballed by marketing because of its positional authority. "We wouldn't touch them with a ten-foot pole, regardless of the price they offered or anything else,'' said the new product manager about a well-known industry supplier. Apparently, these vetoes are not questioned by the other buying influences.

In each of the companies studied, there were cases where a major buying influence objected strongly to the selection of a particular supplier in a new task or modified rebuy situation. In each case, this veto was respected by the other buying influences, even when influences of equal or higher position in the buying organization did not agree.

It is important to note that during the period when marketing and engineering are working to determine the general specifications for a new product, potential suppliers are neither called in nor made aware that the crucial ground rules are being laid for selecting suppliers. The ''center of gravity'' for the procurement process is in these early specification-setting meetings. Thus, a potential supplier may well be eliminated from consideration before he even realizes that procurement decisions are being made. The marketer may be able to do little at the time when some of the most critical decisions are being made. Rather, he is judged according to his past performance and the buying influences' perception and estimates of his capabilities for performing in the future. This, in turn, is partially a subjective, reinforced evaluation of how well he has performed in the past.

Development or Design Engineering

A company may have a development engineering group, a design engineering group, or both. By whatever name, the functional activity is that of product development and modification and is concerned with products and services being commercialized. Advanced design or research and development groups are treated separately.

There is a great deal of overlap between the development-design and manufacturing groups, and they are sometimes combined. There appears to be a logical separation between the two, however, with respect to the roles of personnel as buying influences. It might not be too great an oversimplification to characterize the viewpoint of development-design as ''this is what we *have* to do,'' and that of manufacturing, ''this is what we *can* do.'' If the activities are performed separately, close cooperation is needed between them. Both groups are idea sources which translate general specifications into the actual product. They also hold the final authority on technical matters within their organizations. When involved in a buying situation, their attitudes, opinions, and perspective carry considerable weight. The fieldwork indicates that it is extremely unusual for other buying influences to overrule recommendations of the development or design engineers. The constraints imposed upon this functional group are typified by a predetermined maximum selling price for the final product, make-or-buy considerations, value analysis, "buy American," and similar policies.

It is probably useful to distinguish between the initial introduction of new *products* and the periodic introduction of new *models*. In a new product situation, the buying influences have little if any relevant buying experience and need a great deal of information before decisions can be made with confidence. These decisions are of particular import to marketers because they set the pattern for future purchases. In these new task situations, a precedent is set which will constitute the frame of reference for future purchasing decisions about the same items. While modifications will develop in accordance with new experiences of the buying influences, there are clear advantages to the suppliers who are chosen in the initial new task situations, and it is in these situations that the influence of the development and design engineers is strongest.

The introduction of a new model, or a new product closely related to existing lines, poses substantially different type of buying problem. In this case, the decision makers are already familiar with the general structure and characteristics of the supplying industry. Less information is needed as the procurement process proceeds. These acquisitions are typically handled as modified rebuys, since the broad procurement policies and patterns have already been established on previous occasions.

It appears that the influence of the development and design engineers in modified rebuys is not generally as strong as it is in new tasks. The buying situations studied suggest that this may be because the technical expertise which the development-design engineers have in new task is much more diffused throughout the buying organization in modified rebuys. All of the buying influences may benefit from the company's past experience, although that experience is subject to a variety of interpretations. Consequently, modified rebuys tend to be group decisions to a greater extent than do new tasks.

Whether development-design has the ultimate responsibility for determining the characteristics of the product (as in Companies Able and Charlie), or whether that formal responsibility rests elsewhere (as in Company Baker), the actual development and design work is done by the development-design personnel. In new task situations, their most obvious influence on the procurement process is in the setting of specifications and performance requirements.

In at least two other respects, the development-design engineers strongly influence the procurement process and supplier selection activities that follow. Either alone or with some other group such as accounting, the development-design engineers are usually responsible for preparing estimates of the costs involved in procuring the parts and materials which comprise the final product. Apart from the make-or-buy implications, these preliminary cost estimates tend to set a limit within which prospective suppliers must keep their prices.

The influence of development-design in new tasks was summed up by a director of purchasing who said, "The designers are the real buyers around here. When the drawings come to the buyer from them, 90 percent of the final purchasing costs are already locked up tight." Working with the manufacturing group, the development-design engineers set time constraints for prospective suppliers. Because of the impact of new task buying decisions on the future stream of purchases, the marketer may want to consider staffing his technical sales group with sufficient manpower to handle customer needs promptly and staff to expected peak demands, even if this means being somewhat overstaffed in most periods.

The generally accepted image of the engineer is that of a no-nonsense technical expert who makes completely rational decisions, unhampered by emotional considerations. However, there are definite indications that technically trained buying influences tend to have strong preferences for buying from the large, well-known companies in a given field. One reason may well be that these companies generally do a better job of servicing customers, although several other reasons also appear influential.

This finding appears to be substantiated by Dr. Theodore Levitt in *Industrial Purchasing Behavior*,[1] a recent Harvard Business School study. Levitt concludes:

> ...there is some indication that... purchasing agents, who are usually highly competent as professional buyers, may be less influenced by a company's generalized reputation than technical personnel.... Technically sophisticated personnel seem to be influenced by the seller's reputation to a point that is unexpectedly higher than the influence of that reputation on such technically less sophisticated personnel as purchasing agents.[2]

Why are technically trained men more influenced by company reputation than men without such technical training? Several reasons appear likely. First, technically qualified people may be more susceptible to technically oriented advertising than are other personnel in the buying company. There may also be a more basic reason. The successful, well-known industrial marketers have carefully built their reputations, by advertising and other means, so that their image is one of *capability*. The findings of this study indicate that a company's technical expert, the engineer, believes that mistakes and problems arising from new products purchased are generally blamed on him as much as they are blamed on the supplier. Therefore, to minimize this perceived risk, he tends to favor suppliers who ostensibly have the best reputations.

The chief design engineer at Company Baker said:

> Any time you design a part that is not strictly off-the-shelf, there's

risk involved. Even designing a model that uses standard parts is risky—they may not work together the way they should. So what do I want in a supplier? In one word, *capability*. I have to be sure in my own mind that the supplier has the talent and will stick with it to *make* it work, even if unexpected problems arise, as they always do. My concern is not with what the supplier *promises* to do for me this time. By the time I find that out, it's too late. What I'm interested in is what he has done in the past, for me and to some extent, for others.

Manufacturing

A simple way of distinguishing between the roles of the manufacturing and design development groups is that the former is usually responsible for the development of the characteristics and general specifications for *indirect* goods and services, while the latter is typically in charge of developing specifications for the *direct* items which enter into the final product being manufactured.

The manufacturing group's major responsibilities may be subdivided into three general areas: facilities, production of existing products, and studies preceding the introduction of new products.

Both formal and informal patterns of planning may be observed. In one company, the manufacturing group has technically trained people whose only job is to study general facilities and production methods and standards to determine how and where improvements can be made. In other companies, on a more informal basis, any individual who gets an idea for improving production efficiency brings it to the attention of a responsible individual. Not surprisingly, more new ideas appear to be generated in companies that handle this activity on a formal basis, giving impetus to more new task situations than is the case where informal processes prevail.

Regardless of the planning pattern, however, the manufacturing group appears to be a major factor in triggering new task situations. In new tasks, supplier selection depends largely upon the marketer's reputation for capability. This is especially true when the item being purchased is not a standard item but must be specifically developed to fit the particular needs of the customer. This is the case in most of the new task situations that arise in the manufacturing group.

With respect to facilities' planning activities, the manufacturing group is interested in determining what new capital and other equipment will be needed and the types of goods and services to be produced in the future. The task is one of trying to foresee what the manufacturing operation will look like in the future. Similarly, prospective suppliers should also be able to anticipate the nature of the customer's business in the future. Professor D. Maynard Phelps' notion that the marketer must understand the operation of the customer's business may be expanded.[3] The marketer needs to understand the customer's business not only today, but also five, ten, or even twenty years from now.

With reference to the broad planning aspects of his job, Company Able's director of manufacturing said:

> I'm concerned with establishing people, jobs, systems, and approaches. I keep up with the detailed studies being made to determine if new equipment is needed and if it can pay for itself. I see that the work schedules are outlined, and know the variance from those schedules. Over the years, as a result of experience, you get pretty detailed knowledge of what is happening on the production line. My job is to try to anticipate problems. We used to wait for the operating people to bring problems to us when they ran into them; then we'd approve or disapprove their plans. Now we try to do this on a more centralized basis, in order to anticipate problems and to keep them from arising.

With respect to products currently in production, the manufacturing group focuses its major effort upon reducing operating tie-up and maintaining the work flow. There is a separate planning group in Company Able which plans each step of the operation in order to maximize efficiency. A running account of time and materials costs is maintained, and suggestions for improvement are continually generated within this group. For current production operations, periodic make-or-buy reevaluations may be made, and special cost studies undertaken as requested. When new products or models are being considered, the manufacturing group plays a major role in the related procurement process. Manufacturing is chiefly responsible for studying the feasibility of producing the item, and the closely related economic considerations. What new equipment will be needed? How much will it cost? What will be the impact on current production?

Make-or-buy evaluations may originate within manufacturing. Even when they are made by other groups, such as design and development or accounting, manufacturing personnel are likely to play a major role in the final decisions as to what will be made and what will be purchased from outside sources.

With respect to the parts, materials, components, and subassemblies which actually become a part of the final product, the role of manufacturing is twofold. First, it confirms the decisions made by the design and development group as to the parts and materials to be used and asks such questions as: Is there a better way to make this part? Is this the best material to use? Is there a way to redesign or modify the part to simplify the manufacturing job? The manufacturing group often provides an independent, technical evaluation of the decisions made by design and development. In brief, the manufacturing group is concerned with the manufacturing implications of the design decisions.

A second role of manufacturing is to provide an independent

study of the costs of producing the products in question. It also provides a separate appraisal of the information developed by the design and finance buying influences. In this connection, the value analysis activity in many companies is a part of the manufacturing group rather than the purchasing or design-development groups. With respect to the acquisition of capital equipment and other items that do not enter directly into the final product, manufacturing is typically the dominant influence, with the confirming or reviewing role usually played by the financial and other supporting staff groups.

In the subject companies, the major responsibility for determining what machine tools were required rested with manufacturing. This is quite logical since, for most of these items, manufacturing may be considered to be the using department. In Companies Able and Baker, manufacturing sets priorities for capital spending in accordance with established policies. The initial decisions on individual requests for capital equipment are also made by the director of manufacturing. In Company Able, manufacturing regularly checks existing capital equipment and makes cost studies to determine the timing for acquisition of new equipment and the general type of equipment needed. At Company Baker, the director of manufacturing has established the following priorities for the approval of requests for capital equipment: 1. new product introduction, 2. cost reductions, 3. expansion of current output, and 4. replacement of obsolete or worn-out equipment.

An analysis of the fieldwork indicates that manufacturing personnel may be more receptive to new product ideas than are many design and development men. In each of the companies interviewed, the manufacturing groups regularly conducted pilot tests of new parts and materials and experimented with new production methods and processes. This willingness to experiment may be due to the fact that the manufacturing groups had ready access to testing facilities and could therefore make mistakes without their errors having serious impact on company operations.

Research and Development

This category includes the advanced materials and processes groups and the research and development activities. Although these activities often represent important buying influences, they appear to have been largely overlooked by many industrial marketers. The organizational structure appears to vary substantially, but each of the three companies examined in this study had some internal group responsible for the performance of three basic interrelated activites: 1. the development of products, processes, and technologies, 2. the pre-commercialization work on products, processes, and technologies which are soon to be turned over to an operating unit for introduction, and 3. the setting of broad specifications or requirements within which the design and development people must operate. These general specifications take the form of industry codes, stress and strength criteria, minimum composition standards, and so forth.

At any given time, the advance research and development groups may have a number of projects in varying stages of readiness prior to commercialization. The chief of the research and development group at Company Able said:

> I assign probabilities, in my own mind, as to whether or not the new technologies under study will ever become economically feasible. For each production method, I have to determine whether to design equipment that will require these methods, and then decide the extent to which a particular process or product will be used. We have to really keep on our toes with the new technological developments, because it's mighty easy to be caught flat-footed.

The director of advanced materials group in Company Able turned out to be a strong buying influence, although his involvement was completely informal. In fact, most of the other buying influences in specific purchases were not even aware of his involvement. Because of his past experience and his current job, he had a detailed knowledge of the suppliers in the metals business. Unofficially, the purchasing agent consulted him about general specifications and suppliers. The purchasing agent was a formal participant in the procurement process, along with representatives from the design and development and manufacturing groups. The technical people themselves often had disagreements concerning specifications, designs, and suppliers. The purchasing agent was, in effect, using the advance materials director as his own independent check on the decisions of the technical buying influences. The pattern appeared to work smoothly, with neither the technical men nor the potential suppliers aware that the materials man was involved in the buying decisions.

There appear to be two major reasons why the advanced materials and research and development groups are important to industrial marketers. The first is tied to the marketer's current sales interests. The sooner he can become involved in the customer's procurement process, the greater his chances of getting the particular order. To the extent that people from the supplier company become involved before the product is turned over to an operating group for commercialization, their chances of helping the customer in the problem definition phase are enhanced. Such relationships have both short and long-range benefits for the marketer. Second, a basic knowledge of the areas in which important customers are doing research and development work is perhaps as good an insurance policy as a marketer can have. By understanding the directions in which his customers' businesses are moving, the marketer can better determine the directions for his own business.

Supporting Staff Groups

What is the role of a staff group in the procurement process? In general, it appears that a staff man becomes involved in a given buying situation primarily as a *reviewing* authority. There seem to be three primary reasons for staff involvement: First, the staff man is presumed to have a special information position. He sees the entire corporate viewpoint, and not that of the using or the purchasing department. Second, the "impartial" staff review provides an independent check on the commitments and decisions of the buying influences who are directly involved. Third, a staff review tends to force the using department and the others involved in the procurement process to consider the broad ramifications of their decisions upon the rest of the company.

In addition to the organization and environmental variables discussed in Chapter VIII the type of buying situation appears to be a key determinant of the extent to which supporting staff members become involved. Each of the companies studied has policies requiring that all items which are to be capitalized must go through one or more staff reviews before the purchase takes place. Such procedures do not appear to be based primarily upon the number of dollars involved, although it is true that capitalized items are usually more expensive than other items. In Company Charlie, for example, a purchasing agent may commit the company to purchase several million dollars worth of materials from a supplier without any other authorization. Yet, he cannot spend $75,000 for a conveyor belt without going through a substantial staff and top management reviewing process.

In straight rebuys, there is not likely to be any formal staff group participation. Straight rebuys have been routinized to the point where they are decided in accordance with well-established guidelines and policies. Indeed, the policies themselves may be defined as standardized answers to recurring questions so that there is no need for reviews of each transaction.

Because of the organizational policies mentioned above, modified rebuys need to be broken into capitalized and expensed categories. With respect to expensed goods and services, very little formal staff participation was encountered in the procurement process. Where staff involvement was found, as with the advanced material director in Company Able, it was on an individual and informal basis. The staff man had a special information position rather than a formal stake in the outcome of the decision. In some circumstances, trade relations people might be formally involved in modified rebuys.

It is in modified rebuys and new tasks involving capital equipment that supporting staff people are most likely to become formally involved. Apparently expectations are that it is in these situations where the need for an independent reviewing authority is greatest. Even new tasks are not likely to be of major interest to staff people unless the items being considered are to be capitalized.

In capital goods purchases, the staff buying influences may have, in theory if not in practice, the authority to approve or disapprove the various alternatives being considered. Such is the case in Company Able, where the other major buying influences are aware of, and defer to, the reviewer's authority. Once the reviewer has recommended an alternative, it is almost certain to receive approval from the company president, the final authority.

In Company Baker, by contrast, the staff reviewers are considerably less powerful. There are staff people who review the capital appropriations requests for the line executives who have the approval authority. However, the other buying influences do not feel particularly bound by a negative report from the reviewer. In a number of instances, the using department was able to go around the reviewer and have his recommendations overruled by a line executive.

When capital appropriations are involved, several separate staff reviews may be made at various phases in the procurement process. People from a number of staff groups may all become important buying influences, including accounting, finance, technical services, legal, trade relations, and labor relations. Marketing, production, international, or community and public relations staff reviews may also be called for in particular situations.

To further understand the role of supporting staff personnel as important buying influences, some general remarks made by a technical and financial staff reviewer for capital equipment requests in Company Able are quoted:

My job is to get an unbiased opinion of what the capital request is all about. I've got to take a broad perspective, to give the company a sense of direction. I try to fit all of the requests that come across my desk into an informal, but unified framework.

It's my job to force the operating divisions to consider the long-range implications of their actions. I not only review what the operating people do, but work with them to help determine their real needs. My review is definitely a working review. About 90 percent of the requests that cross my desk are approved, although often in modified form.

I evaluate what the new capital equipment is to be used for. I've got to be convinced that an actual need exists. I want to know how well the new equipment will work with the old. What vendors are being considered? I'm an engineer by training, so I may get into some of the detailed technical features, as well as comparing the features of different vendors. I may even suggest some new sources for them to consider.

I'm also concerned with the risks. What risks have been identified? What's the likelihood of their occurring? How deeply has the requesting department itself looked into this thing? To what extent have they considered all of the alternatives—not only alternative vendors, but alternative ways of doing the job. I can tell pretty accurately just how much time and thought have gone into any request that comes across my desk.

General Management

What role is played in the procurement process by management people at the various horizontal levels within an organization? How actively does top management involve itself in ongoing buying situations?

The analysis revealed four general patterns of top management involvement in, or disassociation from, the procurement processes studied.

The first pattern represented maximum involvement in the buying decision making by members of top management. This was found in new task situations which were somewhat remote from the firm's day-to-day operations. The purchase of an executive airplane, for example, might be handled by top management personally. Similarly, all the buying influences may be from top management when decisions will have major consequences for the firm's operations and its freedom of action in the future. Consistent with this pattern, all of the important buying decisions may be made with relatively few information inputs requested of or received from lower levels in the buying organization.

The second pattern involves major operating decisions which establish general criteria for subsequent buying situations. For example, Company Able's management made a decision to spend $25 million to expand production capacity. This decision, and the staff work that preceded and followed it, established general criteria for the evaluation of purchases and spawned a series of new task and modified rebuy situations to implement management's decision. In these situations, top management is actively involved in establishing the guidelines by which purchases are to be evaluated and may participate in the very early phases of the procurement process. This participation may involve only the initial recognition that a problem exists after which the buying decisions are delegated to others.

The third pattern occurs when the procurement process is activated below general management level in the organization. The original impetus may come from a department head, a staff man, an engineer, or a designer; such situations frequently are sparked by creative foremen and superintendents on the production line. In many of these new tasks and modified rebuy situations, approving authority will have been delegated to a lower organizational level. Top management will not participate, and its role will be that of confirming the buying decisions made at lower organizational levels.

In the fourth pattern, usually applicable to straight and modified rebuys, top management plays no identifiable role in the procurement process, either as an active participant or as a reviewing or confirming authority. This pattern appears to cover the bulk of the purchases made by organizations for its continuing or recurring requirements.

In a study for *Time* magazine of management's role in purchasing, Dr. Emanual Demby concluded that the role of top management in the procurement decision process is generally overstated, while the role of middle management is generally understated. The study states that, "...as United States industrial organizations have grown, top management has been forced to spend more time on long-term considerations and less time on operational problems. The authority for these responsibilities has been delegated to middle management." [4] However, it appears logical to expect that top management will review or participate in the procurement process in those situations where management has additional information which is not known to those at lower organizational levels, or where the results of the purchasing decisions could substantially reduce the company's flexibility or ability to act in the future.

The Purchasing Agent

In assessing the role of the purchasing agent or purchasing department, as compared to the roles of other buying influences, one needs to consider the importance of the transaction and the extent to which management believes that the decision criteria or rules can be clearly established and specified. There is a natural tendency to routinize purchases that occur frequently, so that as the buying company obtains more and more buying experience, the likelihood that the purchasing agent will become a major buying influence increases. What is meant by the "importance" of a purchase to a company? A common measurement is absolute dollar expenditure, although significance will vary among companies, products, time periods, and use-situations. The probability of a shortage or interrupted supply of an item can heighten its importance considerably. Alderson's "power principle" contributes some insight toward measuring the importance of a purchase item. Assuming that the firm will act in such a way as to preserve and enhance its ability to act in the future, [5] the power principle if applied to the buying situation implies that the more the outcome of a buying situation will restrict the freedom of choice of the organization in the future, the higher the organizational level at which the buying decisions will be made.

The purchasing agent's role as a *negotiator* may vary from that of a catalyst to those of an arbitrator or a judge. He must reconcile the internal requirements and personalities with the external situation. He frequently presents and defends the viewpoints of potential suppliers to other buying influences inside of his own firm.

While it is true that purchasing agents serve a screening function, attempts to avoid them frequently boomerang, since the purchasing agent may still exert a strong "blocking" influence even when he cannot influence the outcome of the buying situation positively. It is probably correct to say that in many buying situations purchasing agents, like top management, are involved primarily in a negative way: They can say no. A veto by top management is usually clear and direct. A veto by a buyer may be more subtle. By the information he presents and the way in which he presents it to the other buying influences, it is usually possible for the purchasing agent to eliminate a particular supplier from serious consideration. On the other hand, the purchasing agent may be a "friend in court" for a particular supplier, and statements from the purchasing department may be expected to carry more weight than the same statement made by a supplier salesman.

Another aspect of the purchasing agent's job is to *generate alternative solutions* to procurement problems. This involves the search for potential new suppliers and research directed toward finding new products or methods which improve upon existing ones. This search for new alternatives converts a straight rebuy into a modified rebuy.

One of the fundamental responsibilities of the purchasing agent is to *protect the cost structure of his company*, for those products requiring purchased items. This must be done without impeding the normal production operations. The buyer has the responsibility for *minimizing purchasing costs* by seeking new sources and the development of existing suppliers, systems analysis, value analysis, and other forms of purchasing research.

The purchasing agent also is charged with *assuring long-range sources of supply* and a continuing selection of qualified suppliers. This task often conflicts with opportunities to reduce costs on present orders; hence, the problem is one of balancing these sometime divergent objectives.

Another important job is *the maintenance of good relationships* with suppliers. This activity is not confined to the purchasing department. The more marketing-oriented a company, the more people at different levels and in all departments will be guided toward maintaining good relationships with customers and suppliers. But it appears that the typical purchasing department in a large company is specifically admonished to "be a good customer." In the case of a so-called "soft" purchasing company, the purchasing agent will probably spend a considerable part of his time nurturing supplier relations. The purchasing department in such cases will usually have less influence over the procurement process than its counterpart in the "hard" purchasing company. Major emphasis in the latter is on price reduction with consequent sustaining pressure on suppliers.

The buying company's interest in being a good customer is based upon more than a spirit of altruism. As one purchasing agent expressed, "In the long run, my job is a lot easier if my suppliers think of me as a good customer. I want them to want my business, because when they do they will hustle to get it and to keep it." The

establishment, cultivation, and maintenance of good supplier relationships are considered to be intrinsically more important than the
outcome of individual transactions.

It should be noted that these designated "soft" and "hard" procurement policies only reflect general tendencies and that numerous
inconsistencies will exist in any given company. The distinction
can be supported, however, by actual experience in the fieldwork.

Another major and time-consuming function of the purchasing
agent is to assume responsibility for the *mechanics of the procurement process*. Many parts of the ordering, expediting, inspection,
status reporting, and related activities are handled by the buyer
himself.

Many purchasing agents feel that they spend an inordinately
high percentage of their time with these relatively routine procedures. A distinction is sometimes made between the routine and
the more creative aspects of the job, resulting in the designation
in some organizations of "junior" and "senior" buyers. The
former handle most of the paperwork and the more routinized purchases. Problems and special situations are turned over to the
senior buyers on an exception basis; consequently, they have more
time to devote to the more creative functions which are more likely
to have a significant, long-range impact on the buying organization.

One sagacious buyer summarized the role of the purchasing agent
by saying, "I'm really a generalist among a group of specialists.
Production people, designers, maintenance, accounting, marketing
and legal specialists are all involved in the procurement process,
bringing their special training and viewpoints to bear. I'm the guy
who has to integrate all of these separate entities into a workable
scheme that will meet our needs."

SUMMARY

People become buying influences in specific situations because their
organizational position gives them a formal stake in the outcome,
or because they have a relevant special information position. The
chapter outlined how the particular responsibilities and perspectives
of different buying influences affect their perception of the problem
and their attitudes toward various alternative solutions.

Marketing men tend to look at purchasing as a means of enhancing
the salability of their own items. Design and development engineers
try to minimize the risks of making an error and "play it safe."
Yet the designs and specifications that come from them greatly influence the procurements that follow, since the way in which they
state their requirements eliminates from consideration many suppliers who would otherwise be qualified.

Manufacturing people tend to favor simple items which make the
production job as inexpensive and trouble-free as possible. Re-

search and development people are frequently overlooked but are important because they set the broad criteria within which the other technical buying influences operate. They also provide good clues as to what the company's requirements will be in the future. Supporting staff people get involved because of their special information positions.

In a few cases, all of the buying decisions may be made by general management; usually its role is more limited. When the original need is recognized by management, it sets broad criteria and policies and delegates the buying decisions to lower levels. When the original recognition of the need comes from lower levels, management generally plays no role in the procurement process, although it may always veto whatever has happened up to that point.

The purchasing agent performs a number of specialized facilitating activities which vary in importance across companies and buying situations. Regardless of his formal strength in a given situation, the purchasing agent is usually able to significantly help or hurt the chances of any particular supplier.

X

User-Supplier Relationships

"COMPANIES DON'T MAKE PURCHASES; they establish relationships." This view, expressed by Dr. Charles S. Goodman of the Wharton School of Finance and Commerce, University of Pennsylvania, is consistent with the view of purchasing as problem solving. Although much of the industrial marketing literature stresses making "the sale" as though it were an independent event, both buyers and sellers appear to be primarily interested in establishing long-term mutually beneficial relationships. The central importance of the user-supplier relationship in the industrial procurement situation is stressed throughout this book.

Various policies and practices of different buying organizations were examined in the course of this study. This chapter seeks to analyze some of the more important and to explore and evaluate their impact on user-supplier relationships. Illustrations are presented to suggest how buying company actions and policies affect its relationships with current and potential suppliers and how the nature of these relationships helps to determine the outcome of buying situations. By using examples from the fieldwork, some problems and opportunities for the marketer also are posited.

THE IMPORTANCE OF SUPPLIER RELATIONSHIPS
TO THE BUYING INFLUENCES

The fieldwork clearly indicates that the buying company considers it important to be viewed as a good customer by its suppliers. As one purchasing director expressed it, "It's to our advantage to make sure that our business is important to suppliers. We want them to do business with us." Indeed, the manager of purchasing at Company Baker clearly considers his major responsibility as that of developing and maintaining good relationships with suppliers.

Why are companies concerned about being good customers? The

answer seems to go far beyond the considerations of public relations or assurance of supply in times of a seller's market.
The chief design engineer for one major company explained:

> I'm really very protective of the suppliers who work with us on a
> new product. I have to be, because you can get a reputation among
> the suppliers as somebody who just steals their ideas and then buys
> price. That is no good for the long term. I go to a supplier early
> in the game and tell him we want to work with him. Then he'll
> give his all to help me get a good design. He knows he'll be com-
> pensated for any ideas he has. We have new models coming out
> each year, so I'd be pretty stupid to handle suppliers in any other
> way.

The buying influences take a long-range view of their relationships with present and prospective suppliers. They are generally
willing to forego any immediate windfalls they might obtain by taking unfair advantage of a supplier and are more concerned with the
longer-term benefits that accrue to the company that is respected
and solicited by suppliers. It is possible, however, that smaller
companies may sometimes be forced to take a shorter-range viewpoint.

COMPUTERIZED ORDERING PROCEDURES

There is an increasing trend in the use of computerized ordering
procedures both for individual transactions and long-term relationships. Under such arrangements inventory records are kept on a
computer by the buying company. When the reorder point is
reached, the computer automatically transmits a predetermined
order quantity by data-phone or similar means to a computer used
by the seller. The seller's computer calculates the inventory location nearest to the customer, the means of delivery, prices, and
costs and sends shipping instructions to the relevant shipping department. The user and the supplier periodically (perhaps once a year,
or even less frequently) renegotiate terms and prices. Superfi-
cially, it might appear that such procedures would weaken user-
supplier relationships by eliminating so much of the human element.
In fact, however, there are many indications that the relationships
are actually strengthened. Since the parties commit themselves to
a fairly long-term agreement, each must fully specify his own requirements. The dependence of each party on the other is explicitly recognized. Both gain only if the system operates efficiently
so that there is a large area of shared interest. There are risks
for each which arise from the environmental uncontrollables and
from the actions of the other. Mutual trust and understanding are

vital to a successful program. For these and other reasons, user-supplier relationships generally become stronger.

SUPPLIER INVENTORYING

So-called "stockless" purchasing, where inventories are maintained by the seller rather than the buyer, is a logical extension of computerized ordering procedures. While the supplier incurs greater costs as he takes on more of the inventorying task, such arrangements tend to strengthen the quality of the user-supplier relationships.

In many situations, "understandings" develop which go far beyond those involved in the usual purchasing relationships. Company Charlie, for example, has a number of unspoken agreements with suppliers of frequently purchased items. The supplier will inventory for the buying organization and even save materials although without contractual obligation to do so. Company Charlie normally gives each regular supplier his "rightful share" of business. If circumstances occur which leave the supplier with "dead" inventory that he has held for Company Charlie, Charlie has a gentlemen's agreement to buy that inventory. These understandings, while informal and unwritten, tend to reinforce the interdependence of users and suppliers.

Another type of "understanding" is illustrated by Company Baker which purchases two-thirds of its requirements for a major component from a particular supplier without considering any others. The other third of the business is awarded on a competitive basis.

Similarly, the actual or imagined threat of materials or parts shortages may greatly strengthen the bond between users and suppliers. This seems to be especially true where the total number of potential suppliers is limited. The threat of shortages tends to tie a customer to his existing suppliers, since this appears to be the only way he can assure himself of obtaining a supply of the item in times of scarcity.

MAKE-OR-BUY CONSIDERATIONS

Each of the companies studied has a manufacturing capability and uses its facilities to satisfy all or part of its own requirements for certain items. The policies controlling specific decisions to make an item rather than to buy it emphasize cost factors. An evaluation of specific make-or-buy decisions within these organizations, however, clearly indicates that additional factors are involved which actually may be more important than the measurable cost considerations.

Some companies favor internal sourcing since they consider their skills and technology to be superior to those of outside suppliers. Companies wishing to secrete special processes or procedures may make the relevant items. Other organizations claim, "It's always cheaper to make an item yourself; you spread your overhead costs and keep the supplier's profit." Once a company has made the psychological and physical commitment to internal sourcing, there are a number of organizational and accounting factors which tend to dispose subsequent make-or-buy decisions toward making the item.

For instance, management is usually aware that if items previously made internally are purchased from outside sources, fixed costs may not be covered. Too, the costs of making are often *understated*. Since they are often calculated on an incremental or out-of-pocket basis, only a portion of the actual costs involved in making an item may be recognized.

There is another danger, however, that the costs of buying may be *overstated*. If the company has a history of making its own items, outside suppliers may justifiably foresee little chance of receiving a share of this business. Consequently, when they submit quotations, they may not even be competitive.

In the short run, partial or incremental costs may be appropriate for determining the costs of making to the firm. Long-run cost evaluation should calculate total costs including its full share of joint overhead and administrative costs. In addition, "broad cost" considerations must be recognized, such as an adverse impact on relations with suppliers of other items or decreased market acceptance because the end product does not include a supplier's branded component.

To a large extent, a company's belief that it costs less to make than to buy may be a self-fulfilling prophecy. Company Baker, for example, regularly introduces new models. In the early days of a new product's life, many parts are purchased from outside sources which will later be manufactured internally. In these early phases, when production volumes are low and the risk of failure high, the prices charged by the outside vendors are quite high. After the product has demonstrated that it will be a success, it is brought inside. Naturally, cost savings are realized, and these tend to reinforce the belief that outside sourcing is more expensive than internal sourcing.

Another important factor is the amount of responsibility which an outisde supplier is willing to assume for the proper operation of the item. On the one hand, the supplier may accept full responsibility for the proper operation of a system or component. These circumstances tend to favor the selection of an outside supplier. If, however, the supplier will only guarantee to do the work according to the buyer's specifications, a significant reason for external sourcing is lost. Even where a technical specification is expressed as a composite, stressing what the item must *be*, the buyer's chief interest is still in the performance specifications, or what the item must *do*. This underscores the importance for the marketer to fully understand the use situation and its implications so that he may sell performance rather than products in as many situations as possible.

The term "make-or-buy" tends to imply an either/or type of choice. In practice, there appear to be a number of intervening choices. An operation or item may be split into its components, some of which will be made and some of which will be purchased externally. Even for a given item, it is not unusual for a company to make some of its requirements and to buy the remainder from outside suppliers. The make-or-buy considerations may be applied to designs or processes as well as to goods and services. Similarly, temporary situations sometimes arise when the need for an internally manufactured item will be partially satisfied by outside purchasing. This seems to be the case when new, high risk items are needed, or when periodic capacity overloads occur, or when particular timing demands that items be purchased from an outside supplier.

TRADE RELATIONS

Giving preference to suppliers who are also customers is commonly known as trade relations. Of all the aspects of user-supplier relationships, perhaps none is more subject to strong emotional opinions. It should be noted that trade relations is neither a simple matter of reciprocity nor of rationing purchases from vendors according to what they themselves buy from the subject company. Instead, it is a matter of trying to coordinate all activities of the corporation toward the firm's marketing objectives. At times it may be advisable to do everything possible for a vendor if these activities facilitate the job of selling to him as a *customer*.

Another aspect of trade relations was emphasized by Company Able's director of trade relations, who said, "Most people see only half the picture. But trade relations has defensive as well as offensive motivations. At Company Able, the defensive aspect is the more important. There are a lot of companies who try to sell to us on the basis of trade relations. I take that responsibility off the purchasing agent's back, and in my opinion he is glad to be rid of it."

An increase in the size and diversity of corporations tends to create more situations where trade relations may be employed. However, there are many companies and industries where the issue does not arise, due to to the nature of the products or services involved and the types of supplying industries from which the companies buy. For example, Company Baker, producing a high-priced consumer durable item, has no trade relations considerations. While Company Baker buys large quantities of steel and other materials, these suppliers have no regular requirement for the products of Company Baker.

Two different patterns emerged from the fieldwork with respect to the position of trade relations in the procurement process. At Company Charlie, trade relations tend to enter early in the procurement process, as the determination of the characteristics, quality, and quantity of the needed items are being discussed. The director of trade relations gives the major buying influences the names of relevant customer-suppliers which are to be considered. Most of these will probably already be under consideration, but the specific viewpoint of trade relations is now introduced into the buying decisions.

In some instances, the director of trade relations feels that his only obligation to the customer is to get him on the active supplier list. In other situations, the trade relations director may reenter the procurement process during the evaluation of offers and source selection phases. He reviews the decisions of the other buying influences at this time. In practice, buyers know that if the director of trade relations wants to "review" a decision, the supplier he names should be selected unless there are strong reasons for not doing so. When occasional conflicts do occur, they are usually resolved in favor of the director of trade relations.

In the second pattern, observed in Company Able, trade relations considerations do not enter until quite late in the procurement process, when the supplier selection process has been narrowed down to a final choice between a few vendors. Only at this point does the director of trade relations become involved and suggest awarding the business to a supplier who is also an important customer. However, those suppliers—whether customers of Company Able or not—which have not survived the earlier phases in the procurement process will not have a chance of being selected. Industrial marketers who observe the trade relations influence at this point may tend to exaggerate its role unless they realize that it is not involved in the earlier phases of the buying decision process.

In general, purchasing agents appear to resent the participation of trade relations in the procurement process. This is an understandable sentiment, since an emphasis on trade relations does tend to restrict the freedom of choice of the other buying influences.

An analysis of buying situations studied for this report indicates that trade relations is most likely to become involved when buying relatively homogeneous products at standardized prices. When buying basic commodities, or items which the buying influences see as being "just about alike," trade relations provides a logical means of differentiating among the offers of suppliers. By contrast, when buying highly engineered or customized products, where potential suppliers are easily differentiated on a number of bases, trade relations tend to have little influence on supplier selection.

The breadth of the supplying industry may also influence the involvement of trade relations in the procurement process. In those
instances where trade relations is involved, the fieldwork suggests
that the fewer the number of potential suppliers, the later in the
procurement process trade relations will enter. Where there are
many prospective suppliers, trade relations enters into the procurement process early to ensure that customer-suppliers will receive
consideration. Where there are few qualified suppliers, the cus-
tomer-supplier is almost assured of consideration. Hence, trade
relations can avoid internal conflicts by staying out of the procurement process until the later stages.

COST REDUCTION PROGRAMS

Organizational pressures to reduce purchasing costs appear to be
prevalent in large companies. Purchasing men frequently point out
that a one percent saving in the cost of goods purchased may have
the same effect on net profits as a ten percent increase in sales.
It appears that there are two different types of programs which may
have an impact on buyer-seller relationships, namely, regular and
periodic cost reduction programs. The amount of emphasis devoted
to each program will vary from company to company. In "hard"
purchasing companies, for example, more attention would be devoted to regular cost reduction programs than would be the case in
"soft" purchasing companies.

Regular or recurring programs are those which are in effect
over a fairly long period of time. Most organizations appear to give
some attention to routine control of purchasing costs. The means
of exercising such control usually takes the form of value analysis
and other forms of purchasing research; inspection, testing, and
quality control procedures; and working with suppliers to reduce
costs.

The impact of these procedures on the procurement process, and
hence on the user-supplier relationships, may vary greatly. In
Company Baker, for example, a premium is placed on getting a new
model to market before competitors, thus giving the company a
shorter lead time and an important competitive advantage in the
market. However, the company realizes that it pays a price for
this time advantage. Because of the pressures and disruptive effects caused by any delays, design and development people tend to
"play it safe" and over-engineer the final product, seeking to
minimize the time required to design and build a new model.

After the product or model has been in production for a year,
the value analysis group (which reports jointly to engineering and
manufacturing) begins to examine individual parts and components
in order to effect cost savings. Yet Company Baker realizes that
many changes which the value analysis group suggests cannot be

made without redesigning the product itself, and so suggested changes are frequently not made. The company is willing to pay a premium in the costs of goods purchased in order to maintain a strategic advantage over its competitors.

In Company Charlie, a purchasing-oriented company, heavy emphasis is placed upon value analysis, and the recommendations from this group are rapidly put into effect. In addition, Company Charlie's purchasing agents periodically conduct sophisticated and far-reaching studies of the world supply picture for major parts and materials. Supply and demand projections are made, production and marketing costs analyzed, and general economic trends and environmental factors determined. These studies help to explain the company's ability to maintain an information superiority over suppliers.

Company Charlie frequently helps a supplier get a lower price on a basic part or material used in the manufacture of the item he sells to Company Charlie. This procedure for going to the supplier's supplier is by no means unusual. Nor is it confined to cases where the supplier is a small company. Company Charlie's purchasing agents work closely with major suppliers in order to reduce costs. Ideas are exchanged, tests and trials run, and periodic meetings held with technical and value analysis people from both companies. In selling to a procurement-oriented company, the supplier's success—and his best guarantee that the relationship will continue—may depend upon his willingness and ability to work with the customer company to reduce the costs of the supplier's own items.

In addition to the regular cost reduction programs, companies may face periodic "crash" programs imposed by top management. The scope of these programs is typically much broader than purchasing, since all of the major activities of the organization may be affected. The programs may mean postponing capital equipment and other deferrable acquisitions. Many straight rebuys may be handled as modified rebuys as the company seeks to reduce the prices paid for goods and services. Pressures may be brought to bear on suppliers to develop new cost-saving ideas or processes.

Purchasing research is the major vehicle by which management's cost reduction policies get translated into action. Research initiated by the buying organization may have an impact on the location of the center of gravity in the procurement process. Value analysis may uncover new alternatives, in the form of items or suppliers, to be considered. In each of the companies studied, there was evidence that search was sometimes undertaken as a scavenging activity. That is, the search for new solutions of alternatives may actually *precede* the problem recognition and definition steps. Purchasing research may also help to offset the natural conservatism of some engineers and other buying influences, who may tend to overspecify in order to reduce the risks inherent in the procurement process.

Research initiated by a prospective supplier may improve his reputation for technical competence, thus increasing his chances of being selected as a supplier.

PURCHASING CONTRACTS

Formal contracts between buyers and sellers may be considered in terms of the extent to which the agreement restricts the buying company's freedom to act in the future. A contract to buy all of one's oxygen requirements from one company for a seven-year period obviously restricts the buyer's freedom more than a seven-year contract to purchase ten percent of his polyethylene requirements from a single source, even though the dollar commitment may be the same. It appears that neither the duration of a contract nor the absolute number of dollars involved are the primary considerations when a buying organization is considering a formal agreement with a supplier. Rather, the critical element may be the extent to which the proposed contract will restrict the buyer's freedom of action during the period of the contract.

Why, then, do business firms ever sign contracts? One explanation, as Cyert and March have pointed out, is that many businessmen seek to avoid uncertainty.[1] A contract enables the buying influences to substitute the certainty of the contract terms for the uncertainty as to what the future may bring. These situations typically appear where the important variables are beyond the control of the buying decision makers. Contracts appear to be even more desirable when buyers anticipate that costs will rise in the future. For example, when buying copper the purchasing agent has relatively little control over the factors which determine its price. In view of recent history, he may logically expect the price to rise in the foreseeable future. Hence, he may be quite willing to trade his flexibility for a long-term contract at a favorable current price.

Companies typically prefer to buy parts, materials, and supply items without a long-term contract, unless some important advantage is to be gained by signing such an agreement in a particular instance. The supply situation may change quite rapidly, and buyers want to retain as much flexibility as possible. This is true even when a large number of dollars are involved and in times of rising prices. As one buyer expressed it, "Sure you can miscalculate, but when buying parts and components your mistakes don't hang around to haunt you as they do when you are buying capital equipment." In the case of capital equipment purchasing, certain payoffs are expected. In these situations the buying company tends to want a higher degree of certainty. It may be more willing to forego the chance of a windfall gain in order to minimize the chance of a costly mistake occurring.

In addition to these general factors, there may be specific

organizational policies which determine the types of contracts a company prefers.   These appear to be related to the nature of the buying company's business and the characteristics of the supplying industries.   For example, Company Able is manufacturing on what is essentially a custom-order basis and prefers to retain maximum flexibility.   It has a few formal contracts with suppliers, and those it has are generally for short periods of time, typically one year. Company Baker produces basic models of a mass-produced product for several years without making major changes in the parts and materials used.   Between-model changes tend to be expensive, since product redesigning or new tooling may be involved.   There may also be important implications for the after-sale servicing of Company Baker's products.   Therefore, Company Baker prefers as much stability as possible during the years that a basic model is made, and consequently favors contracts which run for several years.   Company Charlie, buying homogeneous products and materials and operating on a continuous process basis, prefers even longer contracts with suppliers of its basic materials.

Wroe Alderson has distinguished between fully negotiated and routine transactions.   Fully negotiated transactions arise in unique or nonrecurring situations between the buyer and seller.   These transactions are strategic in that they set the conditions which govern a number of subsequent transactions.[2]   In other words, the buyer and seller must agree on the rules or terms which are to govern both parties to the negotiation. Whether buying coal, common stock, or furniture at an antique auction, routine transactions are possible only when the ground rules are known and respected by both parties.

Translated to industrial purchasing, written contracts are likely to be wanted by buyers where fully negotiated transactions are involved.   In these situations, there are no generally agreed upon rules or customs.   As a director of purchasing said, "I'll ask for a written contract only when there is no clearly established precedent. Then there aren't any rules of the game, so it's important to spell out all the terms in detail."   In routine transactions, where the ground rules are known to both parties, written contracts may be found when one party obtains an especially advantageous agreement. As a buyer said, "If I negotiate a price that's better than the published prices in the vendor's industry, I want it to be in writing."

Company Baker tends to favor blanket contracts which have no fixed expiration date but continue in force until one party desires to renegotiate.   These contracts specify the price paid for the particular item.   Anticipated quantities per year are stated, although the buying firm is not bound by them.   Once a blanket contract is in effect, Company Baker's policy is to leave it alone.   This is partially due to the belief that the incidence of attempted price increases by suppliers will be reduced if they are not reminded of renewals and not given the opportunity for a formal reappraisal of the existing agreement.

AN ILLUSTRATION OF THE IMPACT OF CUSTOMER POLICIES ON USER-SUPPLIER RELATIONSHIPS

To illustrate how company buying policies and practices have an impact upon relationships with suppliers, and are themselves affected by the actions of suppliers, an example from the fieldwork follows.

When a new product is being designed at Baker Company, the make-or-buy decisions originate with the designer, who works closely with the project manager who in turn has the responsibility for carrying the new product through the design, development, early production, and testing phases. By the way he designs a part or component, the designer strongly influences the outcome of the procurement processes which follow.

When the preliminary design has been completed, the project manager makes an initial make or buy decision for each part. A parts list is made from the design sheets and contains a column which the project manager marks "make," "buy," or "doubtful." There were approximately 300 items on the parts list studied for this project. The project manager explained:

> About three-quarters of those will be sourced "make" on an almost automatic basis. They show up on almost all our models. We have the facilities, capacity, and skills to make them. About fifty items will be proprietary; and because the supplier has strong marketing, legal or cost protection, we always buy these items. They can be sourced 'buy' almost automatically. That leaves about 25 items which are sourced 'doubtful.' We send a list of these items to purchasing, and ask them to get outside quotes. We also contact the manufacturing and cost people at the plant level and ask: 'Can you make the items? Do you want to? How much will it cost?' If they want to make them and can do it for approximately market price, we let them do it. In practice, most of those 25 items will wind up being made inside, but some will not.

Discussions at the plant level confirmed that its personnel generally prefer to make as many items as they can.

From the industrial marketer's standpoint, it appears that the best protection is to have an item which Company Baker considers to be proprietary. Proprietary items are those for which the supplier has built such a commanding position that it is not considered feasible to make the item internally. Such an impregnable position may have been built by marketing skills, by legal or patent protection, or through the economies of large-scale production.

SUMMARY

The objective of this chapter has been to show how perceptions of the need by both buyers and sellers have an impact on the type of user-supplier relationships which develop. Buying company policies and practices concerning computerized ordering, supplier inventorying, make or buy considerations, trade relations, cost reduction programs, and purchasing contracts affect both the roles played by buying influences and the outcomes of buying decisions. This chapter has examined some of the major factors which have an impact on user-supplier relationships and has explored examples of what is likely to happen when the customer company moves in one of these directions. The marketer who appreciates the impact that such policies may have is ready to consider how he may adapt his own offerings and efforts to meet customers' requirements, and that analysis is the subject of Chapter X.

XI

The Determinants of
Industrial Buyers' Behavior*

BETTER UNDERSTANDING OF INDUSTRIAL BUYERS' BEHAVIOR
requires some conceptual scheme for the analysis of the buyer
behavior and its determinants.

The first section of the present chapter outlines a conceptual
scheme based on existing theories and research findings concerning
human behavior, both as individuals and as members of formal
organizations. Utilizing this framework, the second section discusses some major empirical findings and theoretical concepts
from the literature concerning determinants of buyers' behavior.
Following these generalized theoretical presentations, empirical
findings on the determinants of source loyalty in the purchase of
industrial components are introduced.

A CONCEPTUAL SCHEME FOR THE ANALYSIS
OF INDUSTRIAL BUYERS' BEHAVIOR

Industrial buying decisions, made by human beings as members of
some formal organization, can be viewed as emanating from the buyers' "black box," which in turn is subject to some external inputs
and constraints. Buying decisions and determinants can be examined
in terms of attempting to explain what goes on within the "black
box." Most of the psychological theories of human behavior, in
fact, subscribe to this form of explanation. No consensus has been
reached, however, on one "true" assumption of the determinants of
human behavior. Each discipline and its component schools within
the behavioral sciences have developed their own assumptions of
human behavior. Most of the assumptions and theories were considered by their formulators to be irreconcilable with other theories
yet sufficient by themselves to explain human behavior. This lack

*By Yoram Wind

of a generally acceptable body of knowledge about the process that transpires within the "black box" led the students of cybernetics to solve the problem of understanding the "black box" by:

> . . . discovering the logical and statistical relationships which hold between the information that goes into the box and the instructions that come out.[1]

Similarly, the proponents of the "early behavioristic" school of psychology—Watson (1914), Weiss (1925), and, somewhat later, Skinner (1938)—made no assumptions whatsoever about what went on in the "black box" and believed that any complex behavior can be analyzed into simple stimulus-response units.

This author believes that any comprehensive understanding of human behavior in general or of the buyer in particular presupposes some knowledge about the forces within the "black box," as well as about the exogenous variables affecting the "black box." It is hypothesized that a buyer's behavior is a function of five sets of variables:

1. The buyer's own characteristics, especially his psychological mechanisms and behavioral characteristics, which serve as the major mediating processors between the inputs to which he is subject and his outputs (responses).

2. Interpersonal influences of other organizational members.

3. Organizational variables. The affect of these variables on the behavior of the organization members has been widely recognized by behavioral scientists but almost entirely neglected by marketing experts

4. Inputs from the various sources of supply. These inputs are generally of two types: those supporting source X and those contradicting inputs which attempt to negate the influence of the supporting inputs for source X.

5. Environmental variables, which are of three types:

   a. general variables affecting the value system of the people of the given society

   b. general business conditions

   c. regular business constraints.

These five sets of variables and some of their interactions are presented in Figure 14, a proposed framework for the analysis of the various determinants of buyers' behavior.

The model is basically an extended form of an S-O-R model which takes explicit account of the organizational environment within which industrial buyers make their buying decisions. This can be depicted schematically as:

| Stimuli
(Inputs) → | Organizational Setting
buyer's black box | → Response
(Output) |

The framework is designed to facilitate the identification and analysis of the key decision making units (DMU) in the buying process, the major variables within each of the five sets of variables that affect the decision, and the system of relations involved in the industrial buying situation.

A detailed analysis of the five sets of variables, the relevant theories and findings concerning them, and the hypothesis relating to their effect on buyers' decisions, as well as some of the findings of a case study, are presented in the next section.

THE DETERMINANTS OF BUYERS' BEHAVIOR

Buyer Characteristics as Determinants of His Decisions.

Marketing students have generally accepted the assumption of classical economic theory that industrial buyers' behavior is strongly motivated by rational-economical considerations. The Industrial Marketing Committee Review Board of the American Marketing Association, for example, stated that:

> Rational buying motives appear to predominate in the industrial field (as against emotional motives in the consumer field) but their influence declines with the increase in product similarity.[2]

The exception of product similarity and other empirical evidences, however, has led to an increasing recognition that industrial buyers are influenced by emotional "noneconomical" as well as "rational-economical" considerations. Lazo, for example, in reporting some of the findings of the *Steel Magazine* study, "Emotional Factors Underlying Industrial Purchases,"[3] states:

> In his buying habits, the industrial buyer is more human than industrial marketers have realized. The industrial buyer not only has the same biological needs that you and I have, but he also has the same psychological drives, urges, desires, ambitions. His environment conditions him to express his needs and desires in a certain, perhaps restricted, way because of his vocation. . . .But in the actual buying situation he is human, he is influenced by the same senses and reactions that influence all of us when we buy.[4]

Given the premise that industrial buyers' decisions are subject to the affects of both "rational-economical" and "emotional-noneconomical" factors and viewing rationality as being contingent upon access to information, the computational capacities of indi-

FIGURE 14

A Proposed Framework for the Analysis of the Various Determinants of the Buyer's Behavior

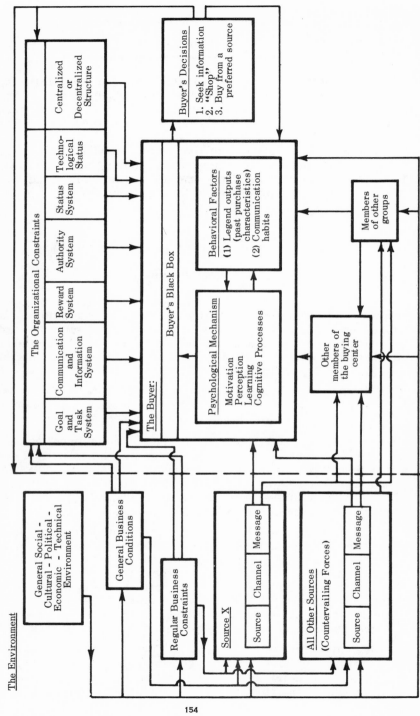

viduals, and actual decision processes,[5] the following analysis summarizes some of the specific buyers' characteristics as described
in the relevant literature.

In a recent study on the determinants of industrial buyers'
behavior, Duncan emphasized the effects of personal attributes,
when defined in the broadest possible way, on the buyer's decisions.
He stated that:

> It is evident that the motivation and behavior of the purchasing
> officer is influenced by such personal qualities as his ambitions,
> his eagerness to learn, his alertness as manifested by his awareness
> and use of "newer" tools and methods, his desire to do a better
> job than the buying executives in competing companies, his educa-
> tion and experience and similar personal characteristics. In ad-
> dition, his family life, including the standard of living he maintains,
> and related—in some cases at least—to his wife's desires and
> motivations including the social activities in which he and she may
> engage, and the extent to which he participates in community affairs
> and church work, all influence his purchasing behavior to an impor-
> tant degree.[6]

A careful analysis of this list of variables indicates that they are of
two types—psychological and demographic variables. It is not intended to elaborate on the demographic-socioeconomic characteristics of the buyer as determinants of his behavior since they are
assumed to be reflected in the psychological variable. The psychological variables mentioned by Duncan are basically concerned with
buyer's motivation. To this, it is necessary to add the learning
mechanism and two psychologically based operational variables—the
buyer's attitudes toward the various sources of supply and his
awareness of them.

The third set of buyer's descriptors that are assumed to affect
his decisions are his behavioral characteristics—the buyer's previous buying decisions and his information handling habits. Following is a brief discussion of the psychological and behavioral characteristics of industrial buyers and their effects on the buying
decisions.

The Buyer's Psychological Characteristics

A. Buyer's motivation as a determinant of his decisions.   The
motives—the inter-striving conditions and states of the organism
having to do with the vigor, persistance and direction of goal directed
behavior[7]—underlying the industrial buyer decisions have been given
far more attention than most other aspects of buyers' behavior.
Generally, these motives can be classified as task and "non-task"
motives. A distinction which is believed to be more meaningful
than the commonly used dichotomy of rational-economical versus
emotional motives.   Liking a salesman and thus buying from him,
for example, can be viewed not only as an emotional, but as a

rational buying motive, given a certain objective of the buyer and under certain conditions. Using the task-non-task dichotomy, on the other hand, enables even in this case a clear classification. The proponents of the task motives assume that the buyer's decisions are influenced only by factors which have direct bearing on the immediate task to be performed (*i.e.*, price, quality, delivery dates, etc.). It follows that the buyer's characteristics have little or no effect on the "rational-economic" decisions made. The non-task motives, on the other hand, are based on the more realistic assumption that the task factors are mediated through a set of non-task factors that characterizes each industrial buyer. If a buying decision is to be properly understood, then, both sets of motives have to be considered.

The non-task motives which affect buyers' behavior have usually been presented either as a specific list of motives[8] or as a generalization of a major motive which determines the buyer's behavior. An example of the latter is what Reed has called the motive of *self-interest*. The effect of this motive, the origin of which was traced back to Bentham's hedonistic doctrine, was defined by Reed as:

> Any offer, the acceptance of which can be proven definitely to advance the immediate self-interest of the (industrial) buyer has in its favor the most powerful selling force known.[9]

The nonoperationality of general motives of this nature, in the case of behavior such as industrial buying, which is determined by many factors on the one hand, and the oversimplified and unrealistic assumption underlying the first approach, that "understanding behavior is simply a matter of consulting 'the' list of motives," on the other hand, necessitate an attempt to identify some major non-task sets of motives which are assumed to be among the factors that affect buyers' behavior. A careful examination of the relevant marketing and purchasing literature suggests that an industrial buyer has two major generic motives—risk reduction motives and achievement motives. It is not intended, however, to include in these two sets all of the various non-task motives which do or might affect the buyer's decisions, such as friendship, "loyalty" to a source where the buyer once worked, "loyalty" to a source that was helpful to the company in the past, etc.

Risk Reduction. The risk reduction motive (if assumed to exist) provides some *a priori* sound explanations of industrial buying. Bauer, who pioneered in applying this motivational mechanism to marketing stated:

> Risk reduction seems to be the predominant process (in explaining behavior) to the extent that risk is in fact involved.[10]

The industrial buyer is faced with two major types of uncertainty (risk) about the consequences of his decisions:

1. Uncertainty about the reactions of others to his decisions. This might be described as uncertainty concerning the consequences of his decisions.

2. Uncertainty due to lack of information concerning

    a. the actual expectations from his job, and

    b. the possible alternative courses of action.

Among the major phenomena which can be explained as being caused (among other things) by the buyer's willingness to "play it safe" and reduce these uncertainties are:

1. Resistance to change from existing satisfactory source to a new source even though the shift might (if successful) improve the company's position,

2. Split orders between two or more sources so as to have an alternative acceptable source constantly available,

3. Buying from well-known sources which are recognized as desired engineering choices,

4. A tendency toward family loyalty. The reasoning is that if source X was satisfactory for components $1, 2 \ldots K$, it is not very likely that it will be a bad choice for component $K + 1$.

The Achievement Motive. Buyers, being human, seek to increase their chances for promotion, status, and recognition without taking too many risks. Morover, it can be hypothesized that buyers tend to make those decisions which they perceive to have the best chances of improving their present situations—a perceived improvement that can be achieved either through some formal organizational recognition or through informal social recognition. More specifically, Strauss hypothesized that:

> The Purchasing Agent seeks to increase his status and power in the organization.[11]

In addition, Sawyer has pointed out that the status motive might lead a buyer to buy from a well-known firm because of the feeling of pride that it gives him.[12]

B. Learning as a determinant of buyers' behavior. Beyond its biological base, human behavior is learned behavior, *i.e.*, behavior (activity) which originates or is changed through reacting to an encountered situation, provided that the characteristics of the change in activity cannot be explained on the basis of native response tendencies, maturation, or temporary states of the organism.[13] Among the learning factors that affect buyers' decisions, "habit"—a connection between stimuli and response that has become virtually

automatic through experience, usually through repeated trials[14]—
has been one of the most commonly considered. Duncan, for example, stated:

> Many purchases of industrial goods are made on a nonrational
> basis as a matter of habit or in accordance with past custom.[15]

Habit is usually assumed to exist in repetitive purchases of a certain
part from the same source. There is no theoretical reason, however, why its effect cannot be extended across products to cause
"family loyalty," (loyalty to a number of products of the same supplier). On the other hand, the importance of habit as a force which
tends to inhibit the changing of source of supply has been exag-
gerated in the literature and should be considered only as one among
many determinants of buyers' decisions. The significance of habit
has been widely recognized; the Industrial Marketing Committee
Review Board of the AMA, for example, stated that:

> Habit, the universal resistance to change in buying patterns, is
> equally important in both industrial and consumer marketing
> fields.[16]

Resistance to change, however, is caused by a large number of
variables of which habit is only one. The force of habit is usually
inferred from observed behavior, but a loyalty to a certain source
can be ascribed, for example, to the motive of risk reduction, *i.e.*,
some risk is always incurred in shifting to a new source, and if the
advantages of shifting do not justify the risk, the buyer tends to
remain loyal to the old source.

*C. The buyer's ATTITUDES toward and AWARENESS of the various
sources of supply as determinants of his buying decisions.* In analyzing the determinants of consumer behavior, Amstutz emphasized
the importance of two operational psychological characteristics:

1. The consumer's attitude toward product characteristics,
   brands of products and retail outlets.

2. The consumer's awareness of brands of products.[17]

The inclusion of attitudes in a consumer behavior model is concurrent with the current trend of social psychologists to emphasize
attitudes as it is reflected in the large number of theoretical and
empirical studies on various aspects of attitude. Applying Amstutz'
concepts to the industrial buying situation, it can be hypothesized
that a buyer's response to the various inputs from his environment
depends, to a degree, on his awareness of the source (sender, trans-
mitter) of the communication and his attitudes toward him. More
specifically, when faced with the decision to select a source of supply, it can be hypothesized that the buyer's decision will depend to

a large extent on his knowledge of the existence of the sources and their areas of specialization, which is the equivalent of knowledge of a brand in the consumer market, and on his attitude toward the various sources. This latter factor was found, in a number of survey studies, to be of considerable importance in determining the buyer's decision. This was stated, for example, by Klass who also specified some of the relevant attributes of attitudes toward a source:

> Industrial purchasers buy—or don't buy—from a particular supplier for many reasons. But when it comes right down to it, the most important reasons are buyers' attitudes toward, or image of your product quality, delivery, price and salesmen.[18]

In addition to these attributes of the buyer's attitude, the communications literature suggests that the attitude toward the source himself, especially his perceived credibility, is one of the determinants of the buyer's decision.[19]   (This is assuming that the credibility is not a function of the above attributes, which can be assumed only in the case where the buyer has no other indications of the product quality, delivery, and prices of the source.) The relevance of attitudes and awareness, however, is not restricted to the evaluation of sources of supply. As buyers are subject to a large number of inputs, their decisions depend also on their awareness of and attitudes toward the sources of these inputs—R & D engineers, other buyers, purchasing managers and any other members of the organization or its environment that transmit some information to the buyer. These attitudes have some effect, in turn, on the buyer's attitudes toward the sources of supply.

The Buyer's Behavioral Characteristics

With the exception of attitudes and awareness, the psychological characteristics of the buyer cannot be measured directly and have to be inferred from some measurable cues. Among the most commonly used cues are behavioral evidences; it is proposed to use these behavioral characteristics directly as possible explanatory variables of buyers' decisions.

The behavioral characteristics to be considered here can be divided into two major types:

1. The buyer's previous buying decisions and their "feedback"— a characteristic equivalent to present product ownership and retail store preference in the case of consumer behavior.

2. The buyer's information handling habits.

To avoid a tautological explanation when using the first set of behavioral characteristics, the buyer's previous decisions are confined to those made at time t and are used to explain his decisions at time $t + 1$. "t" represents any number of purchase trials prior to $t + 1$ and can be either one purchase trial (at time t) or any number of trials (t, $t - 1$, $t - 2$, . . . , $t - n$). The number of observations used in the explanation of buyers' behavior depends on the researcher's assumptions as to the nature of human behavior. For example, the assumptions when using only one purchase trial at t (first-order analysis) to explain the buyer's behavior[20] are obviously different than the ones used in a higher order analysis such as learning model analysis.[21]

The buyer's information habits are the product of a large number of factors such as the individual's personality characteristics, his relations to other organization members, the complexity of his communication flow, his media habits, etc. It is not possible to identify and measure all of these variables, but it was found in the course of this study that industrial marketing people and especially salesmen, can describe the buyer's information handling process quite accurately and can therefore estimate the degree to which the various buyers are perceptive about their information.

Given the two behavioral characteristics of a buyer, it is hypothesized that his decisions depend, to some extent, on the nature of his behavioral variables. As to the direction of the effect of these variables on the industrial buyer's decision, it can be hypothesized that:

> The probability that a buyer will buy from source X at $t + 1$ is higher the greater his positive experience with the source prior to this decision point, the more exposure and access he has to supporting information for source X and the less exposure and access he has to countervailing information.

Interorganizational Interpersonal Variables As Determinants of Buyers' Decisions

The buyer is only one of several persons who influence and decide on the purchase of industrial products. This multiple buying influence is a common practice in industry and is well documented in the literature. After reporting the findings of several studies on this subject, Alexander, Cross, and Cunningham conclude that:

> It is apparent that buying influence is widely diffused among the officials and departments of the average customer firm and that in many cases a sale of industrial goods can be made only after the seller has convinced a considerable number of executive and supervisory officials of the buying firm.[22]

The people influencing the buying decisions can be divided into two groups—those who are members of the "buying center" and, by definition, have a direct contact with the purchase decision and those who are within the organization but outside the buying center, *i.e.*, have only indirect contact with the purchase decisions. The broad definition of a buying center suggests that the relations among the members of this center are of prime importance to the buying decision, whereas the buyer's relations with other members of the organization are of smaller importance. The following discussion will therefore confine its attention to the relations within the buying center. This framework for analysis can also be applied, however, to the analysis of the relations between the buyer and any other member of the organization.

Within the buying center, there is rarely only one decision maker. The buyer, one of the members of this center, can, however, be considered as a KEY decision making unit in selecting a source of supply. The key position of the buyer, although frequently overemphasized, is presented in its proper perspective in the following finding reported by Alexander, Cross, and Cunningham:

> While a number of officials of the buying company often influence a purchase at some point during its development, . . . the purchasing agent usually selects the supplier and negotiates the terms of the contract. This places him in a position of much greater significance than most of the other officials influencing the buying of industrial goods.[23]

The buyer, being in a key position in the buying center, can be regarded, using Lewin's terminology, as one of the "gatekeepers" of the buying process.[24] The advantage of using this concept is that it stresses the communications aspects of the buyer's position and indicates the continuous contact a buyer has with other members of the buying center. It is then likely to assume that the nature and extent of these interpersonal relations affect the buyer's decision. As the other members of the buying center belong to various departments within the organization, the buyer's interpersonal relations are also influenced by the interdepartmental and intradepartmental relations of each of the members of the buying center.

The buying center is composed of two major groups—the buyers and the users. The users may be from various departments and functions within the given operating division, each with somewhat different objectives. At any point of time (t), a buyer (b)—the representative of the purchasing group—is in contact with some user (u_i). Both buyers and users might be in contact with other organizational members (o_i) that can influence the purchase decision (by approving a project, for example). Thus, the performance of the buying center is through a sequence of what can be called negotiations between $b_i u_i$, $b_i o_i$ and $u_i o_i$. Using this notation, a buying center can be described as:

$$\left[\sum_{i=1}^{s} b_i u_i + \sum_{i=1}^{s} u_i o_i + \sum_{i=1}^{s} b_i o_i\right]_{p_j T}$$

when p_j denotes a given project, T the time period over which the process takes place, and the pairs of relations are for all participants in the *relevant* groups—thus, for u_1 to u_s and not u_1 to u_n which would have included all of the members of the group. Dealing only with a subset (1 to s) implies that the buying center is a flexible concept and that its members may change from one case to another.

Defining the relations within the buying center as negotiative, a somewhat simplified and modified form of Walton and McKersie's model of social negotiations[25] can be used. In discussing labor negotiations as an instance of social negotiations—the deliberate interactions of two or more complex social units which are attempting to define or redefine the terms of their interdependence—Walton and McKersie develop an analytical framework which is composed of four distinguishable systems of activities:

1. Distributive bargaining, the function of which is to resolve pure conflicts of interests.

2. Integrative bargaining, the function of which is to find common or complementary interests and to solve problems confronting both parties.

3. Attitudinal structuring, the function of which is to influence the attitudes of the participants toward each other and to affect the basic bonds which relate the two parties involved.

4. Intraorganizational bargaining, which has the function of achieving consensus within each of the interacting groups.

Using these concepts, the negotiative relations between $(u_i b_i)$ $p_j T$ can be presented schematically as in Figure 15.

The distributive-integrative mix of bargaining between b_i and u_i in particular and the whole complex of relations between $b_i u_i$ in general depend on the degree and nature of communication maintained among them. The communication flows among the participants of the buying center, are, in turn, a function of the personal characteristics of the participants, the nature of the job to be done, the overlap between a participant reference group, and the relevant part of the buying center, the organizational environment, etc. This again emphasizes the interdependencies among all the various factors that affect the buyer's decisions.

The negotiative framework (Figure 15) also facilitates the analysis of an alternative form of relation, viz, a paramount unit which dominates the relations between the participants. The dominant department hypothesis assumes that certain individuals and departments exercise controlling influence over some part of the purchasing decisions. It has almost commonly been accepted that the users dominate the decision as to what should be bought as to the type and quality of the parts and that the purchasing people have the prerogative of selecting the source of supply and deciding on the commercial aspects of the purchase.[26] This classification suggests a

FIGURE 15
Negotiative Relations Within a Buying Center

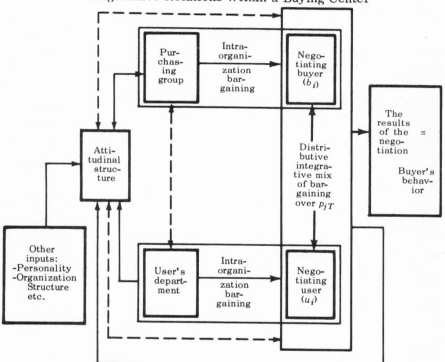

clear-cut division of labor between purchasing and other members of the buying center. (However, other authorities, such as Lewis, indicate that such a division of labor cuts the users off from important market information about the relative economic attractiveness of alternatives.) The findings of the present study relating to the industrial buying process indicate strong dependencies between the various decisions. A decision of an engineer, for example, in favor of a certain part might force the buyer to purchase it from one specific source. It is hypothesized that even in the area in which the buyer is presumed to be dominant, his decisions are affected by the nature and extent of his relations with the other members of the buying center. These relations do not hold, however, for the reverse case, *i.e.*, when considering only the purchase of industrial components, the dominance of the users over the decision on what to buy is clearly evident. As to the decision on how much to buy, it may be in either department or in a special scheduling department based on the specific organizational structure.

The following presentation of the possible organizational effects on buyers' decisions is divided into two sections. The first briefly examines each of the organizational subsystems and their possible effects on buyers' decisions, whereas the second section discusses some of the aspects of centralized versus decentralized purchasing departments.

Organizational Variables as Determinants of Buyers' Decisions

Despite the generally accepted assumption among students of organization behavior that the various organizational subsystems are important determinants of the behavior of organization members, most of the theoretical and empirical studies on buyers' behavior found in the marketing and purchasing literature have not been concerned with the organizational variables as possible determinants of buyers' behavior.

A survey of a few pertinent scholarly and trade journals revealed, however, some recent recognition of the possible effect of the organization system on the buyer's behavior.[27] A summary of the findings of these articles, together with some other scattered pieces of information concerning the effect of some organizational variables on buyers' behavior, are presented next for each of the major relevant organizational variables.

Task Variables.   The buyer's function has been commonly defined as:

Buying materials of the right quality in the right quantity at the right time at the right price from the right source.[28]

Lacking an explicit criterion for "right," this definition is ambiguous and not sufficiently operational. Implied in this and similar definitions, however, is the assumption that the buyer in selecting a source of supply has to take into account four variables—the quality, quantity, price, and delivery. These task elements are, of course, general in nature, and it is to be expected that specific organizations will emphasize different combinations of these elements as the particular task to be performed by purchasing. The specific purchasing objectives reflect the overall company objectives and, in turn, form the basis for the setting of specific purchasing policies. Having such specific goals and policies makes it possible to evaluate purchasing performance and thus provides needed "feedback" that can—and hopefully, will—improve the buyer's decisions. Regardless of the particular emphasis of this task, the buyer is required to act as a screener and clearinghouse of information and is expected to try to match company purchasing needs with what is available on the market.

The Reward System. The types of rewards given by the organization, the criteria upon which the distribution of rewards are based, and the degree to which the criteria for the rewards are clearly specified are significant determinants of the individual's behavior in the organization as long as the rewards are perceived by the individual to be important and desirable.

The Status System. Only a few studies have dealt with the buyer's and the purchasing department's place within the organizational status system. On the basis of buyers' feelings, Strauss, for example, concluded that their capabilities are not sufficiently recognized by management and other departments and that the buyers will strive toward achieving higher status through professionalism[29] and various formal and informal tactics of organizational relations.[30]

The Authority System. This system has received relatively close attention. Duncan, for example, has rated it as one of the major determinants of the buyer's behavior.[31] Authority factors are included as possible determinants of the buyer's behavior because the buyer's formal and informal authority and responsibilities define the scope and intended nature of his activities.

The Communication and Information System. The pivotal role of communication in the managerial process has been recognized, and, as early as 1938, Barnard stated that:

> The first executive function is to develop and maintain a system of communication.[32]

Strauss' study on the tactics of lateral relationship between the buyer and other organization members is only one of several studies on the communication system in general and the methods of communication between the buyers and other members of the organization and other organizations, in particular as related to the buying function. Very few studies have been directly concerned with the effect of the communication and information systems on the buyer's decisions. It can be assumed, however, that the findings of such theoretical and empirical studies as have been conducted by various behavioral science disciplines on this subject apply also to industrial buying.

The *technological state* of the organization, especially the availability of electronic data processing systems, seems to have an indirect effect on the buyer's decisions through its effects on the purchasing procedures and the organizational structure.

The *organizational structure* of the purchasing department and especially its degree of centralization have been described in several of the procurement texts.[33] These descriptions provide, however, little or no explanation as to the specific effects of the organizational structure on the buyer's decisions. Leavitt[34] has indicated that the degree of centralization of the organizational structure (and, hence, of the purchasing department) has some effect on the performance of the organizational tasks. It may therefore be hypothesized that the same individual under the two alternative structures will respond differently to the same stimulus. Some further analysis of the problem of centralization and decentralization is undertaken in the next section of this Appendix.

In summary, it may be said that the formal and informal elements of an organization constrain the discretionary power of the buyers in making buying decisions. The degree of discretionary power that a buyer has is a function of his position on a set of "constraint continua" in which the buyer's position on the first continuum sets the upper limit of discretionary power for the second-order continuum, etc. The buyer's position on the first-order continuum is determined by his authority, status, task to be performed, and control over information flows. Being a member of an organization, the buyer is subject to some constraints (between a totally constrained decision and an unconstrained one) in his decisions. It may be reasonably assumed that the extent of his discretionary decision power will vary from one type of decision to another. For example, it can be expected that he will be more constrained in making decisions concerning capital goods than in those concerning components. This is illustrated in Figure 16.

FIGURE 16
Buyer's First-Order Constraint Continuum

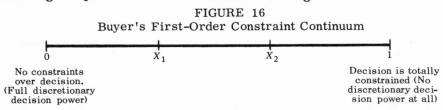

Being subject to limited constraint over decisions to purchase components does not imply that no further constraints are exerted on this decision. The dollar volume of the order, for example, might further determine the degree of constraint on his decision. This is illustrated in Figure 17.

Further constraints can be set by certain organizational variables such as the requirement to use reciprocity buying, to buy only from a subsidiary company, etc. All of these constraints can be analyzed by introducing higher order constraint continua.

FIGURE 17
Buyer's Second–Order Constraint Continuum

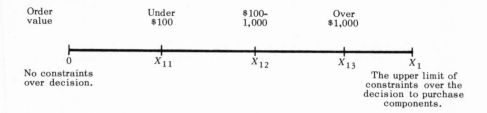

The advantage of the "constraint continuum" analysis is that it clearly demonstrates how each of the organizational variables affects the buyer's freedom to make purchasing decisions concerning certain types of purchase requisitions. It does not, however, offer a general method for analyzing the effects of the organizational variables on the buyer's preference for source Y over source Z as a supplier of a certain product.

Centralization and Decentralization of the Purchasing Function.

This analysis is concerned with the effects of centralization and decentralization of the purchasing function on the buyer's decisions. The alternative of centralization or decentralization of purchasing was stated explicitly by Heinritz and Farrell as:

> Whether to do all purchasing for the entire organization at one central point (centralization) or to set up a separate purchasing department for each operating division or plant location, each with a considerable degree of autonomy in buying (decentralization).[35]

This distinction between the two polar cases of centralization and decentralization is not absolute. The tendency today is toward a mix that will combine the advantages of both organizational structures. Even where decentralized purchasing exists, there is usually a centralized purchasing office headed by a corporate purchasing manager who is responsible for the establishment of basic policies and procedures and is usually the direct manager of the divisional purchasing agents. S. P. Heinritz, for example, reports that a study on purchasing decentralization found that:

> In somewhat more than half the cases, centralization of authority is accepted in principle but adopted to the circumstances by delegating a considerable degree of independent action to the branch purchasing officers while retaining central control through organ-

ization channels, standardized procedures, and systematic accountability to the headquarters purchasing office.[36]

This finding was supported by the results of a later survey which revealed that:

> . . . Industry executives are heading toward a compromise solution of the problem of centralized versus decentralized purchasing—functional and geographical decentralization with centralized control.[37]

On the basis of these findings, three major types of purchasing organizations may be identified which vary from each other as to the location of the formal authority over the buyer and his geographical location. The one extreme is the completely decentralized organizational structure in which the divisional manager is the direct supervisor of the buyer, who is also located with the using department. The other extreme is the completely centralized case in which the purchasing manager is the authority over the buyer, who is located in a centralized office separated from his users. The most common case is the mixed structure in which the buyer is located together with the using department and for all practical flow-work purposes can be considered to be under a decentralized structure. The difference from the completely decentralized case is that his direct superior is the purchasing manager who is located in the corporate headquarters.

Throughout this study, the term ''decentralization'' refers to the (more common) case of mixed structure and not to the uncommon ''perfectly decentralized'' case. The degree of centralization and decentralization of the purchasing function affects the buyer's behavior indirectly through their effects on the elements of the purchasing function (EPF).[38] These elements are:

1. The actual geographical locations where the purchasing functions are performed.

2. The formal authority relations between purchasing personnel and operating personnel.

3. The formal authority relations between the various levels of the purchasing personnel, especially between the buyer supervisor (or purchasing agents) and the purchasing manager.

4. The informal relations between purchasing personnel and operating personnel.

5. The nature and form of the communication process between the purchasing and operating personnel.

6. The structure of group loyalties or the buyer's *loyalty domain*. Whether the factory purchasing personnel, for

example, regard themselves as part of the factory "team" or as part of the purchasing department.

The comparative analysis conducted on a centralized reinforcing. If the lines of formal authority between purchasing and operating personnel, for example, run in the decentralized direction—that is, to the operating division—this tends to strengthen the informal relations with the division, to encourage communication in that direction, to change the nature of communication, and hence, to reinforce the loyalties with the division. Loyalties, which, in turn, will encourage further communication, more informal relations, etc.

As the nature of these six elements is a function of the organizational structure, it stimulates the question:

What are the conditions under which a centralized purchasing structure has more effect on the buyer's decisions than a decentralized structure and vice versa?

This question was considered by Webster, who proposed the following on the basis of his study on industrial buying situations:

The relative importance of the influence of the centralized purchasing department on the buying decision increases as:

a. Market variables become more important relative to product variables;

b. The size of the firm and the spatial separation of its activities increases;

c. The organization assigns specific responsibility to the purchasing department, in a formal sense.[39]

The effect of the organizational structure through the above elements of the purchasing function on the performance of the purchasing system and, especially, the buyers' behavior was the subject of a separate study by the present author. The study concluded that the degree of centralization (or decentralization) of the purchasing department does significantly effect the nature of the purchase decisions, hence enabling, given some information on the organizational structure of the purchasing department, the prediction of some major aspects of the buyers' purchase decisions.[40]

Sources' Characteristics as Determinants of Buyers' Decisions

Industrial buyers are subject to an influx of inputs from various sources. With the exception of a strictly monopolistic market, several sources tend to compete for any buying account. The inputs to which the buyer is subject can be divided broadly into those which support a certain source and those which countervail it. Each of these two sets of inputs can, in turn, be classified into three types of inputs according to their content: 1. the product and service mix, 2. the communication and information mix, and 3. the distribution mix.

Of these three sets of inputs, the first has been the most commonly dealt with in the marketing and purchasing literature. McCarthy, for example, declares that among the product characteristics looked for by buyers are: its "economy, both in original cost and in use; productivity; uniformity; purity; and ability to increase salability of the buyer's final product."[41] To these and other product characteristics, it has been customary to add some of the service factors that are as important (to the buyer) as some of the product characteristics. Among the service factors are, for example, delivery, variety of selection, technical advice, repair services, salesman's help in providing needed information, willingness to help in solving some problems, etc.

The communication and information mix is usually considered to involve advertising, selling and sales promotion. In addition, it seems appropriate to consider under this set of inputs all available information on the source that originates from the source's past or present activities (or lack of activities).

The distribution mix consists of the channels of distribution and the physical distribution complex used by the source. The industrial salesman occupies a central position in the distribution mix, especially as he is often one of the main channels through which the buyer receives information on the product, communication, and distribution mix.[42]

As every source uses some mix of these three sets of inputs, the buyer is subject to multiple inputs. Hence, it is hypothesized that his decision is not affected by a specific input but by the relation between the inputs of source X and the countervailing inputs from his competitors. This can be presented as the following (assumed) functional relation:

$$\text{Buyer's decision to buy from source X} = f\left[\frac{\text{Product \& service mix of X}}{\text{Product \& service mix of X competitors}} + \right.$$

$$+ \frac{\text{Communication mix of X}}{\text{Communication mix of X competitors}} +$$

$$\left. + \frac{\text{Distribution mix of X}}{\text{Distribution mix of X competitors}} + \frac{\text{Other}}{\text{variables}}\right]$$

Environmental Factors as Determinants of
Buyers' Decisions

No business firm can operate in a vacuum. Being part of the general social-cultural-economic-technological-political environment, a firm has to adjust its policies in general and buying decisions in particular to the general business conditions and the external environmental constraints. As the environment continuously changes, buyers have to consider the effect of the environmental factors in making their decisions.

Inasmuch as the buyer's demand for parts and other productive services is derived from the demand for the product which the firm produces, current business conditions and those expected to prevail in the future constitute important factors in determining buying decisions. The general business conditions, regardless of their causes—whether they are technological changes, wars, threat of war, government expenditures, changes in the world markets, etc.—are most likely to affect the availability and prices of needed parts. The buyer's decisions as to whether to buy or not to buy at a particular time are therefore affected to a large degree by his expectations with respect to the stability of price levels. Similarly, his decisions on how much and from whom to buy are affected by the current availability of the parts in the market and his expectations as to the future availability in respect to future needs of his and other firms.

Another set of environmental variables that affects the behavior of the organization members is the general social-cultural-economic-political environment which affects the value systems of the organization members. As this set of environmental factors has its effect on all members of a given society, it is of utmost importance when dealing with international transactions in which the buyer and the seller belong to two different cultures but can be neglected in local marketing to the extent that the buyers and sellers are subject to the influences of similar environmental factors.

SOME EMPIRICAL FINDINGS ON THE
DETERMINANTS OF SOURCE LOYALTY
IN THE PURCHASE OF INDUSTRIAL COMPONENTS

One of the major questions facing any marketing manager (whether in the consumer or industrial goods market) is: Will the buyer who bought my product at time t buy it also at $t + 1$? Given the dynamic quality of every market, fluctuating environmental conditions, and the continuous learning characteristic of human behavior, it is reasonable to assume that some buyers in the *aggregate market* switch from source X to Y, others from Y to X while some remain loyal to their previous sources. When focusing on a single buyer, on the other hand, it is obvious that he can choose either of two alternatives in making a re-purchasing decision:

1. Remain loyal to the previous source, *i.e.*, $S_t = S_{t-1}$ when S denotes a chosen source of supply;

2. Switch to another source, *i.e.*, $S_t \neq S_{t-1}$

In aiming at the most effective and efficient marketing strategies, a marketing manager of source X needs some information on the probability of a buyer being loyal and the major determinant of his decision to switch or not to switch.

This latter decision being a specific case of the more general phenomena of buyer's behavior is likely to be subject to the same set of determinants that effect buyer's behavior in general. Hence the usefulness of the framework presented in the first section of this Appendix is tested by applying it to the case of source loyalty the measures of which are:

. . . Reasonable ways of *describing* purchasing behavior. Not only are they appealing from a conceptual point of view, but they also represent the "best set of dimensions" for describing actual purchasing data by statistical means. Moreover, they tend to be fairly reliable from a statistical point of view.[43]

It is the objective of this section to examine buyer's source loyalty behavior by means of a model of such behavior to which suitable quantitative techniques are applied. The model is derived from the general theoretical framework previously used in analyzing industrial buyers' behavior. It incorporates five sets of variables:

1. Variables associated with the offerings of the various sources of supply as related to the buying requirements. These include the "traditional" variables of price, quality, delivery, quantity and service.

These traditional variables are frequently discussed in the purchasing literature as the sole determinants of the buyer's decisions. In constructing our model, three variables—quality of the products, quantity availability, and delivery capabilities are considered major factors in determining suppliers to be included among potential sources. There is lacking, however, an adequate criterion for deciding which of the suppliers that meet these three basic conditions gets the order. Since these three variables are prerequisites for inclusion in any feasible set of possible suppliers, they can be viewed as constraints that each supplier must accept in order to be considered. Hence, the variables can be excluded as explanatory variables of the selection of supplier X over Supplier Y when both are compatible services.

The justifications for the exclusion of the quality variable from models aimed at explaining source loyalty are twofold: 1. Quality is quite stable over time, especially when compared to price, 2. Buyers are relatively insensitive to changes in quality. On the other hand, buyers are very sensitive to any changes in prices, which, in turn, are less stable and easily identified by objective measures. Thus, it was decided that price, and especially the relative price of source X as compared with other sources, should be included in the model.

The availability of the desired quantity and the capability of delivering on time are the basic requirements for being considered as a source of supply. When no known source can provide it satisfactorily, however, it is likely to expect a split order among several sources, or if not feasible, an attempt to develop a new source of supply.

The service provided by the various suppliers is an important determinant of the buying decision only to the degree that the service of supplier X is perceived by the buyer as superior (or inferior) to the one provided by supplier Y. The perceived service of the various suppliers is, to a large extent, a function of the buyer's past experience with the various sources. It is more appropriate therefore to include this variable in a different set of variables that measures the buyer's past experience with the various sources.

Price has remained the only variable of the "traditional" set to be included directly in the generalized model. According to the hypothesis, all other things being equal, the lower the price of company X, relative to prices of other "acceptable" companies, the higher the probability that the buyer will shift to X (if now buying from another company) or will remain loyal to X (if now buying from it).

2. The buyer's past experience and interaction with the various sources is the second set of variables. It is assumed that a buyer's past experience and interrelations with the sources is summarized and expressed in his *attitude* toward the various sources.

Attitude is a hypothetical or latent variable rather than an immediately observable or measurable one. This being so, attitudes have been most commonly employed in the behavioral science literature to:

. . . Designate inferred dispositions attributed to an individual, according to which his thoughts, feelings and perhaps action tendencies are organized with respect to a psychological object.[44]

A similar definition, but with a stronger emphasis on the action tending component of attitude, is presented by Krech, Crutchfield, and Ballachey who state that:

The social action of the individual reflects his attitudes—enduring systems of positive or negative evaluations, emotional feelings, and pro or con action tendencies with respect to social objects.[45]

This definition stresses the relation between attitude and behavior but does not attempt to resolve the question of a cause and effect relationship between attitude and behavior. Festinger, in reporting on three studies which aimed at answering this question, concluded that:

These few relevant studies certainly show that this 'obvious' relationship (between attitude and subsequent behavior) probably does *not exist* and that indeed, some nonobvious relationship may exist.[46]

This conclusion was supported by McNiven of DuPont[47] who reported the results of an advertising experiment which showed clearly that medium "A" caused more attitude change than medium "B", but medium "B" caused more sales than medium "A."

Although the existing empirical findings indicate that one should not rely on the causality between attitudes and behavior, it is believed that the attitudes are correlated (although not perfectly) with actual behavior. This belief is based on the strength of the homeostasis principle and intuition. It is also supported by DuBois' findings that:

The more favorable the attitude among users, the more users you can hold. The more favorable the attitude among new users, the more you can bring into the user group. Having people up the attitude scale and keeping them there helps your chances of winning them as customers or of holding them as customers.[48]

Given this general hypothesis (that attitudes are correlated with behavior), it is hypothesized that the buyer's attitude toward the various sources is associated with his buying decision. More specifically, the buying decision in general and the source loyalty in particular are hypothesized to be, among other things, functions of:

a. Buyer's attitude level for each source;

b. The difference between the attitude toward source X and the profile of an "ideal" source (this difference is termed "the dissatisfaction gap");

c. The difference between the attitude toward source X and source Y (to be termed the "relative dissatisfaction gap").

3. The third set of variables which are hypothesized as affecting the buyer's decisions are the organizational variables—

variables which are derived from the author's "Reward-Balance" theory[49] and can be specified as:

    a. The pressure for cost savings. It is hypothesized that the greater the pressure, the greater the buyer's tendency to engage in cost savings behavior, and hence increase the probability of changing the source of supply.

    b. The dollar value of the order. It is hypothesized that the larger the dollar volume, the greater the tendency to engage in cost savings behavior, and hence increase the probability of changing the source of supply.

    c. The number of complaints from the using departments to the purchasing manager. The hypothesis concerning this proposition is that the larger the number of complaints, the greater the tendency will be to conform with the objectives of the using department.

    4. The fourth set of variables which are believed to be among the determinants of buyers' behavior are those factors that simplify the buyer's work.

Buyers are under tremendous pressure to complete their routine daily work (of selecting a source, contacting him, etc.) in a given period of time. Because of this heavy work load, which is characteristic of the electronics industry, buyers tend to consider those factors in their buying decisions that might simplify their work and save them extra effort and time (either at the time of making the purchase decision or at any other time between then and the acceptance of the parts by the users). This phenomenon of work simplification is the industrial buyer's equivalent of the consumer's tendency to increase his shopping convenience. Using this analogy, Kelley's conclusions concerning the importance of convenience in consumer purchasing can be cited and thus be used as an *a priori* hypothesis to be tested in the industrial buying situation. Kelley states that:

    Two factors are of utmost importance in understanding consumer shopping behavior. First, consumers making shopping decisions achieve an equilibrium between commodity costs and convenience costs. *Second, convenience costs are assuming* more importance as patronage determinants.[50]

Kelley continues by defining convenience costs as those costs which are:

    . . . Incurred through the expenditure of time, physical and nervous energy, and money required to overcome the frictions of space and time, and to obtain possession of goals and services.[51]

Based on the work simplification tendency, as found in the industrial buyer's case and the similarity to the case of the consumer who aims at minimizing their convenience costs, the following propositions can be hypothesized:

a. Buyers tend to prefer sources which are located geographically closer to them. This simplifies problems of communication between the buyer and his supplier. This is especially important in the purchase of fabricated (nonstandard) parts.

b. Buyers tend to remain with their *favorite source* as long as no strong pressures are exerted for a shift in source. This is due to their previous establishment of working relations with this source. A new order to the established source requires less effort than looking for a new source.

In addition to the above four sets of variables, inclusion of a fifth set of control variables in the models of source loyalty is recommended. The purpose of these variables is twofold: 1. To discover whether or not individual differences among the buyers might account for differences in the degree of source loyalty, 2. To examine the effect of a recommended sole brand (specified by an R&D engineer) on the source loyalty behavior of the buyer.

A General Model of Source Loyalty

The above theoretical discussion can be summarized by the following generalized model of buyers' source loyalty:

$$SL = (X_{11}, X_{21}, X_{22}, X_{23}, X_{31}, X_{32}, X_{33}, X_{41}, X_{42}, X_{51}, X_{52}, \epsilon)$$

Where: SL = Source loyalty

X_{ij} = Specific independent (explanatory) variable

j of set i where $i = 1\ldots5$ for the five sets of variables suggested in a previous section.

Hence: $\{X_{11}$ = Price

X_{21} = Buyer's attitude toward favorite source

X_{22} = Buyer's dissatisfaction gap

X_{23} = Buyer's relative dissatisfaction gap

$$\begin{cases} X_{31} = \text{Pressure for cost savings} \\ X_{32} = \text{Dollar value of order} \\ X_{33} = \text{Number of complaints from the using department} \end{cases}$$

$$\begin{cases} X_{41} = \text{Geographical location of source} \\ X_{42} = \text{Previous purchase history} \end{cases}$$

$$\begin{cases} X_{51} = \text{Change in source as related to change in identity of buyer} \\ X_{52} = \text{Recommendation of specific brand} \end{cases}$$

$$\epsilon = \text{An error term}$$

The Research Methodology and the Major Findings

Both the dependent and independent variables included in the general model can be defined and measured in a number of alternative ways. As there are no *a priori* criteria to determine which of these possible measures is the most appropriate one, a number of alternative measures were proposed and tested. A least squares multiple regression analysis was used to test all of the alternative measures of the five sets of explanatory variables in various combinations of the dependent (source loyalty) and independent variables. Having the results of these regressions, the most appropriate dependent variables and the corresponding "best" explanatory (independent) variables were determined.

Based on the findings of the initial regression study, a "best" explanatory model was constructed and tested by means of a fresh set of data, utilizing multiple regression and discriminant analyses so as to provide some firsthand empirical approximations of:

1. The directions and magnitude of the effect of the explanatory variables on the buyer's source loyalty, and

2. The relative importance of the various explanatory variables.

The data for this study were derived from three major sources:

1. The purchase history cards which provided the information needed for the calculations of all sets of variables with the exception of the attitude and pressure for cost savings variables.

2. The cost savings reports which were distributed weekly to all of the purchasing agents, specified the cost saved by each of the divisions during the foregoing week. These data were used to construct the measures of pressure for cost savings.

3. The buyer's attitudes toward the various sources of supply were derived from an attitude study based on a semantic differential scale.

The findings indicate clearly that all five sets of variables taken together have statistically significant association with source loyalty (R^2 between .86 to .94), regardless of the specific measure of source loyalty used. The association between the explanatory variables, taken separately, and source loyalty was summarized, for expository convenience, in Table 7 by ordering all of the statistically significant variables (t of .05 or better) in declining order of importance (as determined by the standardized b).

A multiple regression with these "best" measures of the various sets of explanatory variables and source loyalty as measured by the number of purchases from a favorite source as a percentage of all purchases, resulted in R^2 = .94 and F = 70.3. Explanatory variables that were found statistically significant by regression analysis were then subjected to a linear multiple discriminant analysis. This revealed that the five sets of explanatory variables capable of discriminating between various degrees of source loyalty.

The scope, consistency, and significance of both the regression and discriminant analysis justify the conclusion that source loyalty is an important aspect of industrial buyers' behavior in the purchase of components. Behavior is influenced by numerous variables however, and no single variable or set of variables can be considered as the sole loyalty determinant. These analyses then, served to emphasize the complexity of the buying process, the multiplicity of factors which affect it and highlight some of the possible determinants of buyers' behavior.

A multiple regression with these "best" measures of the various sets of explanatory variables and source loyalty as measured by the number of purchases from a favorite source as a percentage of all purchases, resulted in R^2 = .94 and F = 70.3. Explanatory variables that were found statistically significant by regression analysis were then subjected to a linear multiple discriminant analysis. This revealed that the five sets of explanatory variables proposed in the conceptual scheme for the analysis of the buyer behavior are capable of discriminating between various degrees of source loyalty.

TABLE 7

Order of Importance of Significant Explanatory Variables

Rank	Variable	Description of Variable	Standardized Regression Coefficient (b)
1.	Cost savings index	The ratio of dollar cost savings one week prior to the time of purchase to the average weekly cost savings for the whole period.	.2626
2.	The dollar value of the order	The number of times in which the dollar value of an order was greater than the critical value above which buyers perceive pressure for cost savings.	.2146
3.	Price index	The average ratio of the price at the time of purchase to the price at the previous purchase for all n purchases.	.2069
4.	Work simpli-fication index	The ratio of the average length of the source run of the favorite source to the average length of all other sources.	.1162
5.	Recommendation of a brand	A dummy variable that takes into account whether or not a specific brand was recommended.	.1145
6.	Attitude toward the source	The weighed attitude ratio (as a measure of the gap) between the most favorite source and the second most favorite source, when the weight is the relative importance of each attribute in the buyer's attitude concerning buying decisions.	.1058

The scope, consistency, and significance of both the regression and discriminant analysis justify the conclusion that source loyalty is an important aspect of industrial buyers' behavior in the purchase of components. Behavior is influenced by numerous variables, however, and no single variable or set of variables can be considered as the sole loyalty determinant. These analyses then, served to emphasize the complexity of the buying process, the multiplicity of factors which affect it and highlight some of the possible determinants of buyers' behavior.

PART THREE

Implications for Marketers

XII

Implications for
Marketing Management of
the Buyphase Framework

AS THE TITLE OF THIS BOOK SUGGESTS, there are many opportunities for creative marketing which derive from a knowledge of the industrial buying processes. Industrial marketers can be creative if they have insight and inspiration to help them in the process of innovation and in the search for differential advantage. This latter notion of differential advantage was stressed in the late Professor Wroe Alderson's last book, *Dynamic Marketing Behavior*,[1] in which he identified and emphasized the continuing competitive struggle which powers the marketplace and separates the leaders from the followers in effective innovation and communication.

The subject of *creativity* in industrial marketing management "has to do with the development, proposal and implementation of *new* and *better* solutions"[2] as opposed to *productivity*, which has to do with the efficient application of *current* "solutions." In this part of the book, a number of implications of the findings reported in the first two parts are identified in a marketing management context. It remains for the individual reader to exploit the research conclusions presented to develop specific proposals for his own firm and to envisage how to implement such strategies productively.

Effective marketing strategies, with respect to both industrial and consumer goods and services, require knowledge of the buying process, the buyer's behavior, and the various influences and motivations that affect this behavior. This study was designed to improve the understanding of these factors by taking into account both theoretical considerations and field observations in evaluating the industrial buying process, buyers' behavior, and the major determinants and influences involved.

As the research progressed, it was apparent that the industrial buying process is often complex and the current state of knowledge of these processes is still in its infancy. It is still too early to assert *conclusive* implications of general applicability to industrial marketing. However, if one assumes that the findings of the studies reported in this book are generally representative of industrial buying processes and buyers' behavior, then, a number of opportunities are identified for industrial marketers.

The present chapter deals with the possible consequences of adapting the marketing effort to buyer's decision points at the various phases in the procurement process. This chapter focuses on identifying the key stages in the Buyphase analysis for communicating and influencing the path of buyer behavior and eventual commitment in the procurement process.

Chapter VIII moves on from the discussion of the eight Buyphases to a review of the three Buyclasses and the various alternatives open to the marketer in handling products, services, promotions, channels, and prices. Moreover, it emphasizes the marketer activities in gathering the required information for formulating these strategies so as to achieve in the most effective and efficient way the firm's strategic and tactical goals.

Chapter XIV supplements the present chapter and Chapter XIII with an analysis of the importance of the determinants of buyer behavior for creative marketers. The chapter combines some suggestions which were derived from the analysis of the determinants of buyer behavior with the BUYGRID model (which in turn combines the Buyphase and Buyclass frameworks). It emphasizes the desirability of achieving insight into, and understanding of, the buyer behavior so as to plan and influence the course of events leading to increased market penetration, improved vendor-buyer relations, and a better matching of the buyer's needs and the supplier's offerings. This chapter concludes with a discussion of direction for future research and development in industrial marketing.

COMMUNICATIVE OPPORTUNITIES

This chapter examines the communicative opportunities for, and responsibilities of, marketers at varying phases of the procurement process. The specific aim of the discussion is to help marketers provide the right people with the right inputs (information, samples, technical service) at the right time.

There are several aspects to the marketer's communicative efforts. First, and most basically, he must respond to concrete requirements which are recognized within the buying organization and endeavor to persuade the potential customer that the marketer's organization is the most advantageous vendor. This basic communicative function must be performed by virtually every industrial sales concern and is dependent upon the personal skills and knowledge of sales people, plus whatever nonpersonal selling means are employed.

For the successful marketer, these requirements are no more than a starting point. Effective communication attempts to anticipate—and even to precipitate—forthcoming needs or changes in customer requirements in order to direct them into channels advantageous to the marketer.

This chapter discusses broad information requirements, since specific requirements of the customer differ in virtually every transaction. An examination of the information requirements and critical phases as discovered from the fieldwork, however, reveals several persisting patterns. In each transaction certain phases of the procurement process are more critical to the buying decision making and more replete with opportunities for the marketer.

Critical phases in the different buying processes varied noticeably with the type of situation, developing later as the procurement process became increasingly more routinized. In new task situations, the early phases of the procurement process seemed to be most significant to the outcome of the buying situation. The basic procurement patterns and direction were generally well established between phases 1 and 3 (between the time of initial need recognition and the specific description of the characteristics of the purchase item). In modified rebuys, the decisions which more vitally affected the outcome of the purchase occurred during phases 3 and 4, when precise specifications were being prepared and sources being qualified. In straight rebuys, critical decision points seem to occur even later, between phases 4 and 6—between the time of initial source qualification and final selection of a vendor.

MARKETING IMPLICATION OF THE EIGHT ELEMENTS OF THE BUYPHASES FRAMEWORK

Phase 1: Anticipation or Recognition of a Problem (Need)

The initial recognition of a specific problem or requirement will most frequently occur within the using department, although it may be anticipated elsewhere within the buying organization or externally by some individual who brings it to the attention of a buying influence. Whatever the particular circumstances, this initial phase eventually culminates in: 1. an acknowledgement by the buying influences that a concrete problem or potential requirement exists which may involve one or more purchases, and 2. a rather loose definition of the problem situation and the general direction(s) of investigation for determining its resolution. These steps represent the first decision points in the procurement process.

The importance of phase 1 activity to the marketer would be hard to overstate. The fieldwork indicated emphatically that the earlier in the procurement process the marketer becomes involved, the greater the probability that he will be selected or retained as a supplier. Marketing opportunities at this initial phase are generally very dependent on problem anticipating abilities and an understand-

ing of the customer's business, problems, etc. Without such understanding the marketer's ability to provide the information which
causes the customer to recognize problems is substantially im-
periled.

In the basic new task situation, a major responsibility of the
marketer at phase 1 is to comprehend the customer or potential
customer's prospective problems and influence him to recognize
their existence.   Problem recognition is largely internal to the
using firm—indeed to the using department.   Salesmen and other
information sources are not yet drawn in. Hence the marketer must
rely largely on seeds that have been sown earlier; these include
ideas planted by empathic, perceptive, and creative salesmen as
well as direct mail and media advertising designed to make prospective customers aware that they have problems which are capable of
resolution.

In the straight rebuy, the initial phase of problem recognition and
definition is less critical from the standpoint of the "in" supplier
since it is recurrent and relatively well routinized. The prime communicative function is to maintain a working rapport with users and
purchasing personnel; this aims to assure continued customer satisfaction with quality and service standards so as to forestall or minimize the extent of shifts into any modified rebuy situation.

Concurrently, the marketer seeks to extend the degree of routinization by the customer.   Communicative opportunities at this phase
may lie in ways to facilitate the customer's work of procurement to
the greatest extent.   In some cases customers may be encouraged
to develop improved and more routinized inventory management and
related procedures, the effect of which may be to tie them more
closely to the supplier.

The "out" supplier's task in the straight rebuy entails maintenance of liaison with the purchasing agent or other buying influences
awaiting emergence of a modified rebuy situation or of conditions
which make such emergence feasible.   A basic intelligence function
exists. Special perception is needed toward the development of circumstances susceptible to changing the established routine. Regular
sources of information and systematized means of interpretation
must be developed in order to detect and respond rapidly to such
events as the development of new facilities, new or modified products, transfer of personnel into new positions of decision making
authority, and failure of a current supplier to meet present or prospective needs.

The "out" supplier has a major task in this first phase when he
has decided to attempt to modify the straight rebuy to a modified
rebuy.   His ultimate goal is to convince the buying influences, directly or indirectly, that a reevaluation of alternative solutions
to the problem would be appropriate.   His persuasive power will
be substantially enhanced by a favorable company image and a solid
reputation as to capabilities, reliability, and credibility of proposals.
A thorough understanding of the customer's business is advantageous

to both in and out suppliers since it makes them better able to recognize opportunities in which they might make a superior service offer.

The more aggressive marketer begins his communicative functions before the customer has even recognized a requirement. To have any influence in phase 1, he must anticipate the customer's problem. In order to do this he must previously have established some measure of rapport with those from whom he can learn about the company and its problems. This rapport is required not so that he can influence them but rather so that he can learn from them. Thus, he will be in a position to perceive presently obscure or emerging problems and help the customer recognize that a concrete problem does or is about to exist which may be possible of solution. He may even be able to anticipate problems on the basis of circumstances and his related experience and advise the customer about how to prevent, confront, or circumvent them.

A more creative approach is applicable to all situational types, but particularly to the new task situation and the modified rebuy. It requires perception, insight, and depth of experience on the part of the marketing organization.

Phase 2: Determination of the Characteristics and Quantity of the Needed Item

In essence this phase represents a technical refinement of the problem and the direction of its resolution. Specific products or services needed to perform the functional requirements determined in phase 1 begin to be defined. This decision point, too, generally lies within the using department. Information is needed which will enable the buying decision makers to prepare broad, often incomplete specifications.

The marketer's responsibility and opportunities in phase 2 lie in providing the customer with information and technical assistance while he is in the process of narrowing down the solution area. In new task situations, the marketer seeks to gain or assure participation in the problem-solving process, obviously to affect the outcome. An opportunity to provide technical assistance or services, however, will be dependent on his reputation for capability which will have been previously established through marketing efforts or actual performance. For consideration, too, he will first have necessarily established channels of communication and recognition by purchasing personnel (who act as source locators) and frequently problem-solving personnel in using departments as well. Advertising intended to have impact at this point in the procurement process might stress the general capability, reliability, and problem-solving skills of the marketer. In some new task situations, the critical buying decisions may have been made before suppliers are even advised that the process is underway. For this reason, industrial advertising may be of special importance to marketers who face a high proportion of new task situations.

Similarly, personal selling activities need to be directed toward the special information requirements of the early stages in the procurement process. Salesmen should be conceptually oriented, imaginative problem-solvers in the broadest sense. In this early stage of the new task situation, suppliers are selected to provide technical assistance largely on the basis of their general reputation for capability and their ability to help the buyers refine and solve problems.

In the straight rebuy situation, the marketing task in phase 2 is basically to provide and maintain a system of information flow and availability so that the buyer need not depart from established routines and thereby become involved in a modified rebuy situation. This is by no means a perfunctory task. To the extent that the regular suppliers fail to provide the quantity and quality of current information which buyers need and expect, buyers will necessarily consider other information sources.

To the "out" supplier trying to effectuate a modified rebuy from a straight rebuy situation, his opportunities closely parallel the new task situation. His primary job is to utilize corporate facilities and expertise, both marketing and technical, to develop offers that add value to the customer so that his "solution" will be considered.

Phase 3: Description of the Characteristics and Quantity of the Needed Item

This decision point may be crucial for the marketer, particularly in the new task or modified rebuy situation. It is at this point that the buying influences usually begin to look outside of the company for specific information about supplier capability, availability of goods and services, and product specifications. To expedite the search, information about the required goods or services will be made available to potential suppliers. For most suppliers, this represents the first knowledge that a buying situation is in process.

At this phase, the major buying influences may change from department heads and staff people to the engineers, designers, or production men who prepare the detailed specifications. In practice, this step cannot be completely separated from phase 4—qualification of suppliers. Consciously or not, specifiers tend to think about suppliers at the same time that they do of products and services. Their primary interest is in securing information on the total offerings available with respect to products and supporting services.

In new task situations, the buyer has now reached the stage of preparing specifications or of choosing among alternative specifications which have been proposed by internal or external sources.

An important job of the marketer is to provide sufficient assurance about his proposal to overcome the strong conservatism of specifiers.

The implication seems generally to be to stress total performance in advertising strategy. Since the decision making "center of gravity" probably has shifted to staff specifiers at a relatively low organizational level, the marketer needs to place greater emphasis on product, technical, and/or merchandising services. Salesmen or technical representatives with a detailed knowledge of the product characteristics and potential applications are in demand, rather than the more conceptually oriented problem solver who is of most value in the earlier phases of the procurement process.

In the straight rebuy situation, the responsibility remains largely the same as in phase 2—to maintain a high level of information flow, availability, and satisfactory customer service.

Phase 3 frequently begins the critical decision stage in the modified rebuy situation. Buyers have some relevant experience with the item being purchased and prior supplier performance. They have a fairly clear idea of what their evaluation criteria are, and these are weighted in importance, either formally or implicitly. Modified rebuys may develop from the actions of buying company personnel, or may be created by a marketer who convinces the buyers that their requirement is new or changed or that the marketer's offer will better fill an existing need than the items presently used.

Industrial advertising for companies selling into modified rebuys might stress two basic appeals. First, the advertising should suggest to the customer that his basic need actually might have changed so that the continued use of his regular suppliers' products might be causing him to lose ground to competitors. Advertising aimed at creating modified rebuys which stresses the features of the goods-and-services offering should not be content to emphasize absolute superiorities unless they are significant to buyers as well as to the marketer. Because of the risks involved in making a change, and the fact that it's always easier to do nothing than to do something different, advertising might subtly stress the dangers of being left behind if the advertiser's offering is not investigated.

The fieldwork suggests that many salesmen trying to convert a prospective customer from a straight to a modified rebuy frequently are not as successful as they might be because they do not fully appreciate the buyer's viewpoint. They stress the superiority of their product and service offerings, but to buyers these differences may seem relatively minor. Since the use of a new supplier involves an element of personal risk to the buyer as well as the risk for his company, he may feel that the advantages to be gained by the new salesman's offer are not great enough to outweigh the risks involved in making a change.

In these situations, the salesman should not stress the absolute superiorities of his own line; rather, he should convince the customer that his need or requirement has changed in at least some significant aspect and that the new supplier's offering is better suited to meet the changed need. In many cases, the salesman may apply the same principle to the service aspects of his offer. The study uncovered a number of examples where this was done successfully. For example, one marketer is able to sell coal at a substantial price premium by maintaining an inventory at the buyer's plant at all times.

Phase 4: Search for and Qualification of Potential Sources

This phase involves the identification of potential sources and their qualification. An elementary task of the marketer is to ensure that appropriate buying influences are convinced that his firm has the capability to meet particular needs.

For new tasks, the demonstration of capability is paramount. Because phase 4 may proceed concurrently with earlier phases, this capability must be demonstrated not only to purchasing personnel but to personnel in the using departments who are involved in solution definition and product description (phases 1 to 3). Here there is no substitute for outstanding prior performance for the using company. Failing this, the marketer may provide testimonial evidence of his performance for others. While advertising may be used to perform a part of the job of assuring supplier qualification in situations likely to involve major commitments, the marketer must be prepared to furnish convincing evidence of performance. The buyer may wish to examine equipment in use or to talk with existing customers of the prospective supplier. In some cases, he may choose to inspect the facilities and observe the processes and quality control procedures of candidate suppliers. The marketing organization must be prepared to cooperate and to provide the necessary services.

The supplier's reputation for competence must extend to his engineers if technical services or applications engineering are important to the customer. This becomes vital in cases in which technical personnel from the supplier company and the customer company work together in the joint determination of problem solutions and product specifications.

In modified rebuy situations, "in" suppliers have similar interest in maintaining performance and capability standards and also in demonstrating the quality and reliability of their past performance. The "out" supplier has quite different problems. It generally is not sufficient for him merely to demonstrate an equal performance capability; his task, rather, is to demonstrate to the customer superior value in some respect and thereby convince him to consider the procurement as a modified rebuy. His offerings might include, for example, faster deliveries, better quality control, more accurate information, etc.

By way of contrast, in straight rebuy situations, the marketer has already established his capability. A primary task now is to ensure that the performance is maintained so that the buyer does not consider alternatives. A smooth working relationship and good buyer-seller communication enhance his position. The center of gravity, or the critical decision point, in straight rebuys is likely to begin at this phase. While the marketer in the new task and modified rebuy situations seeks essentially to secure the customer's business, his job in a straight rebuy is to hold the business. Advertising and personal selling should be directed toward keeping the customer sold. Strong relationships with customers can be stressed. For the buyer's own peace of mind, he should be assured that he is dealing with the most qualified supplier, receiving superior service, and buying the best product.

Marketers facing a high proportion of straight rebuy situations may wish to assign the major part of the task of maintaining the accounts to the individual salesman.

Phase 5: Acquisition and Analysis of Proposals

At this phase potential suppliers already have been identified and qualified. Buyers now seek from them specific proposals and price quotations. In straight rebuys this may involve no more than reference to a catalogue or telephoning a regular supplier to obtain current information about specifications, prices, or deliveries. In complex new task situations, in contrast, this may require detailed information exchanges and negotiating activities, with counter proposals and new offerings, which may extend over months and involve a number of suppliers.

An important obligation of the marketer at this phase in new task procurements is the provision of technical assistance. This may be accomplished by sales personnel who frequently have important responsibilities as communicators between prospective customers and the vendor's technical personnel. At this stage it is important that the salesman understand not only the customer's general problem but the specific details of design and of the problem as seen from the customer's perspective. Unless astute in these respects, effectiveness in communicating to the marketing organization is likely to be limited.

In straight rebuy situations the marketer bears the responsibility for making proposals and quotations with dispatch. The underlying goal is to maintain a sufficiently high level of customer service and information flow so as to preclude any serious consideration by the customer of different suppliers and thereby forestall a shift to a modified rebuy situation. This implies a willingness to share or pass on benefits to the customer (such as cost savings) as such opportunities develop and without waiting until forced to do so by pressure.

An important sales responsibility at this phase in the modified rebuy, in addition to the provision of technical aid, is active willingness to demonstrate the superior value of a particular solution. This suggests that sellers must be prepared to assist in economy studies, in testing, and in evaluations of relative cost.

Phase 6: Evaluation of Proposals and Selection of Supplier

Eventually all offers from potential vendors will be acquired and analyzed, and the supplier will be selected. The role of marketers at this stage is quite limited. There may be some opportunities, however, to convert straight rebuys to modified rebuys by raising such possible questions as the benefits of multiple sourcing, reciprocity, or ''buy local'' policies.

Phase 7: Selection of an Order Routine

The activities involved in this phase are usually directed by the purchasing department and include expediting and trouble-shooting, status reporting, receiving and inspection, and approval of invoices for payment.

Marketers in all buying situations have an important interest in seeing that order routines operate without friction. Although many of these activities do not concern suppliers directly, buyers do need to rely on timely and accurate status reporting. The failure of the marketing organization to perform satisfactorily in this phase by insufficient or inaccurate status reporting, through failure to meet schedules, or by errors in the marketer's production, shipping, or billing departments is likely to have significant impact on future business.

Phase 8: Performance Feedback and Evaluation

Feedback is a continuous element in procurement especially when the latter is viewed as a process embodying continuing relationships rather than as a series of detached events. In some cases, formal appraisal will be made of vendor and product performance. More commonly, such appraisals are made informally and by a number of individuals who will become buying influences in future procurements—most obviously personnel in purchasing or the using departments, but sometimes even within the sales organization, where the supplier's product performance can also affect its marketing operations, favorably or adversely.

The importance of post-transaction evaluation is obvious over the long run. The far-sighted marketer will well recognize the need for a high level of performance in after-service responsibilities. An organization that does not resolve problems promptly and to the customer's satisfaction will soon be burdened with an unsatisfactory image.

MARKETING IMPLICATIONS OF THE CHANGING ROLES OF BUYING INFLUENCES

A major problem for the marketer is that the buying influences are subject to rapid change, with reference to both identify and behavior. For many items, such as capital goods, the buying influences may be quite different in new task and modified rebuy situations, even if the equipment finally purchased turns out to be the same, the situations will be judged according to different criteria. Hence, different types of information will be required.

Even within a given buying situation at a particular time, the buying influences may change as the decision process moves from phase to phase. Analytical people who can visualize how the needed item fits into total company operations are likely to be of major importance in the early problem formulation and definition phases of the procurement process. As the actual specifications are being prepared, designers, engineers, and draftsmen are likely to play the key roles. But, these are not the talents which will be needed most in negotiating with suppliers or in following up and expediting an order. This basic generalization appears to hold in all three types of buying situations, although it is most observable in new tasks. Marketers need to identify the buying influences in a particular instance and to determine their sources and uses of information, an objective which is difficult to achieve until the buying situation is actually in process.

The concept of the creeping commitment suggests that the marketer does not need to personally contact and influence every buying influence involved in a particular situation. General corporate advertising and advertising aimed at the information needs of the buyers in the buying situations of interest may be used to reduce the number of personal sales calls required.

It has been noted that different buyers, and the same buyer in different situations, will respond differently to the various aspects of the marketer's total offering. Buying decision makers do appear to exhibit varying degrees of sensitivity to technical services, merchandising assistance, and price. The fieldwork indicates that marketers are at least intuitively aware of these various sensitivities of their customers. Yet many industrial marketers have only one basic package or offer which they sell to all customers. The determination of which combination of these various components should

be stressed is often left up to the individual salesman. The salesman may be authorized to make adjustments in these elements, within a fairly narrow range, to suit the desires of the individual customer. A conclusion of this study is that industrial marketers
should consider the means by which more flexibility could be built
into the presentations and proposals which are submitted to potential customers. Various proposals might be submitted to one customer so that he could select from several offers of a single vendor.

SUMMARY

The marketer needs to adapt his total offering to respond to cus-
tomer-originated buying situations. He should also be able to
accomplish the more rewarding job of pre-precipitating changes in
the customer's need recognition and buying patterns. It is in this
way that marketing helps to keep the economy dynamic and progressive.

As the procurement process develops, each incremental phase
may be considered to be a decision point in the gradual commitment
to a particular course of action. At various phases in this process,
the identity of the major buying influences is likely to change.
These separate buying influences have differing perspectives and
particular informational requirements. The marketer needs to recognize that what is required of him will change accordingly. He
must recognize, too, the inherent differences in the information
needs at various phases of the procurement process and that these
information needs will vary with each type of buying situation.

XIII

Implications for
Marketing Management of
the Buyclass Framework

THE OBJECTIVE OF THIS CHAPTER is to generalize from the previous analysis and the fieldwork of both the Institute and Dr. Wind's studies and the previous analysis some specific implications for various marketing strategies. These implications are developed for each of the three buying situations (new task, straight, and modified rebuy) for both a marketer who is already an established "in" supplier of a given buying firm, and a marketer who has had no point of entry as yet to the buying firm—an "out" supplier—but who aspires to become accepted. The major subjects to be covered in this chapter can be presented as follows:

TABLE 8

A Framework for the Analysis of the Marketing Effort
Under Various Buying Situations

Marketing Strategies and Tools	New Task	Buying Situations	
		Rebuy	
		Straight	Modified
1. Getting the required marketing information			
2. Channel strategies			
3. Goods and services strategies			
4. Promotion strategies			

The rationale for analyzing the marketing strategies for each buying situation separately is that the three buying situations can

195

be viewed as representing separate market segments, each of which might require different marketing strategies. It is recognized that a firm can maximize its profits by segmenting a market with a heterogeneous demand into mutually exclusive groups with relatively homogeneous patterns within individual groups and by then applying different strategies to the different segments. The specific marketing strategies and tools to be designed for each segment (buying situation) are likely to vary based on the specific characteristics of the marketer and his initial position—whether he is currently an established "in" supplier of the buying firm or only an "out" but aspiring supplier who wants an entrance.

The following suggestions for marketing strategies are developed with the hope that the reader will be stimulated to use them as a framework for developing new opportunities for creative marketing in his own organization by taking into account explicitly the nature of the market (buyers' requirements and needs) and the characteristics of his own organization (resources, capabilities, etc.).

THE MARKETING EFFORT IN A NEW TASK SITUATION

What are the implications for the industrial marketer, facing the opportunities of a new task situation, when the buying influences have little relevant experience and will require a great deal of information about the problem and will also consider a wide range of alternative solutions before making a buying choice?

The ability to understand and solve the problems of the buying company appears to be most critical in new task situations. It is essential that all marketing efforts be directed at:

a. gathering information on the problems of the buying company,

b. interpreting and understanding these problems, and

c. solving the solvable problems.

These functions can be performed either by one person (usually the salesman) or by a number of people. In either case, the relevant marketing administrator must be the coordinator of the total marketing effort required to implement the plan.

It should be recalled that there are numerous variations of new task situations. These situations vary with regard to the supplier's degree of involvement in the problem-solving process. In some new task situations, supplier selection may take place very early in the procurement process. The general solution to the problem becomes, in effect, the selection of a supplier who is qualified to assist in the remaining phases of the procurement process. As the process develops, the problem is progressively more clearly defined and the range of alternative solutions narrowed. This is

most likely to occur when neither the buyer nor the seller can visualize the final product, as, for instance, when new technology is
needed. Here in effect, the company purchases the problem-
solving capability of the selected vendor—a transaction requiring
a great deal of confidence on the part of the buyer in the technical
expertise and reputation of the suppliers. Illustrative situations
are particularly prevalent in defense and space procurement.
Clearly, a military weapons system or a space vehicle poses critical definitional and performance problems.

In other new task situations, the procurement process may have
progressed internally to the stage of drafting specifications before
vendors become aware that a buying situation exists. The problem
may be well defined and the solution area narrowed greatly before
suppliers are contacted.

The marketing tools to be used in these new task situations may
vary both to fit the nature of the marketing segments and their mix
of requirements. The specific marketing tools that can be utilized
to increase the probability of an "out" supplier becoming an "in"
supplier or to strengthen an "in" supplier's hold on the buying
firm (increase his share) are described next.

A. Getting the required marketing information. In industrial marketing the salesman is commonly assumed to know all that is
needed about the buyers' needs and requirements. It is not desirable, however, to leave this information to the salesman and rely on
him to mesh the vendor firm's total marketing efforts with the
specific needs of a particular customer. It seems, from the standpoint of modern marketing management, that the salesman should
transmit his information to the relevant marketing personnel, who,
based on this and other sources of information, design the appropriate marketing strategies.

The marketing manager in turn does not have to be passive and
await the information reaching him but should design suitable channels for information. He must be currently aware of any developments and changes in his market opportunities. The information
gathering function is simplified in the case where a marketer is
currently an "in" supplier for other products or services—given
that he is an active marketer who is anxious to improve his long-
run position with the buying firm. The job of gathering information
on various needs and problems of the buying organization is harder
for an "out" supplier who has to rely either on an active search
for information by the buyer or on indirect sources. In any case,
the information gathering phase, whether conducted in a formal or
informal manner, is a critical first step in any marketing effort
directed at the new task buying situation.

Other functions such as marketing research help with problem
analysis and model building, have to be performed so as to aid the
marketer in designing his marketing strategy. These functions may
be similar for both "in" and "out" vendors and for all types of

buying situations. There appears to be a slight competitive advantage for the ''in'' supplier who may have a better ''feel'' for the possible reactions of the buying organization.

B. *Distribution Strategies*. Direct selling is traditionally considered to be the major channel of distribution in industrial marketing. It should be recalled, however, that distributors and other intermediate organizations can and do perform a number of important marketing functions, and it is one of management's major tasks to select the ''best'' possible channel.

In the new task buying situation, it is essential that the channel member (salesman, distributor, etc.) carry out two major functions:

1. The first and most important function is that of communication with the buying organization. The channel member has to inform (in a persuasive way) the buyers, users, and buying influencers of the existence of the firm he is representing, and of its production and service capabilities. To perform this task the channel member has to be able to interpret buyer problems in a manner that will direct the buyer toward acceptable solutions within the resources and capabilities of the marketing system. If the salesman or distributor can anticipate and identify emerging problems or needs before they are recognized within the buying organization, their influence will be even greater. Equally important, they must elicit buyer confidence in the capabilities of their supply organization to resolve those problems. Since buyers are really seeking *solutions to problems* rather than merely products or services, the marketer should concentrate on selling performance in problem solution.

2. The channel member has to provide the marketer with the needed information (feedback) on the buyers, and as he discerns problem situations. he transmits relevant information to specialists in the supply organization who are qualified to work on particular facets. A large measure of familiarity is required with the operations of the customer organization as well as his own vendor company so that he can bring together appropriate people at various phases of the procurement process.

These two functions of the channel member as a communications facilitator for both information and order flows between the buying and selling organization is of utmost importance to the whole marketing process in the new task buying situation. This role of communication with the buying organization is simplified for representatives of ''in'' suppliers with whom the buyers had favorable past experience. The task of the ''out'' suppliers is harder but with appropriate planning, creativity, and utilization of the various communication vehicles available to the firm there is no reason why they should not be able to reach the buying organization.

As to the selection of the appropriate channel of distribution it might vary according to the characteristics of the product, the buyers, the selling organization, the environment, and the available channel members.

But in all these cases in a new task buying situation the channel to be selected should be the one that will perform the needed communication function in the most effective and efficient manner.

C. Products and Services Strategies. Marketers' offerings often tend to become fairly standardized among competing sellers, although performance and efficiency may vary. Perhaps most significant to both marketer and customer are those distinct or unusual service elements, including engineering capability, design competence, a reputation for imaginative solutions to customer problems, recognition of problems not apparent to the customer, and greater understanding of the customer's operations. To excel in these areas, the marketer must provide superior information that is closely tailored to the needs of the buying decision makers. The buying influences themselves may not be able to specify precisely their informational needs, which sometimes may be disguised because of personal or organizational relationships. A major competitive advantage accrues to the marketer with the most complete knowledge and understanding of customer information requirements and organizational customs. Regardless of the homogeneity of products and services offered by competing suppliers, there are numerous opportunities for the supplier who concentrates on providing information services tailored to the buying company's particular requirements.

Industrial buyers appear to be willing to pay, either directly or indirectly, for marketing services which help to differentiate the offers of various suppliers. For example, suppliers may carry inventory to guarantee delivery or assist in technical applications. These services may be paid for by a higher purchase price on individual transactions. In some cases, separate charges for services will be made. Sometimes it is agreed that the supplier is sufficiently compensated for his marketing services by being awarded a large, continuous participation in the buyer's requirements. Buyers willingly pay for the uniqueness of a supplier's goods and services offerings when their concern is with total procurement costs and not merely with the unit price paid for the physical product.

Both the MSI and Dr. Wind's studies indicated that price as a criterion for selecting suppliers has very little importance in the new task buying situation. Imaginative marketers who provide the needed services are likely to "get the order" almost regardless of price, assuming their prices are not completely out of line.

As the success of goods and services strategies depends on its perception by the "right" members of the buying organization, a "good" "in" supplier has some advantage over an unknown "out" supplier.

D. *Promotional Strategies*. The Buyphase analysis suggested in Chapter X indicates some of the ways in which marketer's efforts may be tailored to the various decision points in the customer's buying process. Hence, promotion, being one of the elements of the total marketing activities, should be tailored and directed at the "appropriate" targets. Promotional activities generally include four subactivities of advertising, sales promotion, publicity, and personal selling. The major importance of the latter activity was emphasized in the discussion of channel strategies and is the subject of MSI's companion book, *Personal Selling in a Modern Perspective*. Publicity—nonpersonal stimulation of demand for a product, service, or business unit by planting commercially significant news about it in a published or broadcast medium that is not paid for by the sponsor—and advertising—any paid form of nonpersonal presentation and promotion of ideas, goods or services by an identified sponsor—should supplement and strengthen the personal selling efforts.

More specifically, Dr. Wind's study suggested that for the cases studied, advertising in purchasing trade journals is not generally productive. The rationale for this conclusion was that the buyers do not, because of time pressure, read many trade journals so that they are not exposed to many of the ads and publicity pieces in these journals. This conclusion suggests that 1. publicity or advertising aimed at the buyers should be transmitted either through general media or direct mail in the form of easy to handle "catalogs" and 2. that advertising in all its form and publicity, be directed at other members of the buying center, especially at those who are actively engaged in search for information (R & D engineers, for example).

Sales promotions are a useful supplement to advertising and personal selling. Dr. Wind's study suggested the use of free samples to the R & D engineers as a major sales promotion activity. The rationale for this is that while designing a system (new task), the engineer tends to use those components that are immediately available to him. Thus, the first place he may head for components is his sample collection. The advantage of having a component in a system is that its probability of becoming a recommended one (for rebuy situations) is fairly high compared with a non-included component.

All the promotion activities are important for both an "in" and "out" supplier. The latter has, however, to rely on this much more than the former who is already a "known quantity" to the buying organization. Hence, the "out" suppliers have to devote more of their resources to promotional activities designed and directed at the "right" decision points in the buying process.

THE MARKETING EFFORT IN REBUY SITUATIONS

A problem handled as a new task will sooner or later be handled as a rebuy if it continues to recur. Regardless of the dollars involved, procurement problems may be handled as modified rebuys if the buying decision makers determine that the gains exceed the added costs incurred in the time and effort required to evaluate alternatives. As these purchases continue to recur they tend to become highly routinized straight rebuys, in spite of complex paper work and even though several individuals may continue to be involved as reviewers.

Straight and modified rebuys are similar in that the problem or requirement of the buying company is one which has arisen before, so that the buying decision makers have some relevant experience to draw upon. The rebuys are distinguishable on the basis of information requirements, and the extent to which new alternative solutions are considered.

From the point of view of the marketer who attempts to sell into rebuy situations, it is useful to distinguish between the marketing effort of an "in" supplier—an approved, regular, and current source—and an "out" supplier—a supplier with no relevant recent experience in selling to the company. The job of the "out" supplier is far more difficult than that of the "in" supplier for two apparent reasons. First, when vendors' offerings are evaluated, the "in" supplier has an advantage in previous satisfactory performance and in any communicatory channels or working relationships which have been established with the buying influences. The "out" supplier is at a disadvantage, since he is an unknown quantity and must rely upon promises and representations concerning future performance.

Second, the addition of a new supplier adds both out-of-pocket costs and risks to the procurement process. Costs take the form of testing, securing approvals, and time. The risks are those of shifting from more certain to less certain relationships; this involves personal risk for the decision maker in addition to organizational risks. If something goes wrong on a purchase from an established source, the error is likely to be blamed on the supplier. If something goes wrong on a purchase from a new source, the mistake may well be blamed on the buying influence who decided to use the new supplier. New sources are generally given serious consideration only when prospective gains in such elements as price, quality or services are significant. Sometimes even then committee action may be invoked to "spread the blame," although, committee action may be divided in some companies, nevertheless they can provide one effective means of introducing review and collective motivation for considering change.

The fieldwork uncovered a number of seemingly paradoxical situations where buying decision makers recognized the superiority of a new supplier's offer, but refused to change from the established suppliers. They were willing, in these cases, to settle for an acceptable solution to the problem rather than to seek out the optimal solution. Even while recognizing some margin of superiority in a new supplier's offering, buyers may decide that the difference is not great enough to compensate them for the risks and uncertainty involved in changing suppliers.

The "out" supplier, then, faces a significant challenge in overcoming the buyer's inertia or his inclination to minimize risk by remaining with established suppliers. This change might be accomplished by increasing the prospective real gains to a point where the buyers determine that potential gains exceed perceived risks. If this is too costly, the out-marketer might try to demonstrate to the buyers that the risks of staying with the old vendor exceed the risks of trying the new. The new vendor could point out that competition is switching to the new offering, and that the change is mandatory to remain competitive.

The objective of the "in" supplier in both the straight and modified rebuy situation can (thus) be stated as directing the marketing effort at developing, maintaining and improving routines so as to reinforce the existing straight rebuy practice, or if the current practice is a modified rebuy, to change it to a straight one.

On the other hand, the objective of the "out" supplier is to deroutinize the buying procedure so as to enable him to get "in." More specifically, under the straight rebuy situation, an "out" supplier will attempt to convert the buying process to a modified rebuy which is more favorable to a prospective new supplier. Similarly, in a modified rebuy the "out" supplier will aim to extend the modification so as to include him as part of the feasible set of prospective suppliers.

These objectives that in turn determine (or should determine) the marketing effort of the given suppliers are summarized in Table 9.

Some specific marketing implications of these objectives are presented next.

A. Getting the required marketing information. A basic prerequisite for successful marketing strategies is the availability of needed information on the buying organization, its other current and potential suppliers and the environment in which the firm operates (general economic, political, legal, technological, and social factors).

Whereas these general classes of information are recognized for both new task and rebuy situations, the specific types of information needed and the ways in which it can be gathered vary to some extent. Moreover, they vary with the specific marketing objective of the given supplier.

Straight Rebuy. The buyer needs very little additional information before making a straight rebuy decision. Hence the "in" supplier's only objective in planning the gathering of information is to keep himself informed of any possible changes in the buyer's satisfaction with his goods and services and the buyer's new needs, if any. The supplier is also concerned with the competitive offerings and other relevant environmental factors.

TABLE 9

The Marketing Objectives of the "In" and "Out"
Suppliers in Rebuy Situations

Supplier Characteristics	Buying Situation	
	Straight Rebuy	Modified Rebuy
"In" Supplier	1. Reinforce the routine rebuy 2. Increase share of market	1. Increase share of market 2. Change the procedure to a routinized straight rebuy
"Out" Supplier	1. Change the buying procedure to modified rebuy	1. Maintain a modified rebuy status 2. Enter the buyer's feasible set of suppliers.

The "in" supplier has easy access to the first two types of information. Despite this, he has to be concerned with designing the right channels for the flow of this information from the marketplace to his firm and within his firm to the right decision influences.

Information on the competitive offerings are not as critical in this buying situation due to two major factors. First, any new offering is likely to be brought to the marketer's attention by the buying firm—it was found that negotiating a change in the offerings of an "in" supplier is perceived by the buyer as cheaper than changing to a completely new supplier. Second, many routine rebuys are based on a standing agreement between the buyer and seller that is not subject to changes in the short run. Despite these two factors, keeping up to date on changes in the buyer's situation should be part of the firm's standard data gathering procedures. In the Modified Rebuy situations, the buyers and buying influences need nonroutine information and utilize a variety of information sources. Hence, irrespective whether the marketer is an "in" or "out" supplier he has to develop and maintain a constant flow of information about the buyer's information requirements, problems and susceptibility to change the nature of the current buying situation.

The marketing effort of an "out" supplier, who strives to become an "in" supplier, are directed at convincing the buying decision makers that their basic requirements have changed or should be interpreted differently. He has to establish the notion that his company can do the best job in filling the modified needs—hence hoping to achieve two objectives of changing a Straight Rebuy to a Modified Rebuy situation and entering into the buyer's "feasible set of suppliers." To achieve these objectives the marketer needs much more information than that required by an "in" supplier. He is in a disadvantageous position with regard to the availability of this information—not having any foothold in the buying organization. Hence the "out" marketer should devote much of his marketing effort and resources for the gathering of the relevant information.

B. *Distribution Strategies.* Selection of the "right" channel of distribution for implementing marketing strategy is a critical decision in the rebuy situation, for both actual and aspiring suppliers. Toward determining the most appropriate channels, salesmen in particular appear to provide a potentially sound information service for planning marketing programs. The current studies indicate that salesmen generally possess accurate information in many aspects of the buying firm, whether they represent a currently "in" or "out" supplier.

The type of product offered has been found to be a significant factor in determining the desired channel in all rebuy situations. Dr. Wind's study further suggests that the channel strategies for standard and fabricated parts should be distinctly different for each given buying situation. The ideal method of distribution for standard parts, specifically, seems to be via a distributor with the following characteristics:

1. Maintain a wide assortment of lines and sufficiently large minimum inventory to meet buyer requirements.

2. Sound reputation (delivery, adjustments, etc.).

3. A sufficient number of phone order recipients to handle incoming calls. (The Wind study revealed frequent buyer source switching when unable to reach the preferred source by telephone.)

4. Physical location near major buyers for ease of communication and rapid service when needed.

For fabricated parts, on the other hand, salesmen and independent representatives appear to be useful distribution channels in the rebuy situations. Engineers were frequently found to rely upon the latter for advice in source selection. Salesmen, however, retained the major critical role of communicating with, and persuading, the buying influences. (In fact, evidence from the Stanford study suggests that salesmen should be used only for this personal selling function—not for order solicitation.)

In the rebuy situation it is usually difficult for channel members of "out" suppliers to reach certain of the buying influences to whom the particular messages should be directed. The "target people" may only be reached by what is commonly termed "backdoor selling"—a procedure usually resented by purchasing. Yet to implement the recognized need for adapting the marketing communications and persuasive activities to the diverse buying responsibilities (as emphasized in Chapter X), it is evident that "backdoor selling" is a necessary tool of creative marketers. The Stanford study indicates more specifically that such selling may be more useful and less offensive if the channel member:

1. Offers something of current interest to the target market (R & D engineer, etc.).

2. Possesses sufficient technical knowledge to fulfill the engineers' needs for information.

3. Inform the buyer on the contact, or even ask him to arrange such a meeting, demonstrating to the buyer that both he and the salesman are "on the same side of the fence."

In both types of rebuy situations, the channel members of the "out" supplier have to devote most of their efforts to promotional activities—chiefly personal selling—directed at the buying firm. As in the new task situation, the salesman will attempt to anticipate and identify problems and needs, and to develop superior solutions. This will require substantially more effort, information and persuasive ability on the part of the aspiring marketer in the Straight Rebuy as compared to the Modified Rebuy situation, since in the former the buying company is not dissatisfied with the current situation and seeks no immediate change. The out supplier must convey the impression of some margin of superiority over the existing supplier's product or total offering to overcome the buyer's natural skepticism about changing from a workable satisfactory arrangement.

Advertising may assist in attracting the attention of the buyer or buying influence(s), and their confidence to some degree, and eventually secure an audience for the appropriate channel member. But this unknown channel member, competing with known personalities, must maintain and extend the supplier's corporate image to one of superior capability to handle the immediate supply situation.

The marketing efforts of the "in" supplier in the Straight Rebuy situation is aimed at reinforcing the routine buying practice, at least in the short run. Harmonious vendor-supplier relationship is cultivated. Channel members of the "in" supplier are enlisted as facilitators for the flow of goods, and to insure that problems are minimized and expeditiously resolved when they occur. They seek to keep the customer satisfied, and to apprise their headquarters of future problems, opportunities and other pertinent information. In the long run, they must anticipate the eventual change to a Modified Rebuy situation and be prepared to handle it when it does occur.

The ''out'' marketers' task in the Modified Rebuy situation is partially alleviated. Having accepted the Modified Rebuy situation, the buying company recognizes the possible wisdom or desirability of changing the current supply situation. The initial barrier then has already been overcome. Different solutions to procurement problems are being sought or at least considered, and the climate is receptive to new suppliers. There may be less need for the dramatic, innovative, ''attention-getting'' strategy, since the matter of securing attention of the buyer or appropriate buying influences is not as severe in this case.

But to maintain the buying company's attention and interest to the point of becoming the selected supplier requires a total offering superior or at least competitive with other marketing firms. Since product modification may be desired, technical and engineering people may provide strategic support.

In contrast to the New Task situation, however, in the rebuy situation the sales idea man, rather than technical idea men, appears to be the most valuable element. To a large extent the outcome of the buying situation may be attributable to the knowledge, empathy, persuasive ability and competence of the individual salesman.

In a straight rebuy situation the ''in'' supplier must recognize the inevitable change to a Modified Rebuy. When it does occur the marketer must be prepared to handle it gracefully, and to direct such modification along lines favorable to themselves. Emphasize previous good relationship, dependability, etc.

C. *Products and Services Strategies.* Any marketer attempts to fit his offerings—the total package of goods and services—to the requirements of his current and potential customers. The major elements comprising his goods and services mix are product quality, quantity, price, delivery and services. Marketers communicate their offerings to potential buyers through their promotional-distribution mix. Hence, buyers' reactions to a product and services mix depend not only on the physical characteristics of the product, but also on their perception of the total marketing mix.

A satisfactory product quality is a minimal requirement for even considering a source as a possible supplier. Similarly, the ability to deliver the necessary quantity at the required time is a critical element in source selection. The importance of these factors has definite implications in the straight and modified rebuy situation for both ''in'' and ''out'' suppliers. The ''in'' vendors having provided or at least seeming capable of providing these requisites in the past, may not neglect their importance to the buyer as major determinants in his supplier selection decisions. Otherwise this may cost him his position as favored vendor thereby stimulating the buyer to make a change from straight to modified rebuy. The "out" suppliers must recognize that ability to meet quality, quantity and delivery requirements is a necessary—yet not sufficient—condition for being included among the buyers' feasible set of suppliers and hence for consideration when the modified rebuy situation does arise.

In all rebuy situations, price has a predominant position, but only after the other, even more basic requirements of quality, quantity, delivery (and possibly other factors) have been satisfied. The studies revealed instances in which low price was assumed to be the principal reason for purchase from a particular supplier, but further analysis disproved this assumption. Buyers, in fact, will sometimes rationalize their purchasing decisions to salesmen who do not get the order on the basis of price. The latter, in turn, report to their sales managers and reinforce the belief that customers are "buying price." The danger in misinformation or misinterpretation of this type is that opportunities for creative marketing may be overlooked or disguised.

In formulating price policies, the marketer should study the buying organization, previous buying patterns, and reaction to various price offerings. The findings of Dr. Wind's study on the purchase of components, suggest a distinction between bidding for the first time and the pricing of a repeat purchase. In determining an original bid, a pricing rule that might increase the probability of getting an order is one that has the lowest per unit cost regardless of the total cost that might be involved in the purchase. The rationale for this rule is that in most bids the fixed and other costs such as maintenance, training, paper work etc. are not considered.

For pricing a repeat purchase, the more relevant price rule is to provide the buyer with some perceived cost savings over the previous purchase.

The implication of these rules is clear; in the first case, a low price per unit has a relatively high probability of getting the bid other things being equal and thus the "out" supplier might secure a foothold in the buying company. The second suggests that a current supplier, whether facing the straight or modified rebuy situation, should from time to time give a buyer some price reductions so as to reduce his motivation to look somewhere else for cost savings and retain his loyalty.

The foregoing conclusions suggest that specific price strategy should be determined in each particular case, based on the marketer's knowledge of the buying process (*e.g.*, how important is price in the given buying situation?), the buyer behavior (how did the buying firm react to previous bids and price quotes?), and the competitive situation (who are the likely competitors? What were their bid practices in the past? etc.)

It appears that special price reduction agreements provide a useful competitive tool to both "in" and "out" suppliers in either straight or modified rebuy situations. The Stanford study indicated that vendors offering "special deal" agreements on all purchases were successful not only in attracting buyers, but in increasing their loyalty across products. The findings further indicated that such "deals" usually by distributors, positively affected a buyer's preference (for purchasing from the particular vendor) not only for purchases in which the deal yielded a reduction in price relative to that of competitors, but also for items in which the real price of the vendor and his competitors was identical.

With regard to services, both studies indicated the importance of providing the required services when they are needed. Under modified rebuy situations both the users and buyers required more services and less routine ones, as compared with the straight rebuy situations. Hence, it is of the greatest importance that the suppliers' technical competence and willingness to provide the needed services be impressed upon the buying influences continually and repetitively, especially in the modified rebuy situation. The services most commonly required by the users were in the form of information, free samples and technical advice. The buyers, on the other hand, required much less service and, when needed, it was in the form of information.

D. Promotional Strategies. The utilization of any channel of distribution by either "in" or "out" suppliers under rebuy and new task buying situations should be supplemented by some direct advertising, publicity and/or sales promotion, in addition to the personal selling activity.

Again, as in all marketing activities, the "out" suppliers must "try harder." This by no means implies, however, that the "in" supplier can afford to treat promotional activities casually. Hence both "in" and "out" suppliers must undertake some promotional activities. Creative effort about the specific buying situation and influences can vastly improve a firm's promotional decisions.

Under both straight and modified rebuy situations the "in" suppliers' main promotional objective is to establish his reputation among all the relevant buying influences so as to reinforce the decision to buy from his firm. In essence he is seeking to provide the buyer with "dissonance reduction" (less confusion and "a clear track to run on") and the buying influences with some reassurance that his firm is a reliable "known" source. Hence, the main reliance of the "in" firm should be on advertising in media that reach all relevant buying influences perhaps including direct mail. In view of the more complex and non-routine information requirements of a modified rebuy situation, it is likely that a marketer under a modified rebuy will have to devote more of his resources to promotion than would be necessary in a straight rebuy.

The "out" supplier has to rely, to a much larger extent, on nonpersonal promotion and advertising. Here the marketer can use simple advertising appeals, such as testimonials by satisfied users (preferably in the buyer's own industry) that may help substantiate his claims of superiority to buyers and other relevant buying influences so as to motivate them to consider a modified rebuy situation with him as a possible supplier. It is not reasonable to expect this promotion to *pull* the product through the procurement process by creating the demand for it. It is reasonable to expect, however, that appropriate promotion will familiarize the buyers and buying influences with the "out" supplier. This, together with the other elements of the marketing effort, may eventually lead to a change in the buying situation from a straight to a modified rebuy and in the status of the supplier from a complete "out" to a potential "in" member of the feasible set of suppliers.

SUMMARY

While the marketer is fully aware of the differences in customer requirements within and among markets, the job of meshing the marketing efforts with the needs of a particular customer has been left largely to the individual salesman—aptly designated "the most flexible element in the marketing mix." On an intuitive basis, varying with the individual, salesmen do tend to classify customers according to their buying behavior. From the standpoint of marketing management, these intuitive and most implicit customer classifications may appear highly problematical and unsatisfactory, since they are dependent upon the ability and perceptions of each individual salesman. In any case, their value is limited because they are so very personalized and informal. Moreover, the salesman's informal classifications, even if possible of verbalization and communication throughout the marketing organization, are unlikely to be of much use to nonsales personnel engaged in other marketing activities, *e.g.*, technical service men, specification drafters, proposal writers, advertising planners and copywriters, budget makers, policy formulators, etc.

The primary operational value of the buying situation classificatory scheme proposed in Part One is that it provides a means for translating these judgmental categories derived from experience into more formal terms and making them generally meaningful to the varying marketing activities.

Assuming that each buying situation leads to somewhat different behavioral response, the three buying situations can serve as a basis for market segmentation, and hence lead to different marketing implications as the ones suggested in this chapter.

Using the three Buyclass buying situations as a basis for market segmentation does not rule out further modification of the segmentation policy, such as the introduction of the "in" and "out" suppliers' concept, or any other basis. But even when the major basis for segmentation is some characteristic of the buying firm that is not related directly to the buying firm—such as the organizational structure of the purchasing department that was suggested by Dr. Wind's findings—the distinction among the three buying situations is useful in designing the marketing strategies of the creative marketing firm.

XIV

Understanding Buyer Behavior
for Creative Marketing

UNDERSTANDING THE BUYING PROCESS whether by the use of
the Buyphase framework (that was developed and verified in Part
One of this book) or any other suitable model, suggests some distinct
advantages for marketing management as demonstrated in Chapter
XII. The knowledge of various possible buying situations (new task
or rebuy situations for various types of products) provides some
additional guidelines to the creative marketing manager in formulating his marketing strategies as prescribed in Chapter XIII.
The marketer who concentrates also on understanding fundamental buyers' needs and determinants of their decisions, rather
than relying solely upon identifying and persuading those who
purportedly influence the buying decisions will be able to perform
much more effectively in the central activities of industrial marketing. This emphasis can help by resolving existing problems and
needs, and anticipating and fostering changes in customer requirements. Since even the buyers themselves may not completely
understand, or want to disclose, their basic needs, the marketer can
do a better job if he does not have to rely solely upon the buyer's
statement of his requirements.
Hence, the purpose of this chapter is fourfold:

1. To reemphasize the importance, for marketing management,
   of understanding buyer behavior in general and under dynamic
   changing conditions in particular.

2. To suggest an approach that will enable marketers to translate the concept "understanding buyer behavior" to an
   operational managerial tool.

3. To suggest some major marketing implications of the improved knowledge of buyer behavior.

4. To propose some potential developments in the analysis of
   buyer behavior that are likely to aid creative industrial
   marketers.

BUYER BEHAVIOR AND CHANGE

It is a basic principle of good marketing that to be successful those in charge of the distribution policy of a company should know as much as possible about the buyers: who they are, what they want, where they are, how best to reach them, the motives which induce them to buy, the prices they are willing to pay, and so on.

Accepting this premise, it was the purpose of this book to analyze the industrial buying process and to emphasize buyer behavior as the basis upon which marketing strategies can and should be formulated. Focusing on the buyer requires that a creative marketer will recognize the buyer needs which in turn are a function of the specific buying situation and the various determinants of the buying decision. Moreover the greatest opportunities for the creative marketer lie in anticipating and fostering changes in those requirements.

Recognizing Changed Customer Requirements

It is a clear-cut, relatively easy job to reply to a request for sealed bids for a large quantity of a standardized material such as carbon paper, and this is also likely to be the least profitable type of marketing effort. It would be much more difficult to convince the buying company that its routine requirements for carbon paper should be changed by, for example, discontinuing the use of carbon paper and making photocopies of all materials that require duplication. But the potential rewards for recognizing the true nature of an ill-defined need are likely to be great.

The fieldwork strongly suggests that even marketers of basic, commodity-type goods and materials sold on an industry standard basis have numerous opportunities for modifying customer requirements. It is clear that the marketing effort can encompass a great deal more than simply product-price-delivery options, which tend to become highly similar in all industries. Even in the marketing of standard items like potash, flour, and sulfuric acid, there are opportunities to differentiate the offer and to shape the basic nature of the customer's requirements through marketing services. These services can take many forms, e.g., problem-solving, providing information keyed to customer need, inventorying, technical and merchandising assistance, assuming more of the responsibility for the final performance of the item, etc. While there are risks involved in such a strategy, the rewards appear to be commensurate with those risks. Indeed, playing it safe may be the riskiest course of all for the industrial marketer as well as for the buying organization.

In a sense, customer requirements undergo change with every purchase. No two transactions are likely to be identical in terms of the needs, wants and priorities of the buying decision makers. On a transactional basis, then, the marketer must attempt to adapt his effort to the specific requirements of each individual procurement rather than to rely upon perfunctory approaches that remain static in the midst of dynamic buyer decision processes.

Yet, the changes of greatest potential impact on the marketer are those of a magnitude to cause buyers to consider seriously modifying what or how they buy a particular item. Changes in the basic nature of the customer's requirements may occur in response to environmental condition, as discussed in Chapter VII. Changed requirements may result from a revised perception of the problem on the part of the buying decision makers, as when a new buying influence enters the picture. A new perspective also may be stimulated through various information sources available to the buying influences.

A change in requirements may be caused by a reorientation in the customer's buying patterns. The buying activities may be newly centralized or decentralized, thereby amalgamated or spread among several groups. Even if the buying influences remain constant, fundamental differences will be reflected in the quantities purchased, delivery times and locations, and needs for different types of marketing services at various using locations.

Changes in company goals and policies may cause shifts in the basic nature of the needs for goods and services. The buying company's niche in its industry may change. The company may upgrade or downgrade its product line; products, models, features, or colors may be added or dropped from the line. Similarly, changes in the organization, offerings, or technology of the supplying industries may cause a reevaluation of requirements to be made by the buying influences.

From the buyers' standpoint, few of the intra-organizational and external environmental variables which determine the nature of the requirements are ever fixed for very long. Many of the changes will not be perceived by the buying influences as significant enough to warrant a reevaluation of the basic requirements. When the reevaluation of a need is initiated by the buying influences, a given supplier will have less influence on the outcome than if he had recognized the changed situation before other suppliers were brought into the picture.

The vendor's own marketing program must be adapted to the *customer's* marketing program with changes in it, since the customer's buying patterns and marketing patterns are closely correlated. The marketing programs of Company Able, for example, have changed substantially over the past few years as its customers have become less interested in standardized pieces of capital equipment. Able has adapted to customer demands for larger, more expensive pieces of equipment which incorporate new technologies and offer substantially greater capabilities. Yet the Company has not been able to move as rapidly as it would like because many of its own regular suppliers have not been willing to modify substantially their offerings to meet Able's changing requirements. As a result, Company Able has been forced to seek out new sources of supply, and has increased its purchases from foreign suppliers which it considers to be more willing to adapt than the domestic suppliers.

Anticipating and Fostering Change

While recognizing changes in customer requirements and devising imaginative ways to capitalizing on them present real opportunities to the alert marketer, still greater opportunities may arise from being a *change agent* himself.

How does the industrial marketer go about anticipating and fostering changes in the requirements of customers? The general answer is found in the theme of this entire study—he must thoroughly understand the basic informational and other needs of the customer in each buying situation, the roles of the major buying influences, the organizational procedures in the procurement process, and the environment in which the customer company operates. The results of this study suggest that the marketer consider his customers' requirements in the analytic framework of three basic types of buying situations. It appears that the nature of the customer's requirement may be understood and predicted by focusing on the buying situation as modified by environmental considerations.

UNDERSTANDING BUYER BEHAVIOR:
AN OPERATIONAL TOOL

The central theme of the book is the application of the "marketing concept" to industrial marketing—*i.e.*, the emphasis that successful marketing strategies have to be based on knowledge of the buyer's wants and requirements as well as his decision process and its major determinants.

In order to make the abstract notion of "understanding buyer behavior" more operational, it may be helpful for the industrial marketing manager to have in mind a profile of the buying habits, patterns, and influences of each major customer or potential customer. Although a profile will not enable the marketer to predict precisely the identity of all buying influences, the magnitude of the effect of all the determinants of the buying decision, or all the criteria used in customer buying decisions, it can be of great value in providing the marketing staff with a reasonably explicit blueprint of the customer's buying processes.

This procedure in constructing a profile of the buying organization forces the marketing manager and the sales staff to think
through, define intelligibly and render applicable to others, their
subjective experiences with a particular firm and its key decision
makers. By maintaining these profiles, the accumulated knowledge
and experience about a customer company can be systematically
organized and made readily available to the marketing group.
Moreover, it provides a guideline as to the type of information
required and motivates the firm to engage in active search for and
organization of this information. Preparation appears practicable
for most industrial marketers; especially those for which a few
large customers account for a high percentage of total sales.

Many existing customers of the industrial marketer are likely
to buy particular goods and services on a rebuy basis, straight
and/or modified. The marketer of standard parts and components,
subassemblies, chemicals, or commodities is not likely to face
many new task situations unless he creates a new market or develops a new product. By contrast, a marketer of machine tools,
engineering services, aerospace or computer/communication systems may find that most of his customers are in a new task situation each time they buy or lease.

Whatever the distribution of situational types faced by the marketer, his customer profiles should specify distinguishing elements
about each customer's requirements as he is confronted with the
three different buying situations. The marketer should be able to
answer questions such as the following: In what proportions are
the different types of buying situations likely to arise in this company? How will each situation be handled inside the buying company
once it arises? Who are the major buying influences likely to be
in each case? Under what conditions is each buying influence likely
to play a key role in the product/supplier selection process? What
information and factors are of major importance to each buying
influence? Answers to these questions can be of great help to the
seller in directing his search and retrieval of information and in
programming the elements of his marketing effort.

UNDERSTANDING BUYER BEHAVIOR: SOME GENERAL IMPLICATIONS FOR CREATIVE MARKETING

Creative industrial marketing management can be defined as the
development and implementation of new and better marketing
strategies. It is the contention of this book that understanding the
buyer behavior is the major key for any creative marketing activity. The BUYGRID framework and the framework for the analysis of the determinants of buyer behavior claim no monopoly on
aiding understanding, but they do provide a useful additional tool
for the industrial marketer in analyzing customers' needs. The

models are particularly useful frame of references because they focus directly, rather than indirectly, on the basic nature of the customers' requirements. To this end, the profile of customer requirements may materially assist the marketer in the understanding which must precede any effort to anticipate or foster changes in customers' requirements.

More specifically, the customer profile as the operational representation of the buyer's requirements and the overall "marketing concept philosophy" which focuses on the buyer as the *raison d'etre* of the whole marketing system can provide a guideline for the analysis of the whole marketing management function.

Any managerial process includes four major elements: setting objectives, planning, organizing and controlling.

Setting the Marketing Objectives

It is suggested to set the marketing objectives on the basis of both the intraorganization constraints (corporate objectives, resources, etc.) and the general nature of the buyers' needs and requirements.

The *planning* of the specific marketing strategies—product and service, promotion and distribution—should be aimed at the satisfying of the marketing objectives and the specific functional subobjectives. Some specific implications for these strategies were suggested in Chapter XI and it is hoped that they indicated the usefullness of basing them on knowledge of buyers' behavior.

Organizing the marketing operations. It is suggested to organize the marketing staff in "groups of specialists." This suggestion is based on the analysis in Parts One and Two of this book. If the marketing effort is to service the various decision points in the customer's buying process, it must be organized accordingly. Such an approach would seek to utilize the appropriate specialists in the marketing organization in the most effective way, while retaining the flexibility which is needed to reckon with the fact that the next opportunity, perhaps even with the same customer, may entail a different buying situation.

One possible application of this approach would have customer contacts made by an "account executive" or customer man who would coordinate the various aspects of the marketer's program and represent his supply organization to all buying influences within the customer company. As various customer problems and requirements arose, this customer's man could call upon specialists from his own company. The marketer's team could be composed of relevant problem-defining, problem-solving, technical, negotiating, and servicing personnel. Each specialist would be charged with developing and maintaining close personal relationships with his counterparts at a variety of organizational levels and locations in the customer organization. From this group of specialists, appropriate individuals would be consulted as particular problems arose. Occasionally they might travel together in concert to meet with buying influences from the customer company.

The group or team approach stresses the marketing advantages of establishing and maintaining close personal relationships with those people in the customer organization who can and do modify basic requirements. These buying influences are likely to have diverse backgrounds, training and interests. Moreover, they appear in the buying process at various times and for various purposes. This approach represents a direct attempt to organize the marketing effort to deal specifically with the diverse influences of different people at different phases of the buying process.

There is today a growing recognition among industrial marketers that diversity in advertising (by type of influences, for example) is useful. The same notion can be extended to other elements of the marketing mix. Personal communications tasks, for example, can be handled most effectively by salesmen who specialize in selling into particular types of customer buying situations.

Many companies now build specialization into the allocation of their marketing effort. Certain salesmen may be specialized in both training and assignment, handling lines or products different from those of other salesmen. They may be differentiated according to type of account, in turn reflecting differences in customers' applications or in the types of services needed. Salesmen may be "specialists" in geographic areas. Technical representatives or applications engineers have specialized functions when compared to regular salesmen. This study strongly suggests that salesmen can also profitably "specialize" according to the type of buying situation, the nature of the customer's needs and the resources of the marketing organization.

Similarly it might be useful to organize the whole marketing effort (including the organizational structure) along relevant classification of customers.

Controlling the marketing effort is critically important for the long-run success of the business firm. The basis of control (given that the goals and standards of the system as well as the specific program were determined) is the measuring of the program's results and the initiation of corrective actions if the goals are not being achieved. Both these elements of the control process, as well as the planning and organization functions require the marketer to have *information* on the buying organization its buying influences, their needs and determinants of their decision. This information can come from active search for information by members of the buying organization, or from solicitation and service activities of vendors supplying data and proposals. This market information has to reach the relevant marketing decision makers, hence it is necessary to design effective channels for the internal flows of information within the firm.

The importance of the information flows for all the marketing activities suggest that the marketer should design and plan the channels of information required so as to avoid cases in which needed information is not available or too much information is floating around and hobbles the manager's work. See MSI's recent studies, *Experiments on the Value of Information in Simulated Marketing Environments* and *Management Information and Control Requirements*.

SOME POTENTIAL DEVELOPMENTS IN THE ANALYSIS OF INDUSTRIAL BUYING AND THEIR MARKETING IMPLICATIONS

Among many possibilities which lie ahead, two promising developments stand out for the application of new scientific aids to industrial marketing management. Both of these new approaches have come to light during the course of this project, and one has already been developed and put to practical use in a related MSI research study for which suitable information was available.

Shortly after the inception of this project early in 1964, the idea of classifying and comparing transactions led to the development of MSI's so-called cluster analysis computer program. In concept the idea is relatively simple, but in application there can be a problem of obtaining suitable data since standard accounting and sales records are not altogether suitable. Each industrial transaction must be described by a number of consistent measures (including factors such as economic, technical, end-use, service requirements, physical characteristics, etc.). Then for each transaction an endpoint comparison of its "nearness" or tendency to "cluster" with other similar transaction points is possible.

For example, in MSI's Comparative Analysis for International Marketing study this same cluster analysis procedure permitted the systematic grouping of countries having many characteristics in common. The international marketing management implications of this analysis impinge on organization and policy formation in many ways that were not previously obvious, but have become clear after cluster analysis. Likely, the implications of transactions' clustering can be just as profound for industrial marketers. In this study we have classified all industrial purchases in one of three categories: new tasks, modified rebuys or straight rebuys. As has been shown in the earlier chapters this scheme is based upon the primary characteristics of the individual buying situations. The relevant characteristics for this classification being newness of the problem, information required to make decisions, and the extent of consideration of new alternatives. These classifications were found to be extremely useful. In particular the scheme demonstrated that the purchases of different products by different buyers might have a great deal in common if they were representative of essentially the same buying situation.

Such diverse products as metals, drills, flanges and fittings, stainless steel bars, forgings, pipe and fabricated parts and assemblies were all purchased in pretty much the same way, given a straight rebuy situation. Similarly, the general properties of the modified rebuy were found to apply to such diverse products as industrial bags, hydraulic pumps, machinery engines, piping elbows, chemical raw materials, steel wire, metal stampings, and screw machine products. This is not to say that all modified rebuys are identical but rather that they have more in common with each other, despite the particular item involved, than they do with similar or even the same product when purchased under new task or, alternatively, under straight rebuy circumstances.

Some differences will of course be observed between procurements. The BUYGRID classification scheme serves largely to point up that the various procurements within a general buying situation have more in common with each other than the differences among them.

Further development of the idea of buying situations offers additional promise of shedding more light on the industrial buying process. In this connection the so-called cluster analysis technique may be useful in examining, analyzing, and relating various buying situations. One might expect that individual procurement situations will have some of the properties of one general type of buying situations, at the same time exhibiting some of the properties of another, and perhaps even some properties of a third. Cluster analysis techniques may provide a way of isolating the relevant factors for distinctive analysis and may thus provide the opportunity to develop subgroups within the general ideas of new task, modified rebuy and straight rebuy.

Perhaps the most promising characteristic of the cluster analysis technique is the fact that it facilitates classification and analysis of complex systems (such as industrial buying behavior) with the aid of electronic data processing equipment. The technique thus enables the analyst to compare and differentiate procurement processes and buying situations in terms of several dimensions or characteristics.

Aside from these potentials for MSI's cluster analysis approach (and for other similar cluster analysis computer programs that have been developed elsewhere and are now available for general use) there is an attractive prospect for developing a computer simulation of the industrial buying process.

Development of this simulation should provide market management with a new analytical and diagnostic tool based on the "creeping commitment" flow-diagrams and buying influence decision networks as presented graphically in this report. The simulation should consist of a dynamic decision model of industrial buying processes which can be tested and manipulated by industrial marketers (and buyers) to better understand and plan offerings of industrial goods, services and information for prospective buyers.

This simulation should permit tests of various assumptions through the use of sensitivity analysis (*i.e.*, trial-and-error variations in assumptions and factors with successive "dry runs" of the simulator to see what differences such changes create and preparation of "PERT-type" charts of coordinated vendor efforts). Such a simulator should also provide a flexible computer-based training device suitable for varied demonstrations and operational gaming (*i.e.*, a dynamic model of activities with participation by the people concerned). This type of extension of the present analyses should help detect and diagnose buying influences, information inputs and their timing under realistically modeled conditions, preparatory to field applications.

Annotated Bibliography

The purpose of this annotated bibliography is threefold:

1. To provide the interested reader with supplemental reference material on each of the three major portions of the manuscript and some general references on industrial buying and industrial marketing.

2. To present the findings of a systematic review of relevant articles that appeared in major business journals since 1957. Works published prior to 1957, and from other periodicals—particularly trade journals—also have been sampled.

3. To suggest subject areas that lack adequate coverage in the literature and that offer useful opportunities for industrial marketing investigation and research.

In preparing the bibliography, a framework was developed to incorporate topics suggested by the manuscript, explicitly and implicitly. The bibliographical outline, having been designed specifically to supplement the text, is not intended to provide comprehensive coverage of industrial buying or industrial marketing, or any facet thereof. Restricted in objective to the industrial area, references to retail, military, governmental or institutional buying and selling are not included.

Due to space and other limitations, much relevant material has necessarily been omitted. Bibliographical coverage is not intended to be exhaustive either as to subject matter or source citations. Rather, it seeks to broaden the reader's perspective on the various topics under examination.

Each annotated document is listed only once in the bibliography, categorized according to the author's emphasis in the particular work. For example, certain industrial advertising studies are concerned with motives underlying buyer behavior. In this case, if the author's emphasis is on advertising implications, the study will be categorized under the heading "Industrial Marketing: Promotion Policy." If the emphasis is on the buyer's motivation, it will be categorized "Buying

Determinants: Personal Characteristics.'' Since a number of selections are related to several subject headings, it is suggested that readers interested in specific subject areas refer to all relevant sections of the bibliography to secure more adequate coverage.

Four major sections, with their respective subdivisions, comprise the bibliography:

General Reference.   Texts and Bibliographies on Industrial Buying and Industrial Marketing.

Part One: The Industrial Buying Process. A sampling of the literature, supplementing Part One of the manuscript, that deals with various facets of the industrial buying process and the purchasing function:
    Purchasing Practices
    Organization for Purchasing
    Purchasing Policies, Procedures and Decisions
    Evaluation of Purchasing Performance
    Improving Purchasing Performance
    Related Purchasing Practices

Part Two: Determinants of Industrial Buyer Behavior. A sampling of relevant works, complementing Part Two of the manuscript, concerning some of the major determinants of industrial buying decisions:
    Identifying the Buying Influences and Decision Makers
    Personal Characteristics as Determinants of Buying Decisions
    Intraorganizational Relations and Organizational Characteristics as Determinants of Buying Decisions
    Environmental, Vendor Characteristics and Other Factors as Determinants of Buying Decisions

Part Three: Industrial Implications for Marketers. A sampling of the literature, supplementing Part Three of the manuscript, concerning marketing implications of existing knowledge and theory about industrial buying in the following general areas:
    Industrial Management-General
    Market Analysis
    Product, Service and Price Policy
    Distribution
    Promotion Policy
    Industrial Marketing Research

General References

1. INDUSTRIAL BUYING

a. Texts

Alijian, George W. (Editor). *Purchasing Handbook*. New York: McGraw-Hill Book Co., Inc., 1958.

A standard reference work on purchasing policies, practices and procedures, contracts and forms. Reflects the thinking of experienced purchasing executives, contributions from hundreds of practitioners. The book provides a comprehensive authoritative source of practical information and guidance for all persons involved in procurement. Contains a host of facts, principles, methods, data and illustrative material on purchasing routine—selection of sources of supply, quality and quality control, price considerations and evaluation, value analysis, forward buying, inventory control, performance evaluation, etc.

Colton, Raymond R. *Industrial Purchasing: Principles and Practices*. Columbus, Ohio: Charles E. Merrill Books, Inc., 1962.

This book provides fundamental information regarding procurement principles, procedures, and tools. It examines in detail the procurement process and introduces the reader to established principles which guide the purchasing professional. The author also treats on a number of specialized functions including expediting, value analysis, research, materials management, traffic management and the use of data processing in purchasing. Ample case studies and illustrative materials are included.

England, Wilbur B. *Procurement: Principles and Cases*, 4th edition. Homewood, Illinois: Richard D. Irwin, Inc., 1962.

This book is a revised edition of earlier volumes bearing the same title by the author and Professor Howard Lewis, standard undergraduate texts since 1948. This new edition incorporates the most current principles, practices and recent developments in procurement. It gives a complete step-by-step picture of the procurement process and related activities. Text material is skillfully combined with actual case studies, 74 in all.

Heinritz, Stuart F., and Farrell, Paul V. *Purchasing Principles and Applications,* 4th edition. Englewood Cliffs, New Jersey: Prentice-Hall, Inc., 1965.

A standard text and reference work by the editors of Purchasing Magazine analyzes and explains every important phase of the industrial procurement process and its interaction with other organizationl areas. Emphasizes recent developments in industrial purchasing and their applications. Case studies, relevant to each chapter, follow the text. This new edition reflects current thinking in the field, with in-depth discussions of materials management, negotiation, EDP, purchasing forecasting, and other relevant topics.

Lee, Lamar, Jr., and Dobler, Donald W. *Purchasing and Materials Management: Text and Cases,* New York: McGraw-Hill, 1965.

This book deals with the purchasing and materials function in the context of the total business operation. It emphasizes purchasing as a primary materials activity and integrates the purchasing activity with all other materials activities. The authors have provided a complete basic introduction to the purchasing and materials function, as well as a useful working tool, with advanced discussions and cases, for the sophisticated business practitioner.

The volume contains 25 chapters, divided into six parts. Part One, Function of Purchasing, views purchasing's place in modern business and in an organization. Part Two, Fundamentals of Purchasing and Materials Management, deals with quality, quantity, and price considerations, sources of supply, negotiation, timing, value analysis, capital equipment, make or buy. Part Four is concerned with Management of Purchasing—planning, basic policies and procedures, organization, appraisal and control, automation, legal aspects, etc. Parts 3, 5, 6 deal with Auxiliary Functions, Government Purchasing, and cases for study and analysis.

Pooler, Victor H., *The Purchasing Man and His Job.* New York: American Management Association, 1964.

This book is written from a managerial perspective, viewing purchasing as an important profit-productive center in industrial concerns. Emphasis is given to the human relations aspects of purchasing as well as to techniques and practical solutions of problems which confront the purchasing executive. Offers information on such general topics as organizational structure and relationships, communications, planning, performance evaluation. Also discusses problems specific to purchasing: pricing, trade relations, negotiating techniques, value analysis, inventory control, relations with suppliers, materials management, etc.

Westing, J. H., and Fine, I. V. *Industrial Purchasing: Buying for In-dustry and Budgetary Institutions.*   Second Edition. New York: John Wiley & Sons, Inc., 1961.

This is a revised edition of an earlier volume bearing the same title. *Industrial Purchasing* is a standard reference for practicing purchasing agents, and was prepared in close collaboration with experienced procurement specialists. The authors give major at-tention to purchasing policies, rather than procedures.

The usual purchasing subjects are fully and adequately covered. Current information is presented concerning materials manage-ment, value analysis, quality and quantity control procedures, ad-ministered pricing, etc. At the end of each chapter two short case studies focus on specific problems.

b. Bibliography

"A Basic Purchasing Library" *Purchasing,* November 4, 1965, pp. 83-84.

Lists 32 books and pamphlets on purchasing and materials man-agement, plus additional works on allied subjects with which Pur-chasing Agents should be familiar. Also notes films and film-strips available for use from various sources in training programs for purchasing department personnel.

Lewis, Howard T. (comp.). "Bibliography of Purchasing Literature," in *Guide to Purchasing,* New York; National Association of Pur-chasing Agents, 1965, (Appendix).

Provides a basic list of current references dealing with the broad field of industrial procurement, specific and related aspects of the subject. This is the latest revision of earlier editions, also com-piled by Mr. Lewis, entitled *Where to Find it! Bibliography of In-dustrial Purchasing,* New York: National Association of Purchasing Agents, 1945, 1955, 1961.

2. INDUSTRIAL MARKETING

a. Texts

Alexander, Ralph S., Cross, James S. and Cunningham, Ross M. *In-dustrial Marketing.*   (Rev. ed.) Homewood, Ill.: Richard D. Irwin, Inc., 1961.

Particularly useful in teaching, this comprehensive text deals with the special problems connected with the purchase and use of in-dustrial goods which complicate the planning and execution of effi-cient marketing programs. Chapter headings include: Marketing

Planning and Marketing Information, Marketing Channels, Management of Pricing, Getting the Goods Sold, Managing Customer Service and Relations, and The Control Function.

Corey, E. Raymond.   *Industrial Marketing: Cases and Concepts,* Englewood Cliffs, N. J.: Prentice-Hall, Inc., 1962.

The book is a collection of 32 industrial problem situations with commentary, concerning concepts in industrial marketing.   No solutions are offered; rather the student of marketing is provided an opportunity to work with actual problems showing the complexity of industrial markets and to develop a broadened knowledge of industrial marketing.

b. Bibliography

Staudt, Thomas A. and Lazer, William (Comp.). *A Basic Bibliography on Industrial Marketing.*   Chicago: American Marketing Association, 1958.

An annotated listing of books and articles in industrial marketing. Specific section devoted to references on industrial procurement and buying behavior.

PART ONE

The Industrial Buying Process

1. PURCHASING PRACTICES

a. The Purchasing Practices of Market Segments

Buckner, Hugh. *How British Industry Buys*. A study sponsored jointly by the Institute of Marketing and Industrial Market Research Limited. London: Hutchinson & Co., Ltd., 1967. This book is offered as a guide for those engaged in marketing and purchasing of industrial goods in the United Kingdom. Purchasing procedures are examined among 924 industrial companies representing a variety of manufacturing industries. The intention of the study was to provide a reliable, empirical analysis of how functions are assigned and carried out and authority delegated in industrial purchasing, in order that both marketing and purchasing strategies and activities might be based on realities. "Only (in this way) can these complementary activities, buying and selling, be effectively organized, accurately timed and smoothly executed." The findings reveal that industrial purchasing is carried out in a structured and defined manner throughout the majority of British industrial companies. Though the pattern of specialist involvement may alter fundamentally, a pattern emerges in all cases and for each product group.

How Small Manufacturers Buy, Volumes I, II. Prepared by the School of Business Administration, University of Connecticut, under the Small Business Administration Management Research Grant Program, June, 1964.

This monograph examines the purchasing practices of small manufacturers. Summarizes the results of a research study concerning buying habits of 604 small manufacturing firms and 60 marketers selling to manufacturers. The study was designed to develop some guides for small manufacturers through improving the effectiveness of their purchasing practices. Tabulated results of the survey are included in the Appendices (Volume 11.)

Lusardi, F. R. *Purchasing for Industry.* New York: National Industrial Conference Board, 1948. (Studies in Business Policy No. 33).

Study reviews the purchasing organization policies and procedures of nearly 300 companies in 25 industry classifications. Case studies describe in detail the experience and practice of six companies.

Metaxas, Ted. "Purchasing's Part in Capital Goods Buying," *Purchasing,* (September 11, 1961), p. 84. Results of *Purchasing* magazine survey of 78 purchasing departments concerning the extent of purchasing's part in capital goods buying. In 84 percent of plants surveyed, capital goods buying is reported to be a mutual manufacturing-purchasing project, purchasing to be a substantial to dominant influence in selecting sources of supply.

Mulvihill, Donald F. *Purchasing Problems of Small Manufacturers in Alabama and Some Suggestions to Solve Them.* Prepared by the School of Commerce and Business Administration, University of Alabama, under the Small Business Administration Research Grant program, 1961.

This research report summarizes the results of a study of purchasing practices and problems of the small plant based on interviews with 94 small manufacturers in Alabama. Reveals that principal suppliers generally are those who seek out the buyer on their own initiative—not necessarily the sources which the buyer has determined most suitable on quality-price considerations.

"A New Survey of Industrial Buyers." *Industrial Distribution* May, 1958, pp. 113-132.

Survey reveals significant changes in industrial buying practices over a six year period.

Paul, Samuel. *Small Sellers and Large Buyers in American Industry.* Syracuse, New York: Business Research Center, Syracuse University, 1961.

A study of relationships between small suppliers and large buyers, involved primarily in industrial transactions.

Skinner, Wickham. "Procurement for International Manufacturing Plants in Developing Economies," *Journal of Purchasing,* Vol. 3. (Feb., 1967), pp. 5-19.

Research into the experiences of thirteen U. S. firms operating plants in six developing nations confirms the expectation that procurement can be an immediate and major source of difficulty.

"Small Company Purchasing," (Special Report), *Purchasing,* (September 26, 1960), pp. 89-97.

Special report on the scope and responsibilities of purchasing in the small firm.

Stuart, Robert Douglass. *Purchasing in Worldwide Operations*. Management Bulletin No. 75. New York: American Management Association, 1966.

A concise informative report which discusses the problems and practices involved in creating a worldwide procurement organization. Based on interviews with a selection of large and small companies engaged in international operations. Reflects top management recognition of the importance of the purchasing function and increasing purchasing responsibilities in international operations. Worldwide purchasing policy guide of a major U. S. company is reproduced in the Appendix.

Thain, Donald H., Johnston, Charles B., Leighton, David S. R. *How Industry Buys: With Conclusions and Recommendations on Marketing to Industry*. Sponsored by the Business Newspapers Association of Canada and the Canadian Chapters of the National Industrial Advertisers Association, 1959.

This research report written primarily for industrial marketing executives, describes and analyzes the industrial purchasing process. It is based on a sample of some 108 industrial purchases involving 36 Canadian manufacturing firms. Emphasis is given to the functions, procedures and people involved in the purchasing process in different types of industrial companies and the factors which influence purchasing decisions, such as salesmen, advertising and trade information. In addition, comments are offered upon the application of these generalizations to the marketing concept as applied to the industrial marketing field.

" 'Typical' Purchasing Agent Sees 16 Salesmen a Week, has 200 Suppliers," *Industrial Marketing*, March, 1966, p. 86, 88.

A survey by McGraw-Hill Research discloses that the typical industrial company has 200 active suppliers, yet the chief purchasing officer sees only 16 salesmen a week. Also presented are: findings relating number of suppliers to size of purchases; statistics on visits to other purchasing personnel; and findings on sales visit restrictions.

United States News and World Report. *How Business Buys*, Sections II, III. Washington, D. C.: United States News Publishing Corporation, 1957.

Detailed tabulations and overall findings on a series of research studies on the buying patterns of American corporations. Develops information on 3 basic steps in major business purchases: 1. the levels of responsibility most likely to generate thinking toward a major business purchase; 2. the levels of responsibility most important in the direct approval of a major business purchase; 3. the degree to which members of the "decision team" are available for direct personal contact by the seller.

b. Purchasing Practices of an Individual Firm

Ammer, Dean & Francisco, C. D., "The Forward Look in Purchasing," *Purchasing*, (January, 1959), pp. 69-83.

Special report takes an intensive look at Chrysler's purchasing
operations.

Judice, Peter F. "Purchasing Changes at Mobil." *Sales Management*, August 2, 1963, pp. 40-41.

New purchasing chief at Socony Mobil Oil Co. introduces fresh
ideas to improve the purchasing function.

McLean, Herbert E.   "The Biggest Buying Job in the World," *Purchasing*, (July 15, 1965), pp. 70-94.

Special report features the gigantic, complex purchasing operation
at General Dynamics in connection with the F-111 program.

"Profiles in Purchasing," *Sales Management*:

A project series on how large manufacturers buy. Features executives who determine broad procurement policy and make the important buying decisions in major companies.   Emphasis is on
purchasing executives who set the pace in new and scientific procurement practices in the following companies:

Allegheny Ludlum Steel, Kearfott Division of General Precision,
National Cash Register, United States Steel, (January 18, 1963),
pp. 37-43.

Cleveland Electric Illuminating Company, (April 5, 1963), pp.
44-46.

Kaiser Aluminum and Chemical Corporation, Pittsburgh Steel
Co., Resistoflex Corp., Sperry Gyroscope Co., (February 1,
1963), pp. 38-43.

Socony Mobil Oil Co., (August 2, 1963), pp. 40-41.

Thompson Ramo Wooldridge, Inc., (May 17, 1963), pp. 121-22.

Westinghouse Electric (January 4, 1963), pp. 27-29.

"Purchasing Case Studies." *Purchasing*:

Special reports feature the purchasing operations of major firms:

Carrier Corporation, (February 29, 1960), pp. 70-79.
Dow Chemical's Texas Division, (May 11, 1959), pp. 69-71.
Esso Research, (April 11, 1960), pp. 70-79.
Ford Division, Ford Motor Co., (May 23, 1960), pp. 53-84.
Kaiser Aluminum, (March 16, 1959), pp. 73-86.
Rheem Manufacturing Company, (September 15, 1958), pp. 69-77.
Swift & Company, (April 13, 1959), pp. 69-76.

Schmelzlee, Robert. "Work Study in Purchasing—A Case Study," *Journal of Purchasing*, Vol. 3 (Feb., 1967), pp. 42-51.

This article reports the results of a work study done on specific jobs within a purchasing department. Concern is only with duties of personnel and not with procedures, policies, layout, or equipment.

Swartwood, G. L. "How Standardization Helps Everybody," *Purchasing*, (July 4, 1960), pp. 54-57.

Describes the materials standardization program at Bryant Electric Co., and its accomplishments.

Van De Water, J. "Systems Contracting; New Concept in Procurement," *Purchasing*, (November 18, 1963), pp. 70-77.

Carborundum's revolutionary buying technique has eliminated inventories, made the purchase order virtually obsolete, is saving millions of dollars.

2. ORGANIZATION FOR PURCHASING

a. Purchasing's Role and Place in a Corporate Structure

Anyon, G. Jay. *Managing an Integrated Purchasing Process*. New York: Holt, Rinehart and Winston, Inc., 1963.

This book, part of the Modern Management series, views purchasing as an integral part of the total business operation and expresses its concepts, principles and techniques from the managerial point of view. The author describes each step in the purchasing process in relation to overall management planning. Illustrative material links principles with actual company practice and experience.

Bethel, Lawrence L., Atwater, Franklin S., Smith, George H. E. and Stackman, Harvey A. Jr. *Industrial Organization and Management*, 4th edition. New York: McGraw-Hill Co., 1962.

This book presents "an overview of the operations of an industrial organization, the interrelationship of functions and the fundamental principles of management which lead toward effective coordination and control." It incorporates latest developments in industrial technology, organization and management. Relevant topics include research, engineering, plant engineering, quality control, production control, methods, finance and accounting. Two chapters are devoted to the four phases of materials control: 1. Procurement (purchasing) 2. External transportation (receiving traffic & shipping) 3. Internal transportation (materials handling) 4. Inventory control (store-keeping).

Denton, J. C. "The Functions of Purchasing," *Journal of Purchasing*, Vol. 1 (August, 1965), pp. 5-17.

A sophisticated survey of 500 employees of SOHIO (most of whom had direct or indirect contact with the purchasing department) requesting definitions of various purchasing activities and their importance has provided a framework for thinking about the organization and control and has led to some valuable practices and procedures.

Hackamack, Lawrence C. "Reward," *Journal of Purchasing*, Vol. 1 (May, 1965), pp, 16-23.

Management must awaken to the competitive realities of their procurement situations and the impact of these procurements upon the economic survival of the business. Without constant and unrelenting pressure from informed buyers for lower costs, there is little incentive for the prompt introduction and utilization of more efficient manufacturing methods or more effective cost control measures. Several techniques for evaluating "worth" are presented: "value analysis," pioneered by Lawrence D. Miles, and the "learning curve."

Henderson, Bruce D. "Purchasing's Part in Corporate Strategy," *Purchasing*, Vol. 60 (January 13, 1966), pp. 76-78.

Uniting the marketing and procurement concepts, "corporate strategy development" means that each company must identify its own unique characteristics and determine how best to use them in the future environment. The author explains how the purchasing executive can participate in corporate strategy development, translating his firm's competitive advantages and procurement alternatives as related to the environment into potential courses of action.

Hodges, Henry G. *Procurement: The Modern Science of Purchasing*. New York: Harper and Row, Publishers, 1961.

This handbook describes purchasing practices and principles and shows their applicability to various forms of business enterprise, public and governmental institutions. Emphasis is given to the effective integration of procurement in the activities of production, sales, research and other divisions.

The author presents a systematic analysis of purchasing department operations, quality control, value analysis, negotiations, record-keeping, etc.

King, Martin L. "In Search of an Intellectual Home for Purchasing," *Journal of Purchasing*, Vol. 3 (Feb., 1967), pp. 64-69.

This article briefly reviews the historical emergence of purchasing as a separate business activity, discusses the problem of finding a conceptual body of knowledge appropriate to this function, and concludes by suggesting a course of action designed to overcome existing limitations.

Kotler, Philip. "Diagnosing the Marketing Takeover,"*Harvard Business Review,* (November-December, 1965), pp. 70-72.

The author is concerned with the pervasive marketing orientation of business which affects sound performance in purchasing and other profit-making areas. He presents the case for coordinating company actions that affect the customer and to the need for some mechanism to eliminate the conflicts that inevitably result between other departments and marketing.

Lewis, Howard T. "Industrial Procurement and Marketing," *Harvard Business Review,* XXVIII, (September, 1950), pp. 49-58.

Observes a marked trend toward the increasing importance of the purchasing department and functions, with emphasis on inventory control.

Logler, Robert F. *A Critical Look at the Purchasing Function.* Management Bulletin #13. New York: American Management Association, 1961.

Appraises the generally restricted purchasing function, current trends in procurement patterns, and implications for the rigorous business climate ahead. Outlines means by which purchasing can meet the challenge of the future, more effectively contribute to corporate goals and management.

Morse, Leon. "Purchasing: From Rags to Riches," *Dun's Review and Modern Industry,* (May, 1963), p. 54.

Discusses the vastly expanded role and stature of purchasing and how it has a direct affect on marketing when used intelligently. Through the use of advanced procurement techniques, the new purchasing executive is transforming the profit picture of many industrial marketers.

Van De Water, J. "Is Purchasing Meeting Its Responsibilities," *Purchasing,* (January 14, 1963), pp. 75-77.

A critical look at a potentially dangerous trend in purchasing—confusion about the procurement role in our competitive economy. The author warns against an overly pronounced marketing orientation on the part of purchasing executives which, if carried to the extreme, would threaten purchasing's *raison d'etre*.

————————. "What's Behind the Big Change in Purchasing," *Purchasing,* (January 13, 1964), pp. 74-78.

The PA must lead the purchasing revolution to retain his influence. Systems contracting and materials management are two ways to cut operating costs.

b. The Organization of the Purchasing Department

Berry, Harold A. *Purchasing Management.* Waterford, Connecticut: National Foremen's Institute, 1964.

In his foreward the author indicates he seeks "to inform management men in all fields of business activity as to the function, organization, and operations of a purchasing department." He suggests too that the book serve as a guide in establishing or evaluating a purchasing department. Brevity is the keynote, and the book provides reliable, easy to read information on the essentials of purchasing.

Haas, George H., March, Benjamin, and Krech, E. M. *Purchasing Department Organization and Authority.* Research Study 45. New York: American Management Association, 1960.

This research report provides comparative statistical data on the purchasing departments of 147 companies.

McLean, Herbert E. "Switch to Centralized Buying Saves Ampex $500,000," *Purchasing,* (October 7, 1963), pp. 60-63.

Consolidating three separate purchasing organizations at Ampex proves a difficult but rewarding task.

"Mack Truck Tries Centralized Buying," *Purchasing,* (September 23, 1963), pp. 70-74.

Tells how Mack Truck made the switch to a centralized purchasing department and to good advantage.

Pegram, Roger M. and Thompson, G. Clark. "A Drift Toward Decentralized Purchasing." *Business Record.* June, 1956, pp. 257-63.

This empirical report indicates a slow and partial move in the direction of decentralized purchasing. Advantages of centralization vs. decentralization are discussed.

Van De Water, J. "Centralize and Save," *Purchasing,* (November 6, 1961), pp. 89-93.

Director of purchases for the Commonwealth of Virginia makes a strong case for centralized purchasing.

c. Interdepartmental Relations

Barnett, H. C. "Purchasing is more than Just Buying," *Purchasing,* (February 2, 1959), pp. 66-68.

A report on the important service functions which purchasing can perform for operating executives and for management is illustrated at Mead-Atlanta Paper Company.

Denton, J. C. & Prien, Erich P. "Defining the Perceived Functions of Purchasing Personnel,"*Journal of Applied Psychology*, (October, 1963), pp. 332-38.

Results of an employee questionnaire survey to identify the relative importance of the various functions performed by the purchasing division of a large manufacturing concern.

Dyer, H. M. "Ways Purchasing Can Help the Sales Department." *Purchasing*. October 22, 1962, p. 88.

Spells out ways in which purchasing departments have helped in their own firms' marketing endeavors.

Liston, Scott. "Engineers Need the P. A.'s Help," *Purchasing*, (March 25, 1963), p. 75.

A successful standardization program requires cooperation between engineering and purchasing. The author pleas for better communications to alleviate the "cold war."

Metaxas, Ted. "Capital Goods Buying: Teamwork's Essential," *Purchasing*, (August 27, 1962), pp. 70-73.

The author stresses the essentiality of cooperation between purchasing and engineering in the development of performance specs for capital equipment buying.

"Purchasing and Engineering: Can They Work Together?" (Symposium), *Purchasing* (August 12, 1963), pp. 51-57.

Three views of the purchasing-engineering relationship by qualified observers. First, a purchasing executive stresses the need for clearly defining the specific responsibilities of each function. Next, an engineer cites specifications as the common ground between purchasing and engineering where cooperation is essential.

Strauss, George. "Tactics of Lateral Relationship: The Purchasing Agent" *Admin. Sc. Quarterly*, Vol. 7 (September, 1962).

An impressionistic discussion about an exploratory study into the broad range of tactics used in interdepartmental conflict in which each department seeks to impose its specialized point of view on others and is struggling for greater authority and status. Illustrates the day to day techniques, formal and informal, used by PAs to influence the behavior of other functional departments and the requisitions they receive.

_____. "Work-Flow Frictions, Interfunctional Rivalry, and Professionalism: A Case Study of Purchasing Agents" *Human Organization* Vol. 23, (Summer, 1964), pp. 137-49.

Continues the discussion of the purchasing agent and his relations with other departments, concentrating in this article on the overall strategy used by PAs to enhance their position. Illustrates the forms which interfunctional rivalry can take, and examines some of the implications, among which is the increasing trend to "professionalizing" the PA's job.

Weigand, Robert E. "Identifying Industrial Buying Responsibility." *Journal of Marketing Research*, Vol. III, (February, 1966) pp. 81-84.

This empirical study adds to the evidence concerning how individuals in an institution perceive their responsibilities. In particular, they demonstrate the disparity between how a group of purchasing agents see themselves and how others in a firm see them.

3. PURCHASING POLICIES, PROCEDURES AND DECISIONS

a. Make, Buy or Lease Decisions

Baumes, Carl G. and Thompson, G. Clark. "A Cautious Trend Toward Leasing." *Conference Board Business Record* November, 1958, pp. 493-500.

Survey of manufacturing companies on their policies concerning "leasing or buying" of real estate and equipment. Article reviews advantages and disadvantages of leasing, from the perspective of both lessor and lessee.

Culliton, James W. *Make or Buy?* Boston: Harvard University, Graduate School of Business Administration, 1942. (Research Study No. 27.)

Subtitled: A consideration of the problems fundamental to a decision whether to manufacture or buy materials, accessory equipment, fabricating parts, and suppliers. Evaluates make or buy alternatives in relation to procurement objectives. Considers cost, quality, quantity, timing, external factors. Throughout the thesis, the author makes reference to actual experiences of business organizations, generally presented in the form of cases. Concludes that buying is generally preferable to making.

Gross, Harry. "Purchasing Procedures for Make or Buy Decisions," *Journal of Purchasing*, Vol. 2 (Nov., 1966), pp. 63-73.

The author recommends that certain stringent purchasing procedures be instituted and applied on a continual basis in conjunction with the make or buy decision. Such efficient procurement practices, which lead to cost reduction and anticipate major problems, readily may influence this ultimate decision.

Hackamack, L. C. "Make or Buy Can Make or Break," *Purchasing*, (April 22, 1963), p. 67.

Outlines a technique for analyzing make or buy problems, enabling a more scientific decision and eliminating much of the risk.

Higgins, C. C. "Make or Buy: Reaching a Sound Decision," *Management Review,* Vol. 44 (August, 1955), p. 525.

Reviews cost and non-cost considerations involved in weighing make-or-buy alternatives.

"New Life on Leasing, A," *Dun's Review and Modern Industry,* (April, 1963), p. 65.

A general discussion on the lively field of leasing and its favorable impact on corporate balance sheets.

Oxenfeldt, A. R. and Watkins, M. W. *Make or Buy: Factors Affecting Executive Decisions.* New York: McGraw-Hill Book Co., 1956.

A study of cost and non-cost considerations in make-or-buy decisions. The authors use a negative approach to make-or-buy problems, concentrating on the errors most commonly made and the factors frequently overlooked or improperly evaluated in decisions to make what might be purchased.

Quinn, J. B. "How to Analyze Capital Equipment Purchases," *Purchasing,* (June, 1957), p. 93.

Demonstrates a cost analysis system which is applicable to equipment replacement problems, to new equipment decisions in which alternate facilities are available, and to the "make or buy" question when making would require capital facilities. Distinguishes between cost and return factors and intangible factors.

Vancil, Richard F. *Leasing of Industrial Equipment.* New York: McGraw-Hill Book Co., Inc., 1963.

An examination of the economics of leasing industrial equipment. About half of the chapters are concerned with lease-or-buy decision making, describing analytical procedures used in evaluating alternatives. The remaining chapters are for the analyst who evaluates leasing plans.

b. Supplier Selection, Evaluation and Development

Ammer, Dean. "Know the Facts about your Vendor," *Purchasing,* (November, 1957), pp. 131-33. Describes the techniques at Avco's Lycoming Division for objectively rating vendor's performance on price, quality, delivery, and service.

Busch, G. E. "New twist on supplier evaluation," *Purchasing,* (September 9, 1963), pp. 102-03.

Describes a system in which requisitioners rate supplier performance, subject to purchasing review.

Bushnell, J. M. "What makes a Good Supplier?" *Purchasing*, (June 20, 1960), pp. 102.

States the basic qualifications of a good supplier and principles the PA should follow towards a satisfactory relationship with his primary source and alternate sources of supply.

Dickson, Gary W. "An Analysis of Vendor Selection Systems and Decisions," *Journal of Purchasing*, Vol. 2 (February, 1966), pp. 5-17.

The study of firm vendor selection practices and the opinions of purchasing agents in four vendor selection cases lead to similar conclusions about what factors are important in the decision to select a supplier. Nonetheless, implications of the findings cast some serious doubts on the development of a universal system for vendor analysis that is appropriate over the entire range of purchasing situations.

Dillon, Thomas F. "How to Select Vendors for Stockless Purchasing," *Purchasing*, (March 10, 1966), pp. 89-92.

Selecting a vendor to participate in a stockless purchasing program is more critical than selection of a regular vendor since the alignment is for an indefinite period of time. The article sketches the evaluatory approach of Detroit Edison Company which involves vendor meetings, plant visits, and a nine-category rating system to cut chance of error.

Dowst, Somerby. "How Purchasing Agents are Rating You," *Sales Management*, (June 19, 1964), pp. 30-32.

Purchasing agents are increasingly setting up mathematical systems to rate suppliers in performance, quality and price. This article describes some of these systems and tells how the marketer can benefit from an awareness of them.

Dowst, Somerby. "How to Spur Vendors to Peak Performance," *Purchasing*, (July 29, 1965), pp. 53-57.

Hard-hitting program to strengthen vendor-purchasing ties shows tangible benefits at Sperry Farragut Company. Educational campaign keyed to suppliers makes them aware of what the company expects from them in the way of quality, delivery and cost reduction contributions.

Edwards, Marshall G. "Supplier Management Evaluation," *Journal of Purchasing*, Vol. 3 (February, 1967), pp. 28-41.

In the belief that a long-term supplier is a company's most important procurement decision, the author discusses such long-term relationships. A comprehensive evaluation plan originated by the Boeing Company is described, in addition to nine case examples illustrating problems of management evaluation of suppliers.

Hafner, R. A. and Humhauer, H. J. "Vendor Rating: Get the Quality You're Paying For," *Purchasing,* (February 15, 1960), pp. 82-85.

Explains IBM's quality conformance program based on sample inspection of incoming material lots from suppliers. Evaluation formula compares the percent defective in the first sample with an Acceptable Quality Levels assigned by a quality engineer and expressed as percent defective.

Hickey, John V. "General Foods' Recipe for Good Vendor Performance," *Purchasing,* (March 10, 1966), pp. 93-98.

Giant food processing firm supplements its buying expertise with thorough supplier briefings and vendor evaluation program.

"How to Measure Supplier Performance," *Purchasing,* (September 29, 1958), pp. 68-69.

Vendor rating system used by Whirlpool Corporation goes far beyond conventional vendor evaluation programs. It covers product quality, suggestions for improvement, integrity, service, pricing and packaging standards.

Kellner, William D. "Evaluation of Supplier Performance." *AMA Proceedings,* Winter, 1963, pp. 503-12.

The Cost Ratio Plan is described as a way of vendor-performance evaluation. The plan includes objectively derived ratings for quality, delivery, and service.

Kellogg, Ned. "Selecting and Evaluating Vendors," *Purchasing,* (February 16, 1959), pp. 80-81.

Republic Aviation's program ensures it selects only vendors who can meet exacting quality standards and follows through to be sure supplier quality doesn't slip. Rigorous check-out system screens potential suppliers; highly effective vendor evaluation program gives purchasing an up-to-date analysis of vendor performance.

Leenders, Michael R. *Improving Purchasing Effectiveness Through Supplier Development.* Boston, Massachusetts: Harvard University, Graduate School of Business Administration, 1965.

This research study explores the role of supplier development as an increasingly valuable procurement tool. Based on a survey of Canadian manufacturing companies, the research concentrates on the creation and development of new sources of supply by the purchasers. Identifies the basic elements and considerations of supplier development and illustrates its use, successful and unsuccessful, with suppliers of small, medium and large size firms.

_____. "Supplier Development," *Journal of Purchasing,* Vol. 2 (November, 1966), pp. 47-62.

The value of supplier development in cases of necessity generally is recognized by procurement executives, but its wider scope as a potential contributor to profit is not as fully appreciated. The author defines the concept of supplier development and offers bases for deciding upon such course of action.

Metaxas, Ted. "Unique Vendor Evaluation Program Boosts Quality, Cuts Costs," *Purchasing,* (March 9, 1964), pp. 76–80.

Using a novel Quality Assurance Program, Cummins Engine Company determines the real price of the castings it buys by adding its costs of labor, rework and salvage costs to the invoice price. Buyers rely on the true cost rather than "raw" price to award orders. Vendors get regular reports showing their quality rating. This system can be used for any goods bought for fabrication.

O'Connell, D. J., and Benson, J. J. "Sourcing Abroad for Domestic Profit," *Harvard Business Review,* (March–April, 1963), pp. 87–94.

Illustrates the profit possibilities of international sourcing, revealed by an increasing number of companies who seek materials, assemblies, finished products, plus personnel and partners—overseas.

"Personal Approach to Vendor Evaluation, The" *Purchasing,* (March 10, 1966), pp. 99–102.

Describes Young Radiator Co.'s approach to selecting suppliers, enlisting their cooperation in product improvement and cost reduction projects, and rating their ability to meet the company's quality-reliability-price standards.

"Plant Visits Pay Off . . . If You Know What to Look For," *Purchasing,* (August 17, 1959), pp. 72–73.

Pertinent items to be remembered by the buying company's inspection team when visiting a potential vendor's facilities.

Pooler, Victor H. "Can Vendors Really be Rated?" *Purchasing,* (June 18, 1962), pp. 60–62.

Discusses a number of supplier evaluation programs and some of the problems involved in vendor rating.

Porter, W. E. "How to Get Better Vendor Quality," *Purchasing,* (November, 1957), pp. 87–90.

A program aimed at developing a closer, more effective relationship with vendors. Stresses the importance of making sure the vendor can do the job, via formal survey and capability analysis, before awarding a contract. Suggests mutual agreement on specs and standards of measurement, preproduction run and checking procedures, vendor training in quality control procedures, early evaluation of selected vendors, and a certain amount of working assistance as necessary.

"Put a Dollar Sign on Vendor Performance: *Purchasing*, (January 27, 1964), pp. 87-90.

Borg Instruments uses a unique rating system in which suppliers' bids are weighted in dollars and cents according to past performance on quality, reliability and service criteria. Using a special formula, buyers convert vendors' monthly ratings on 12 performance standards into cash values. They add these amounts to suppliers' bids as handicaps or fines. The poorer a supplier's performance rating, the higher the bid handicap he gets. Vendors are given the right of appeal. They receive a monthly Supplier Evaluation Report which pinpoints their weaknesses and enables buyers to help them improve.

Sloane, Leonard. "Financial Reports: What They Tell About Suppliers," *Purchasing*, (Pt. I, May 20, 1963), pp. 50-54; (Part II, June 3, 1963), pp. 94-97.

Two-part series explains how financial reports can be used to evaluate a supplier's financial strength. The first article analyzes the balance sheet; the second, the income statement.

"Rating System Improves Vendor Performance," *Purchasing*, (December 18, 1961), pp. 84-86.

J. M. Huber Corp. buyers use a simple printed form in evaluating suppliers' service, products, and sales personnel. Aim is to help them recognize and eliminate weaknesses.

"Vendor Rating Aids Buyer and Supplier," *Iron Age*, (October 21, 1965), p. 162.

Describes one of industry's most advanced rating programs, employed by General Electric Company's Re-Entry Systems Dept., Philadelphia. System is basically a weighted scale, measuring a complexity of factors on quality, delivery, service, cost. A valuable means of communications, advising vendors where their performance should be upgraded.

c. Purchasing Procedures: Negotiations, Reciprocity and Trade Relations

Negotiations

Bowers, W. B. "Who's Afraid of the Learning Curve?" *Purchasing*, (March 24, 1966), p. 76.

Case history illustrates how company buyer uses the learning curve as a negotiating tool with a subcontractor.

De Rose, Louis J. *Negotiated Purchasing: The Key to More Profitable Buying.* Boston: Materials Management Institute, 1962.

Critically reviews buying procedures and practices. Develops in detail the techniques for more effective purchasing performance. Discusses areas for negotiation and techniques of negotiation especially price cost analysis. Evaluates factors influencing both the buyer and the seller in the negotiating process. Examines vendor and vendor performance ratings.

"Do's and Don'ts of Negotiation," *Purchasing*, (November 18, 1963), pp. 86-87.

Thirteen basic techniques of successful negotiation are posited by the author.

"How to Negotiate," *Purchasing*, (Pt. 1, February 12, 1962), pp. 70-74; (Pt. 11, February 26, 1962), pp. 84-87; (Pt. 111, March 12, 1962), pp. 87-89.

Three-part series covers the nature of negotiation, planning for negotiation, personal characteristics of a good negotiator, and successful negotiating tactics.

Lewis, Howard T. "The Art of Negotiation," *Purchasing*, (August 13, 1962), p. 70.

Noted procurement authority tenders guidelines for one of purchasing's most important functions.

Newman, Richard G. "Some Comments on Negotiation." *Journal of Purchasing*, Vol. 2 (May, 1966), pp. 52-66.

Recent writings in the area of negotiation and bargaining are explored and then placed in a purchasing context and discussed. The author concludes that the purchasing agent's ability to negotiate for greater value depends on the information he is provided, on his ability to develop a strategy for the process, and on the capability of assessing the added value of new information.

Reciprocity and Trade Relations

Adams, Velma A. "The Rise of the Trade Relations Director," *Dun's Review and Modern Industry*, (December, 1964), p. 35.

The need by large industrial complexes for a more formalized and sophisticated approach to trade relations grew increasingly urgent during the 1950's as manufacturing capacity—and competition—increased. This article discusses the complexity of functions of that new breed of executive, the trade relations director, whose basic job is to bring order to the often controversial corporate problem of buying from and selling to its friends.

American Management Association. *Trade Relations Defined: The Concept Legal Aspects, Ethical Problems*. Management Bulletin No. 19. New York: American Management Association, 1962.

Selections define the trade relations concept and function in modern business. Others discuss the legal and ethical aspects of reciprocity, including antitrust.

Austin, Arthur D. "Reciprocal Trading and the Anti-Trust Laws," *Journal of Purchasing*, Vol. 2 (May, 1966), pp. 5-17.

Any possessor of substantial purchasing power who overtly engages in reciprocal trading can anticipate litigation under one of the few trade regulation laws discussed in this paper. The firm, however, which decides, under no external pressure and for the sake of good will, to buy from a company with large purchasing power is not violating any law and will remain a permanent problem for both anti-trust enforcement agencies and the purchasing agent.

Lewis, Howard T. "No Matter What You Call It, It's Still Reciprocity," *Purchasing*, (January 15, 1962), p. 74.

Professor Lewis rejects the arguments generally given in defense of reciprocity, deplores its excesses. Semantics don't change the essential character of reciprocity.

Mandell, Melvin. "Industry's Secret Sales Weapon," *Dun's Review and Modern Industry*, (September, 1960), pp. 32-34.

Expresses industry executives' concern over the steady rise in reciprocal pressures and examines causative factors.

McCreary, E. Jr., and Guzzardi, W. Jr. "Customer is a Company's Best Friend," *Fortune*, Vol. 71 (June, 1965), p. 180.

Describes the expansion of reciprocal relations throughout U. S. business, accompanied by new techniques and formal organization. Over one-half of America's largest manufacturers employ a trade relations manager.

Meade, E. D. "Changing Concepts of Trade Relations," *Purchasing*, (June 1, 1964), pp. 75-76.

The author distinguishes between reciprocity and trade relations, praising the latter as a valuable communications function.

Sloane, Leonard. "Reciprocity: Where Does the P. A. Stand?" *Purchasing*, (November 20, 1961), pp. 70-79.

Special report on the role of trade relations in different industries and its demands on purchasing. Includes results of *Purchasing* magazine survey in which 300 PA's express their views on the trade relations problems.

Stocking, George W. and Willard F. Mueller, "Business Reciprocity and the Size of Firms," *Journal of Business*, Vol. XXX (April 1957), pp. 73-95.

Aspects covered on reciprocity include conditions conducive to reciprocal buying and economic significance of reciprocal dealing.

Several examples of this activity are described in detail with regard to such large firms as duPont, General Motors and U. S.
Rubber.

"What's Good and Bad About Reciprocal Buying," *Industrial Marketing,* (July, 1962) pp. 118-20.

IM found "Top Management Forum" members reluctant to discuss the subject of reciprocal purchasing. Only three made formal
statements, reproduced in this article, reflecting diverse views and
perspectives on the controversial subject.

d. Miscellaneous

American Management Association. *Systems Contracting: A Stream-
lines Purchasing Technique with Companywide Implications.* Management Bulletin No. 63. New York: American Management
Association, 1965.

Contributions from experts who explain and examine various aspects
of systems contracting technique, also known as stockless purchasing or contract buying. Includes selections on the applicability of
systems contracting, selecting and negotiating with suppliers,
difficulties from the perspective of both customer and supplier
of this long-term single source approach.

Brooking, W. J. "Expediting the Professional Way," *Purchasing,*
(May 11, 1959), p. 84.

A complete expert analysis of the expedition process.

"Buying Divorced from Expediting," *Iron Age,* (June 27, 1963), p. 107.

Reports on the successful separation of the buying and expediting
functions at Philadelphia Gear Corporation. Primary reason for
the differentiation is that most new orders require special engineering and production attention.

Collings, William B. "The Big Small Order Problem." *Journal of
Purchasing* (February, 1966) pp. 43-63.

Orders of small dollar value are a significant problem for any
purchasing agent. The author describes some procedures used to
simplify and systematize such purchases differentiating basically
between recurring or repetitive purchases of the same item, and
nonrecurring or one-time purchases.

Dowst, Somerby. "Buying Without Requisitions," *Purchasing,* (October 7, 1963), pp. 64-66.

Purchasing agent substitutes preprinted spec sheets for individual
requisitions in a successful, standardized, requisition-less buying
system.

"Expediting," *Purchasing,* August 25, 1966.

A five-article section details various successful expediting techniques used at different companies. Included: "Expediting—Purchasing's Answer to Tight Deliveries," "Advance Expediting Puts Deliveries on Schedule," "Outside Expediter Speeds Deliveries," "How Towmotor Beats the Shortage Problems, etc."

Henderson, Bruce D. "Coming Revolution in Purchasing," *Purchasing,* (April 20, 1964), pp. 70-73.

The systems procurement concept has revolutionary implications for purchasing. Repudiating the arms-length relationship between supplier and user, it substitutes a policy of cooperation and even integration of facilities and services, drastically changing the purchasing operation.

"How Should Purchasing Report to Management?" *Purchasing,* (September 10, 1962), pp. 85-88.

A discussion of information essentials which purchasing should provide to management.

Koch, A. P., and Walters, S. G. "Good and Bad Sides of the Blanket Purchase Order," *The Controller,* (November, 1960), p. 534.

In appraising the blanket purchase order, the authors identify advantages and disadvantages occuring to both buyer and seller, plus means of circumventing possible hazards to the supplier.

MacKinnis, Frank. "Five Tips on Expediting," *Purchasing,* (August 26, 1963), p. 77.

A check-list is suggested to bring about more effective expediting.

McMillan, A. L. *The Art of Purchasing: A Modern Textbook for Training Personnel in Purchase and Supply.* New York: Exposition Press, 1959.

This readable text explains the fundamental principles that the Purchasing Agent must expect to follow as he procures materials supplies, the limitations of the purchase and supply activity, and the problems which will confront him. Views the human side of purchasing, as well as the broader economic aspects, and the methods for cooperating with other departments in their areas of joint interest.

"PA's Look Hard at Contract Buying, Symposium" *Steel,* (May 11, 1964), pp. 25-26.

Purchasing Agents express their views on the benefits and hazards of contract buying.

Spivack, J. "How to Set Up a Blanket Order Program," *Purchasing,* (November 5, 1962), pp. 76-78.

Discusses the advantages of blanket orders, ways to set up a program, and how to determine items best suited for blanket order contracts.

Van De Water, John. "Good Communications Boosts Purchasing's Value," *Purchasing*, (January 27, 1964), pp. 70-74.

Frequent informative reports and informal meetings help industrial firm's purchasing department tie in with both management and production, achieve better cost control and on-time deliveries.

_____. "Kearfott's Blanket Order Breakthrough," *Purchasing*, (July 16, 1962), pp. 74-79.

Examines the blanket order system at Kearfott, unusual in several respects.

4. EVALUATION OF PURCHASING PERFORMANCE

Ammer, Dean. "How to Measure Purchasing Performance," *Purchasing*, (October 27, 1958), p. 59.

The author identifies four basic steps towards measuring purchasing performance: 1. Define the limits of the purchasing job, 2. Determine the desired objectives to be achieved within these limits, 3. Develop a program to meet these objectives, 4. Compare progress on the program with objectives. He then examines how these theoretical principles have or have not been put into practice in industry, with some specific examples.

Bussard, W. A. "A Study In Purchasing Effectiveness," *Journal of Purchasing*, Vol. 2 (May, 1966), pp. 76-94.

The author presents a descriptive model which attempts to combine into one most all previous approaches to developing a sensible yardstick for measuring purchasing performance.

Farmer, Samuel C. *A Look at Purchasing Through the President's Eye.* Management Bulletin No. 33. New York: American Management Association, 1963.

Discusses methods for evaluating purchasing performance and measures which can be taken to improve the purchasing operation.

Foster, Ray R. "The P.A.'s Problem: How to Measure Performance," *Purchasing*, (October 22, 1962), pp. 76-80.

Hughes Aircraft has devised a novel self-comparison method to measure the effectiveness of its many specialized buyers.

Hayes, F. Albert, and Renard, George A. *Evaluating Purchasing Performance.* New York: American Management Association, 1964. (Research Study 66)

A research study concerning methods used by top corporate officers to measure purchasing effectiveness and the extent of such evaluation in 201 companies. Reflects the opinions and practices of more than 7,500 purchasing department personnel, with extensive illustrative material.

Loen, R. O. "Purchasing Audits Itself," *Purchasing,* (June 17, 1963), p. 62.

Describes a study by an internal auditing team at Fibreboard Paper Corp., solicited to give an objective appraisal of purchasing performance.

Pearson, A. G. "Evaluating Purchasing Performance," *Purchasing,* (June 20, 1960), pp. 86-87.

A discussion of the complexities of purchasing evaluation, here defined as "value analysis applied to purchasing management." The author stresses the importance of the purchasing climate.

Pooler, Victor H., Jr. "Can We Measure Purchasing Efficiency?" *Purchasing,* (January 18, 1960), pp. 74-76.

The author suggests various "indicators" which might be used to measure purchasing performance.

_____. "Trend: A Total Approach to Measuring Performance." *Purchasing,* (May 19, 1966).

"Total Recognition of Environmental and Numerical Development" is the basis for this new approach to gauging purchasing's effectiveness within the company operation.

Van De Water, J. "Measure Buyers by Vendor Performance, *Purchasing,* (August 26, 1965), pp. 70-75.

Mennen Company's numerical rating system measures buyers more on suppliers' performance than on personal qualities. Buyers are judged 90 percent on how their vendors do (on price, quality, service factors), 10 percent on personal qualifications.

5. IMPROVING PURCHASING PERFORMANCE

a. Cost Reduction Methods

American Management Association. *Purchasing for Profit: Practical Guides for Purchasing Cost Reduction.* Management Report No. 20. New York: American Management Association, 1958.

The report contains 16 selections by purchasing executives which discuss the scope, administration and organization of the purchasing function. Tools and techniques for increasing purchasing's efficiency are described, as are approaches to cost reduction in the area of vendor relations.

Ammer, Dean S. "Purchasing for Profits,"*Harvard Business Review*, Vol. 39 (May-June, 1961), pp. 135-43.

This article highlights principles of organization and planning which will enable purchasing to help top management reach many important goals. Differences which good purchasing can make are illustrated in terms of reduced costs and unreached profits. Some of the new techniques used to improve and measure performance in the purchasing departments of progressive companies are also discussed.

Blumenthal, Lassor. "How to Cut Purchasing Costs," *Dun's Review and Modern Industry*, (March, 1964), pp. 53-54.

Examines four new cost-cutting systems being used to reduce the cost of processing purchase orders and which entail distinctly new relationships between vendor and customer.

Kneitel, J. "It's Easy to Take the Guesswork Out of Buying," *Purchasing*, (February 2, 1959), pp. 62-65.

Illustrates several basic techniques which can supplement the buyer's judgment towards securing maximum return on the purchase dollar.

McLean, Herbert E. "Cost Reduction Goes Formal: Two Case Histories," *Purchasing*, (March 24, 1966), pp. 68-76.

Case histories of cost reduction plans at TRW Systems and Link-Belt. The former's highly successful program combines definite goals, progress reports, intra-company competition, and vendor cooperation. Report cards on buyer accomplishments key Link-Belt's cost reduction plan.

_____. "Holding the Cost Line," *Purchasing*, (January 27, 1966), pp. 50-60.

Two-part feature contains case studies of purchasing at West Instrument Corp., and Furnas Electric Co. Shows how both departments—one with manual systems, the other automated—have kept purchasing costs down in growth companies. Focuses on different techniques used by each purchasing agent towards cost containment: blanket orders and value analysis in the former, automation and EQO in the latter.

Taylor, Richard W. "Undeveloped Gold Mines in Purchasing," *Dun's Review*, April, 1969, pp. 51-53, 120-21.

Several effective but often neglected ways of reducing procurement costs are described.

b. Value Analysis

Ammer, Dean. "Value Analysis—Purchasing Leads the Way," *Purchasing*, (Value Analysis Issue), (April 23, 1962), pp. 36-50.

Purchasing has the greatest need for Value Analysis since it spends about 50 percent of the sales dollar (usually about twice the value added by manufacturing, its closest competitor) in the typical company. In this keynote article, the author reviews basic value analysis principles and discusses techniques used in eliminating nonfunctional costs.

Bullen, H. Jay. "Value Analysis: Marketing Men Take Notice," *Industrial Marketing*, (August, 1963), pp. 86-90.

Spells out some implications for industrial marketing of VA's rapidly-spreading adoption by industry. Describes the typical VA procedure in which the PA brings together the VA "team" and acts as a "catalyst" in the buying process. Predicts declination of the "old fashioned" salesman as VA becomes a more finely-honed buying and selling technique.

Fallon, Carlos. "Value Analysis: A Definition of Terms and Concepts," *Journal of Purchasing*, Vol. 2 (November 1966), pp. 16-40.

Metaxas, Ted. "Where You Can Go Wrong on Value Analysis," *Purchasing*, (January 27, 1964), pp. 78-79.

Emphasizes purchasing's responsibility for the value analysis program. Spells out ground rules for a sound value program, and recognizable flaws which can cause its failure.

Van De Water, J. "RCA's New Concepts in Value Buying," *Purchasing*, (Value Analysis Issue), (May 18, 1964) pp. 35-75.

This issue is devoted to an intensive study of RCA's use of value analysis techniques for holding costs down while improving products. Examines the company's VA philosophy, organizational setup and program specifics. An important facet is the emphasis placed on vendors' critical part in cost reduction.

—————————. "The Tools of Value Analysis," *Purchasing*, (Tools of Value Analysis Issue), (May 6, 1963), pp. 33-57.

Value analysis is now purchasing's top cost-reduction technique. This keynote article is devoted to the question "how to get the most out of value analysis," reflecting upon opportunities newly open to purchasing since it no longer faces general hostility or skepticism from other departments. Discusses specific techniques and considerations for developing a value analysis program in any size/type of company.

"Value Analysis," *Purchasing*, (May 5, 1966).

Special issue devoted to value analysis features the VA program at Westinghouse Electric Corporation—the scope of the program, its methods and results; purchasing's contributions to an effort that extends into every department; how VA teams enlist supplier aid; how value research boosts division profits. Also, hundreds of VA case histories.

c. Use of Computer Technology

Dowst, Somerby. "What the Computer Can Do for the Small Company," *Purchasing* (September 9, 1963), pp. 74-77.

Illustrates the utility of automated purchasing at Dixie Mercerizing, where a computer is used to buy 900 stock items.

Judice, Peter F. "Salesman's Nemesis: The Computer." *Sales Management* (April 5, 1963) pp. 44-46.

Purchasing agent discusses the rapidly accelerating revolution taking place in industrial purchasing, as exemplified by the new breed of purchasing agent and the mushrooming application of automation to the buying function.

Metaxas, Ted. "EDP Can't Do It all," *Purchasing* (July 15, 1963), p. 70.

Tells about the purchasing department reorganization at Automatic Electric Co. Buying methods have been modernized, but decisions are made by men, not machines.

Plant, Harold. "What Can EDP Do for Purchasing," *Purchasing,* (April 22, 1963), pp. 60-62.

This article examines some of the problems and opportunities purchasing faces in the use of electronic data processing. A helpful general guide to the whole subject of EDP in procurement.

"Purchasing and the Computer," *Purchasing,* July 28, 1966.

A four-article study of the impact of EDP on current and future buying. Included: "Planning for a computer," "Computer cuts buying job to size," "Small department makes move to automation look easy," and "How to buy a computer."

Widing, J. W., Jr., & Diamond, C. A. "BUY by Computer," *Harvard Business Review,* (March-April, 1964), pp. 109-20.

A comprehensive discussion of electronic data processing as applied to purchasing and purchasing activities. Great potential for reducing material costs, financially and in less tangible ways, eventually as an integrated part of a total EDP system of control.

Wright, J. "What Will Automation Do to Purchasing?" *Purchasing,* (January 14, 1963), pp. 83-85.

Purchasing expert believes automation will provide the opportunity for purchasing executives to reach top management status if they are prepared to meet its challenges.

d. Use of Models and Quantitative Methods

Ball, Roger E. and Gilbert, Allan A., "How to Quantify Decision-Making", *Business Horizons* (Winter, 1958), pp. 73-79.

Management consultants outline some advanced techniques for major business decisions. Illustrate the use of a decision matrix in case study involving a question of equipment replacement.

"Learning Curve, The," *Purchasing*, (Pt. 1, March 11, 1965), pp. 70-75; (Pt. 11, March 25, 1965), pp. 80-83.

Two-part series offers a general description of the learning curve, how to set it up and apply it to negotiations, make-or-buy decisions, and scheduling. Two methods of setting up the curve are compared, and their respective results.

"PERT and CPM: New Planning Tools for Purchasing Management," (Special Report), *Purchasing*, (June 3, 1963), pp. 71-90.

Special section devoted to new scheduling and cost control techniques. Explains critical path methods in general terms and interprets their usefulness for the P. A. Describes technical aspects of PERT planning, the part PERT plays in purchasing, and practical uses of PERT illustrated by three case histories. Contains charts, diagrams, graphs and forms employed in a PERT system.

e. Purchasing Research

American Management Association. *Purchasing Research: The Concept and its Value.* Bulletin No. 17. New York: American Management Association, 1962.

A purchasing research expert discusses the growing concept, steps towards establishing a purchasing research program, and profit opportunities which might be thereby exploited.

Fearon, Harold E., and Hoagland John H. *Purchasing Research In American Industry.* Research Study 58. New York: American Management Association, 1963.

This research study is based on the experiences of 304 firms which have used purchasing research to increase profits. A major portion of the report discusses specific projects which have been conducted, with varying degrees of success, by purchasing research departments.

Metaxas, Ted. "Purchase Research Section Gives Big Boost to Buyers," *Purchasing*, (August 26, 1963), pp. 67-69.

Purchase Research and Analysis group provides technical expertise for purchasing operations at Eaton Manufacturing Co.

Smith, Spencer B. "Linear Programming: New Tool for Purchasing
Problems," *Purchasing*, (Pt. I, November 9, 1959), pp. 67-76; Pt.
II, November 23, 1959), pp. 80-84; (Pt. III, December 7, 1959), p. 69;
(Pt. IV, December 21, 1959), pp. 69-73.

A series of articles on the applications of linear programming to
basic purchasing problems. The first article explains what linear
programming is and how it can be applied to a problem in source
selection. The second article treats on the purchase of commodities
subject to wide price fluctuations. The third article describes the
application of linear programming for the most economic solution
to make or buy problems. In the last article, linear programming
is used to find the optimum mix for given product specifications
and raw material prices.

6. RELATED PURCHASING PRACTICES

a. Materials Management

American Management Association. *Managing the Materials Function*.
Management Report No. 35. New York: American Management
Association, 1959.

Most of the selections comprising this report were originally
presented at an AMA conference on "Integrated Materials Management," New York, 1959. The first section contains an appraisal
of the integrated materials management concept, basic organizational principles and practices. The second section describes a
number of advanced techniques and tools for materials planning
and control. Finally, the purchasing engineering relationship is
spotlighted and suggestions offered for its improvement.

Ammer, Dean S. *Materials Management*. Homewood, Illinois: Richard
D. Irwin, Inc., 1962.

In this basic text, materials management is treated as an integrated activity of business. In the author's words, he approaches
it as a "specialized application of fundamental principles of economics and management," and he relates discussion to these fundamentals throughout. Similarly, materials organization is closely
related to general business organization theory. The author presents a detailed analysis of the three basic materials functions: inventory control, purchasing and traffic. Other topics include materials management objectives, sourcing (make, buy or lease),
finding qualified suppliers, purchase price analysis, supplier relations and negotiations, performance evaluation, etc. The latest
concepts and current developments in materials management and
industrial purchasing are represented in this volume.

"Four Approaches to Materials Management," *Purchasing*, (June 17, 1963), pp. 55-59.

Case histories in which materials managers discuss four differing types of materials organizations, pro and con. Controlling factors are considered to be type of company, group objectives and kind of materials used.

Harmon, George M. "Purchasing and Logistics Management,' *Journal of Purchasing*, Vol. 2 (February, 1966), pp. 32-42.

The proper province of purchasing is examined in light of "logistics management" (akin to materials management)—a newly developing management concept which has been made practical by improvements in computer and communications capabilities.

Van de Water, John. "How K&E Moved up to Materials Management," *Purchasing*, (November 4, 1963), pp. 70-75.

Reviews a classic study of a firm's transformation from decentralized purchasing to a centralized materials organization, part of the modernication program at century-old Keuffel and Esser.

b. Quality Control

American Management Association. *Quality Control in Action*. Management Report No. 9. New York: American Management Association, 1958.

This report is comprised of articles by managers experienced in the field who discuss top management responsibilities and functions in quality control. They describe organizing for quality control, quality control cost reduction, product quality design, plus other applications of quality control.

Buck, Vernon E. "Too Much Control—Too Little Quality." *Business Horizons*, Vol. 8, No. 3 (Fall 1965) pp. 34-44.

Study suggests that management should reconsider its reliance upon specialized quality control systems. Findings support job enlargement as one approach to the reduction of the negative consequences of present job designs and for increasing individual job control.

"Buyer Gets Bigger Quality Role," *Iron Age*, (November 16, 1961), p. 156.

Quality control approach at Westinghouse Electric's Atomic Fuel Department stresses prevention of defects in purchases goods rather than just detection. Prevention control involves greater teamwork and direct contact between buyer (quality control and engineering) personnel and vendor (manufacturing) personnel, from drafting the specifications through production. Results in lower prices, lower inventory costs.

Hansen, B. L. *Quality Control: Theory & Applications*. Englewood Cliffs, New Jersey: Prentice-Hall, Inc., 1963.

This reference book is designed for persons in quality control and related fields. It provides a comprehensive, systematic exposition of the quality control process, stressing the fundamentals of statistical and economic analysis and their applications.

c. Inventory Control

Brown, Robert G. "Less Risk in Inventory Estimates," *Harvard Business Review,* Volume 37 (July-August, 1959), pp. 104-06.

Explains a well designed inventory control system, using in combination the expected demand, the distribution of forecast error, and decision rules, to minimize the uncertainty facing a firm.

Crook, Gordon J. "Inventory Management Takes Teamwork," *Purchasing,* (March 26, 1962), pp. 70-72.

An expert in inventory control makes a strong case for cooperation between purchasing and production control in setting order points and determining economic order quantities.

Groot, A. M. and Groot, A. M., Jr. "How to Make E.O.Q. Really Work," *Purchasing,* (Pt. I, August 26, 1963), pp. 63-66; (Pt. II, September 9, 1963), pp. 78-80; (Pt. III, September 23, 1963), pp. 80-83.

Three part series on modern inventory control techniques. Two articles explain a way to calculate economic order quantities which is simpler but more accurate than many now in use. The last article discusses lead-time and safety stocks.

Hirschmann, W. B. and Brauweiler, J. J. "Curing and Preventing Surplus Inventories." *Business Horizons,* Spring, 1963, p. 87-98.

Offers a precise method for evaluating the maintenance inventory and employing a decision making rule to identify and liquidate surplus.

Morgan, James I. "Questions for Solving the Inventory Problem." *Harvard Business Review,* July-August, 1963, pp. 95-110.

This article discusses the inventory process and an adaptation of the scientific method of studying it. An approach to inventory problem solving is presented based on the answering of certain key questions at six differentiated phases—consideration, analysis, synthesis, control, action and evaluation—of the inventory process.

Pooler, Victor H., Jr. "ROI—'King' of Inventory Management," *Journal of Purchasing,* Vol. 1 (November, 1965), pp. 24-31.

With the importance of inventory from the point of view of both profitability and company performance, the purchasing man should help control inventory and not stand in the way of better inventory performance. Discussed here are some existing concepts and guidelines regarding inventory size, control techniques, and effects of turnover on investment.

d. Various Purchasing Functions and Problems

Ammer, Dean. "How to Make Your Own Forecast." *Purchasing,* Dec. 17, 1962, pp. 70-72, 117-19.

Starting with a professional's general forecast, the purchasing agent can adapt the macro-economic estimates to his own industry.

——————————. "Forecasting is Purchasing's Job," *Purchasing,* (January 1, 1962), pp. 65-69.

Guides for the purchasing executive in business forecasting.

Dobler, Donald W. "The Challenge of Proficiency in Small Company Purchasing," *Journal of Purchasing,* Vol. I (May, 1965), pp. 53-61.

Purchasing can perform as a profit-making activity in small firms when the buying activities are planned and managed carefully. The author discusses certain managerial techniques which facilitate the performance of routine purchasing activities, maximizing time available for the creative, profit-making activities which purchasing must exploit.

Goubeau, Vincent de Paul. "How to Get the Most out of Standardization," *Purchasing,* (November 9, 1959), p. 90.

In rebuttal to critics of standardization, an authority on the subject expounds its value as a purchasing tool. Among the advantages of using standard products, the author emphasizes its cost reduction potential and its utility in vendor negotiations in that it eliminates the unproductive aspects of negotiation and provides a value analysis tool that enable the PA to negotiate intelligently.

"How a Buyer Feels about Pricing," *Iron Age,* (September 11, 1958), p. 224.

Purchasing Vice President at Westinghouse Electric Corporation advises buyers to support price structures which permit supplier expansion and insures adequate supply.

"How Much Should You Tell the Vendor?" *Purchasing,* (January 13, 1964), pp. 84-87.

Staff report studies the problem of price secrecy in purchasing-sales relations. Suggests a franker approach to vendor relations may help the buyer.

Lee, Lamar, Jr. "Six Problems Purchasing Agents Are Thinking About," *Purchasing,* (April 27, 1959), pp. 69-74.

Research report summarizes opinions and experiences of 36 purchasing executives on 6 subjects of concern: 1. Representation for
purchasing; 2. Performance Evaluation; 3. Leasing vs. buying
equipment; 4. The decision to make or buy; 5. Forecasting and
purchasing and 6. The learning curve?

Levine, N. P. "The Hidden Threat of Standardization," *Purchasing,*
(March 2, 1959), p. 69.

The advantages of standardization as a cost reduction tool outweigh the disadvantages, but some evidence has been misdirected.
The author expresses the view that too much standardization might
reduce the effectiveness of the purchasing executive by nullifying
his role as negotiator.

Metaxas, Ted "What Does Purchasing Owe to its Vendor?" *Purchasing,*
(January 14, 1963), pp. 78-81.

This article offers some contrasting views on the mettlesome problem of "free engineering" resulting from the competitive bidding
system as applied to custom engineered equipment.

Rottman, Dick L. "The Purchasing Agent's Role as a Risk Manager,"
Journal of Purchasing, Vol. 2 (August, 1966), pp. 52-60.

As the purchasing manager is often responsible for buying insurance for his firm, the concept of risk management is examined with
regard to its nature, significance, elements, and role in the firm.
Risk management's objective is the conservation of the firm's physical and human assets and future income against accidental loss
arising from the pure risks faced by the business.

Ryan, Leo V. "Business Ethics and Purchasing," *Journal of Purchasing,* Vol. 2 (Nov., 1966), pp. 32-40.

Since the advancement of purchasing as a profession depends on
ethical conduct by every purchasing practitioner, specific problem
areas are cited and criteria are offered for evaluating the ethics
of a decision.

Treadway, Lyle E. "How Much Should You Pay," *Purchasing,* (July 31,
1961), pp. 54-56.

Discussion of the aspects of "open price" orders, legal escalation
clauses or other terms and conditions which permit the supplier
to increase the price before the time of shipment.

Van Schaak, Herbert, "Human Relations in Purchasing" *Journal of
Purchasing,* Vol. 2 (November 1966), pp. 5-15.

The premise underlying this article is that the purchasing manager
can be more effective in his job by understanding other people's
behavior. Thus the author explains the roots of perception and
how it might be developed and used in dealing with subordinates
as well as those outside the department.

Watson, Clifford and Smith, W. A.,   "Input-Output Analysis and Industrial Purchasing," *Journal of Purchasing,* Vol. 2 (May, 1966),
pp. 67-75.

Every purchasing professional might give serious thought to the
use of Input-Output Analysis as an economic tool through which
he can make a direct contribution to the management of his company and establish himself as an individual with significant economic decision making potential.   A review of the "literature" is
also included in this article.

PART TWO

Determinants of
Industrial Buyer Behavior

1. IDENTIFYING THE BUYING INFLUENCES AND DECISIONS MAKERS

Harding, Murray. "Who Really Makes the Purchasing Decision?" *Industrial Marketing* (Sept., 1966), pp. 76-81.

Study on nonrepetitive purchases by ten industrial firms confirms the complexity of the industrial buying process and notes some unexpected influences on the final decision.

"Helping Salesmen Identify Points of Buying Influence," *Industrial Marketing,* (May, 1962), pp. 104-06.

Marketing and sales executives tell how industrial salesmen can better identify and contact the individuals who actually make the important buying decisions.

Kernan, Jerome B. and Sommers, Montrose, S. "The Behavioral Matrix—a Closer Look at the Industrial Buyer," *Business Horizons,* (Summer, 1966), pp. 59-72.

While it may be recognized that industrial buyers are subject to behavioral influences the same as consumer buyers are, practical application of this maxim to industrial selling demands an operational scheme. This article tells how to systematically combine certain behavioral notions to produce such a scheme.

Kotler, Philip. "Behavioral Models for Analyzing Buyers," *Journal of Marketing,* (October, 1965), pp. 37-45.

The author contrasts five buyer behavioral models, of which one—the Hobbesian model— applies to the case of industrial buying. This model suggests that organizational buyers can be appealed to on both personal and organizational grounds, since Hobbesian man is seeking to reconcile individual gain with organizationanl gain. The marketing strategist must appreciate these goal conflicts in approaching the organizational buyer.

Walsh, Charles E. "Reaching those 'Hidden' Buying Influences," *Industrial Marketing* (October, 1961), pp. 165-168.

Research on industrial buying patterns confirms the complexity of the industrial buying process, and points out the large number of buying influences missed by vendor salesmen. The author concludes that the manufacturer must advertise to survive. In many cases business publication advertising is the only contact the manufacturer has with important buying influences.

Webster, Frederick E., Jr. "Modeling the Industrial Buying Process." *Journal of Marketing Research,* Volume II (November, 1965), pp. 370-76.

This article presents an analytical framework of the industrial buying process, identifies some critical variables, and makes some statements about their interrelationships. The author constructs a preliminary descriptive model that divides the industrial buying process into four elements: 1. problem recognition, 2. organizational assignment of buying responsibility and authority, 3. search procedures for identifying product offerings and for establishing selection criteria, and 4. choice procedures for evaluating and selecting among alternatives.

2. PERSONAL CHARACTERISTICS AS DETERMINANTS OF BUYING DECISIONS

Blumenthat, Lassor. "The Hidden Influences on Buying" *The American Salesman,* (August, 1959).

Suggests some methods for ferreting out hidden buying influences.

"Close Look at Why Buyers Buy," *Iron Age,* (December 24, 1959), pp. 24-25.

Reports on a study by the Industrial Advertisers Research Institute which used motivation research to probe for buyers' image attitudes towards sellers and hidden motives in industrial purchasing. Interviews were held in 24 companies with 58 industrial buying influences: Purchasing Agents, engineering, production and management personnel.

Clohesey, J. E. "The Polished Purchasers." *Sales Management,* (August 7, 1964), pp. 32-33.

Descriptive article tells how profit-oriented purchasing professionals, armed with the tools of modern procurement, are changing industrial selling, and offering new opportunities for the creative industrial salesman.

Copeland, Melvin T. "Buying Motives for Industrial Goods" in *Principles of Merchandising,* Chapter VII, A. W. Shaw Company, Chicago, 1924.

Examines factors that influence the purchase of industrial goods, differentiating between 1. buying motives, which induce a customer to buy a particular commodity in type of articles; and 2. patronage motives, which induce a customer to trade with a particular firm. Maintains that rational motives undoubtedly predominate heavily in industrial goods selling.

Dichter, Ernest. "The Human Being in the Job of Buying," *The American Salesman,* (January, 1959), pp. 42-53

The purchasing agent is influenced by the same motivations which affect any human being as customer, but additional considerations enter into the industrial buying situation. The author discusses some of the various factors which complicate the P.A.'s task and affect his buying behavior.

Duncan, Delbert J. "What Motivates Business Buyers." *Harvard Business Review.* 1940, pp. 448-54.

A classic study of buying motives for industrial goods: their rational or irrational basic, specific buying motives, and the general influences which cause industrial buyers as a whole to buy or not to buy at a particular time or during a particular period.

"How to Use Emotional Factors that Trigger Industrial Sales," *Steel,* (April 6, 1959), pp. 104-109.

Summarizes major findings of Dr. F. Robert Shoaf's study to explore factors that motivate that industrial buyer. Concludes that a large majority of buying decisions are made on an emotional basis. To the extent that products and services become more objectively alike, the buyer's final decision is based more and more upon subjective emotional factors.

James, Bert. "Emotional Buying in the Industrial Market." *Scientific Business*, (Spring, 1966), pp. 326-30.

This article presents an analysis of the industrial purchasing function and its position in organization structures. It suggests that the nature of the activity, its relationship to other functions, and the work flow could be the source of irrational behavior.

Lewis, Howard T. "What motivates the Industrial Buyer? Don't Overlook his Human Emotions," *Printers' Ink,* (April 11, 1958), pp. 44-45.

A critique of the hard sell theory of "nuts-and-bolts". Industrial advertising strategy frequently fails to convey any image of the advertiser. Lewis stresses the importance to the buyer of both tangible and intangible motivation, the need to enhance product quality with a favorable corporate image, thus giving him further assurance.

Marino, Sal F. "Five Hidden Obstacles to Industrial Selling" *Industrial Marketing* Vol. 51, No. 5, (May 1966), pp. 53-54.

Talks about ways to overcome major roadblocks to industrial sales-ignorance, indifference, inertia, fear and procrastination-in business publication advertising.

McPherson, J. H.   "Does PA's Ego Get in Way of his Job?" *Iron Age,* (March 17, 1966), p. 120.

A psychologist addresses himself to the emotional processes of the purchasing manager.   Says purchasing executive's effectiveness is enhanced if he is problem centered—*i.e.,* highly involved in problems, less involved in ego needs.

Robertson, George M.   "Motives in Industrial Buying," *AMA Proceedings,* Summer, 1960, pp. 266-276.

Study reveals various personality factors which must be considered and perhaps overcome before a sale is made.

Sawyer, Howard G.   "What Does the Industrial Buyer's Emotional Involvement Mean to You?" *Industrial Marketing,* (May, 1959), p. 132.

Examines the implications for industrial advertising of the *Steel* magazine study conducted by R. F. Shoaf.   Discusses the types of emotional factors—favorable and unfavorable—that admen should understand and attempt to capitalize on or compensate for in their selling strategy.

Shoaf, Robert F.   "Here's Proof—the Industrial Buyer *is* Human!" *Industrial Marketing,* (May, 1959), pp. 126-28.

Motivation research consultant summarizes findings of his study commissioned by *Steel* magazine to determine the extent that psychological factors extend into the industrial buyer's business life.

Tofte, Arthur R.   "They Don't Buy Bulldozers the Way they Buy Beer," *Industrial Marketing* (March, 1960), pp. 86, 89.

Emotions have nothing to do with industrial buyer's purchasing decisions, explains the author.   The best industrial advertising provides a factual and pertinent guide to buyers.

3. INTRAORGANIZATIONAL RELATIONS AND
ORGANIZATIONAL CHARACTERISTICS
AS DETERMINANTS OF BUYING DECISIONS

Duncan, Delbert J.   "Some Basic Determinants of Behavior in Industrial Purchasing."   *Pacific Purchasor,* XLVII (May, 1965), pp. 17-22; (June, 1965), pp. 19, 22-28; (July, 1965), pp. 37-40, 48-49.

Discusses forces within the business firm which influence the behavior of buyers of industrial goods.   Focuses particularly on the purchasing agent, the environment in which he operates, specific company policies related to purchasing activities, and organizational factors.

Howard, John A., *Marketing Theory*, Boston, Massachusetts: Allyn and Bacon, Inc., 1965.

This book is a revision of the author's earlier work, *Marketing: Executive and Buyer Behavior*, published by Columbia University Press in 1963. He has incorporated in the text many of the current developments relevant to marketing and shows some of their interrelations. The book discusses organization theory and influences upon the decision premises of the executive, and provides a normative view of the executive's choice principles.

Perlmutter, I. "Purchasing and Motivation," *Purchasing*, (July 1, 1963), pp. 56–57.

The author states that interpersonal relationships, so important in purchasing, can be improved through a better understanding of human motivation. He discusses a few of the more complex needs of man in a social/business situation.

Wind, Yoram, *Industrial Buying Behavior: Source Loyalty in the Purchase of Industrial Components*. Ph.D. Dissertation, Stanford University, Graduate School of Business, 1966.

A theoretical and empirical investigation of determinants of source loyalty in the purchase of industrial components. The study presents an organizational explanation of the decision to purchase components and tests the relative effectiveness of the organizational factors and other relative variables in determining the degree of source loyalty.

4. ENVIRONMENTAL VENDOR CHARACTERISTICS AND OTHER FACTORS AS DETERMINANTS OF BUYING DECISIONS

Ahl, G. W. H. "What American Buyers Want," *Purchasing*, (May 21, 1962), p. 79.

The article is abstracted from an address given by the author at the Swedish Export Advertising Conference in Stockholm, March 9, 1962. Ahl submits that one out of three U. S. purchasing agents buy from foreign producers items which could be procured from domestic suppliers. He poses a challenge to Swedish manufacturers who would sell in America, spelling out requirements and strategies for competing in the rigorous U. S. market, purchasing agents attitudes and apprehensions concerning foreign sources of supply.

Duncan, D. J. "External Forces Influencing Purchasing Behavior," *Pacific Purchasor* (August, 1965), pp. 15–21.

This article presents a discussion of some of the important external forces that affect the behavior of the purchasing executive and influence purchasing decisions. Included are such factors as general business conditions, technological change, the existence of "emergency conditions," vendor activities, and the policies and practices of competitors.

"How Do You Decide What to Buy?" *Iron Age*, (December 19, 1957), p. 101.

A. O. Smith reveals its formula for deciding whether a new piece of equipment is a good buy. After a purchase, records are kept to check accuracy of estimated cost savings.

Klass, Bertrand. "What Factors Affect Industrial Buying Decisions?" *Industrial Marketing*, (May, 1961), p. 33.

This article presents the results of an extensive interview survey of 300 executives in 208 industrial companies. The study focuses on factors (such as advertising, salesmanship, delivery and service) that affect an industrial buying decision and the importance of each factor. It also touches on participants in the decision-making process.

Levitt, Theodore. "Communications and Industrial Selling." *Journal of Marketing*, Vol. 31 (April, 1967), pp. 15-21.

Reports on communications simulation research that focuses on the interrelationship between the industrial firm's generalized reputation and its ability to launch new products. Examines the relative importance of salesman efforts and the quality of direct sales presentation, the role of personal risk in buying decisions, the influence of customer "competence," and the durability of vendor reputation on buying decisions.

Levitt, Theodore. *Industrial Purchasing Behavior: A Study of Communications Effects*. Boston, Massachusetts: Harvard University, Graduate School of Business Administration, 1965.

Reports on an experiment designed to test applicability to purchasing decisions of concepts taken from communication theory and to distinguish among the effects on various purchasing groups of the many aspects of the selling communication. The differential effects revealed by the experiment show the relevance to marketing managers of the varied elements of selling efforts and how they need to be considered in the formulation of marketing strategy.

Metaxas, Ted. "Can You Trust the Lowest Bid?" *Purchasing*, (May 4, 1964), pp. 70-73.

The PA at ITT Kellogg has devised a system that takes the risk out of accepting low bids.

"PA's Look at Cash Discount," *Purchasing*, (September 9, 1963), pp. 90-92.

Summarizes PA attitudes about problems surrounding the practice of giving cash discounts for prompt payment.

Page, Eugene S. "A New Look at—Quality, Service and Price," *Purchasing*, (December 7, 1959) pp. 84-86.

Suggests performance and cost—not quality, service and price—as the basis for sound buying decisions, and discusses the complexities of each.

Reck, Dickson. "The Effect of Buying Policies on Products and Prices—II, *The Journal of Marketing*, (April, 1952), pp. 409-22.

Using typical examples, the author traces the effect on products and prices of policies used by the federal government and industrial buyers in the purchase of differentiated products.

PART THREE

Industrial Implications
For Marketers

1. INDUSTRIAL MANAGEMENT—GENERAL

Adams, Velma A. "Can You Beat the System?" *Sales Management,* (June 15, 1966), pp. 35-38.

The wave of the future in industrial marketing may well be a form of total selling that delivers a multi-product, multi-service operation that is wholly self-sustaining. The author discusses the concept, advantages to the customer, potential pitfalls and complexities facing the vendor.

Alexander, Fred C. "Is Industrial Marketing Ready to 'Go Consumer'?" *Industrial Marketing,* (December, 1964), pp. 74-77.

The author traces seven stages of marketing development in consumer products and finds five parallel stages in the marketing of industrial products. He contends that the latter is in a transient stage of a maturing pattern of growth which will inevitably lead to the mass distribution practices of consumer marketing. He predicts the development of 'mechanized' industrial selling and a marked evolution in distribution patterns.

Allen, Heber E. "Organizing Industrial Sales for Profit," *Journal of Marketing,* (Jan. 61) pp. 22-24.

The article discusses some objectives and pitfalls in the "hazardous journey" of getting an industrial product to market. Emphasizes the vital role of the salesman in discovering market opportunities that require technical development.

Christian, Richard C. "Innovate for Success." *Journal of Marketing.* Vol. 27, No. 2, (April 1963) pp. 78-79.

Some thoughts on the significance of innovation in industrial marketing, historically found in three distinct categories: 1. Creative innovation—doing what has never been done before, in product, service or method, 2. Adaptive innovation—combining or modifying familiar elements in novel ways, 3. Administrative innovation—improving operating results in a familiar setting by a major advance in administrative effectiveness.

"Fourteen Big Complaints About Industrial Selling, The" *Sales Management*, (June 1, 1962), pp. 40-41.

Records the most common complaints concerning the industrial salesman and the industrial supplier's headquarters operations, voiced by more than 3,000 industrial buyers and as recorded over a five-year period.

Fullerton, Baxter. "Industrial Selling," *AMA Proceedings*, Winter, 1961, pp. 200-02.

Considers characteristics that differentiate industrial customers from ordinary consumers, and discusses the abilities and guidance needed by industrial salesmen.

"Fundamental Differences between Industrial and Consumer Marketing," Industrial Marketing Committee Review Board, *Journal of Marketing*, (October, 1954), pp. 152-58.

Spells out differences in marketing patterns, motivation and requirements in the industrial versus the consumer goods sphere.

Hagler, James A., "How are Marketers Meeting the Import Challenge?" *Harvard Business Review* (September-October, 1960), pp. 107-14.

Study queried U.S. marketing execs to discover what use representative American companies of both industrial and consumer products are making of the marketing tools at their disposal to meet the challenge of foreign competition in present domestic markets. Article contains an evaluation and critique of questionnaire responses.

Hirsch, Werner Z. "Decision Making in Industrial Marketing," *Journal of Marketing*, (January, 1960), pp. 21-27.

In industrial marketing, scientific decision making is slowly replacing conventional methods which rely upon "intuitive judgment" or "considered opinion." Some examples are developed by the author of the scientific approach to industrial marketing decisions—specifically linear programming, empirical demand projections, and input-output analysis.

"Innovate—That's Your Real Job," *Steel*, (June 21, 1965), pp. 25-27.

Symposium for industrial marketers about changing patterns in industrial marketing and purchasing behavior.

Kelly, Eugene J. "Contributions of the Behavioral Sciences to Industrial Marketing," *AMA Proceedings*, Winter, 1959, pp. 77-84.

Considers the perplexities inherent in attempting to integrate numerous and often conflicting explanations of behavioral scientists into practicable industrial marketing problem solutions or a better understanding of industrial marketing.

Lewis, Marshall C. "A Leap into the Future of Industrial Marketing," *Journal of Marketing,* Vol. 30, (April, 1966), pp. 56-58.

Suggests that marketing is on some kind of threshold, golden or otherwise, and makes some predictions concerning the industrial marketing process as it will be affected by increasing computerization and better educated buyers.

McIver, Colin. "Selling to Industry? Basic Principles Are the Same," *Advertiser's Weekly,* (October 5, 1962) p. 50.

Despite important differences, fundamental requirements are similar for the marketing of industrial and consumer goods.

McManus, G. J. "How 'Marketing in Depth' Works for the Basic Metals," *Iron Age,* (July 16, 1959), p. 63.

United States Steel's success in sales programs organized along market lines rather than product lines suggests that horizontal selling might become the trend of the future in the metalworking industries.

Morse, Leon. "Can Industrial Marketing Match Production?" *Dun's Review and Modern Industry,* Vol. 83 (February, 1964), p. 41-42.

Though highly efficient with regard to production, industrial goods manufacturers have lagged in marketing efforts over the years. Industrial market research is belatedly adopting techniques well established in the consumer field and pushing to close the gap.

——————————. "New Look at Industrial Marketing, A," *Dun's Review and Modern Industry,* (December, 1962), pp. 28-30.

The interplay of increased competition, overcapacity and technological change is transforming the conventional concepts of industrial marketing. The shotgun wedding of marketing and technology, in particular, is reshaping the very nature and techniques of the industrial selling system. Industrial marketers are taking a closer look at the integrated marketing concept, calling for distinctly new relationships between manufacturers and suppliers.

——————————. "Systems Selling: Industrial Marketing's New Tool," *Dun's Review and Modern Industry,* (October, 1964), p. 51-52.

Discusses the growing trend toward systems selling in the industrial market, precipitating a quiet revolution in business patterns and some remarkable corporate gains.

Tracy, A. J. "How Industrial Accounts Change—and What G-E Does About it," *Sales Management,* (March 6, 1959), p. 86.

Fluctuating business climate confronts industrial marketers with a number of challenges. Rapidly changing customers (expanding, diversifying, automating, etc.), plus growing competition and costs make the industrial marketer increasingly vulnerable to mistakes. Discusses implications and demands on suppliers—the marketing concept, customer orientation, specialized selling efforts, internal communications, and so forth.

2. MARKET ANALYSIS

Eggert, F. John "Are You Selling at the Drawing Board?" *Industrial Marketing*, (July, 1963), pp. 113-15.

Industrial sales literature frequently ignores the fact that the original selection of equipment is made by the man on the drawing board. This article spells out what the engineer and draftsmen seek from manufacturers' sales literature for planning, laying out, and selecting industrial production equipment.

Groves, Richard H. "Pinpointing Industrial Buying Targets," *AMA Proceedings*, Summer, 1960, pp. 253-57.

A promising area for market research is the examination of specific roles played by various groups influential in the purchase of industrial products. A study by *Iron Age* is discussed.

Henderson, H. Russell. "Relating Company Markets to SIC," *Journal of Marketing*, (April, 1963), pp. 42-45.

To relate company sales data to SIC, the author suggests that a useful approach is to begin with the company's products and known markets.

Hummel, Francis E. "Pinpointing Prospects for Industrial Sales," *Journal of Marketing*, (July, 1960), pp. 26-31.

This article describes an organized research approach to determine new prospects for an industrial firm. It is based on use of the standard Industrial Classification System to predetermine those industrial firms that afford the greatest potential of becoming future consumers.

Kofron, John H. "How to Apply and Use SIC Data," *Sales Management*, (December 16, 1960), pp. 61-72.

Contributors from six business publishing houses discuss various applications of SIC, the benefits of the SIC system, and fresh areas for development.

Lieberman, Alfred. "Further Pinpointing of Prospects for Industrial Sales." *Journal of Marketing*, (April, 1961), pp. 64-68.

The author attempts to extend Francis E. Hummel's analysis on pinpointing industrial prospects. This article describes a means for improving on a company's limited knowledge and judgment of those markets not previously open to it.

"Sixteen Case Histories of Plant and Employment Data," *Sales Management,* (December 16, 1960), p. 40.

These case histories were written by marketing executives in companies that have used SIC codes to solve a variety of sales/ advertising problems. They spell out the benefits and limitations of SIC in application to their particular problems.

Yankelovich, Daniel. "New Criteria for Market Segmentation," *Harvard Business Review,* (March-April, 1964), pp. 83-90.

The author proposes that market segmentation analysis can be enriched by considering nondemographic factors such as differences in buyer attitudes, values, patterns of usage, aesthetic preferences, and susceptibility to change. He shows how ten different markets for consumer and industrial products are affected by seven different modes of nondemographic segmentation.

3. PRODUCT, SERVICE AND PRICE POLICY

Christian, Richard C. "A Checklist for New Industrial Products." *Journal of Marketing,* (July 1959), pp. 70-73.

Offers a new product checklist which can be specifically tailored to the individual firm. This handy tool can provide the company with a ready list of pertinent questions to apply against products and product ideas.

——————————. "Increasing the Success-Odds in Marketing New Products," *Journal of Marketing,* (January, 1961), pp. 74-76.

Toward improving the success-odds in marketing new products, the author examines several of the most critical areas in new product development.

Clohesey, J. E. "It Pays to Worry About Customers' Problems." *Sales Management,* (April 3, 1964), pp. 81-82.

Marketing strategy case study tells how a small manufacturing firm holds its own in the booming complex chemical coatings industry with a customer-oriented strategy that pinpoints sales opportunities.

Cook, Paul W. Ja. "Fact and Fancy in Identical Bids," *Harvard Business Review,* (January-February, 1963), pp. 67-72.

A realistic appraisal of business practices concerned with competitive bidding. The author concludes "that identity of bids is not necessarily worse than the alternatives actually available, given the structure of the American economy; that identical bids are no more suspicious by their very nature than any other kind of bid, and that a wholesale and discriminatory attack on businesses engaging in identical bid practices is illogical, unwarranted, and very possibly unwise in view of the alternatives.''

Day, Cameron. ''Service: the 'Something Extra' in Industrial Selling.'' *Sales Management* (May 15, 1964), pp. 25-27.

Based on a cross-country check by *Sales Management* of a range of industrial companies, this article reveals that industrial companies are fostering a dramatic change in the entire concept of service. Today's competitive picture calls for the furnishing of more elaborate and expert assistance—ranging from immediate on-the-job help to long-range planning and product development.

Edelman, Franz. ''Art and Science of Competitive Bidding,'' *Harvard Business Review*, (July-August, 1965), pp. 53-66.

The author describes an approach to the highly complex process of formulating a specific competitive bid. Combining executive judgment and computer analysis, his method is designed to assist in weighing payoff against risk in the light of future uncertainties. It leads to a specific bid price which represents the optimum trade-off between profitability and success probability. A hypothetical case study illustrates application of the approach.

Hauk, James G. *Technical Service in The American Economy,* Ann Arbor, Michigan: University of Michigan, 1962.

A comprehensive study of the role of technical services in industrial marketing. In addition to the manufacturer's legal and ethical responsibilities, technical service can be extended as a profit-maximizing tool.

McGuire, E. Patrick. *Technical Service Handbook.* Mountainside, New Jersey: Padric Publishing Co. 1962.

An up-to-date view, written for the industrial marketer, of this increasingly important element of non-price competition.

Morse, Leon. ''The Something Extra in Selling,'' *Dun's Review and Modern Industry,* (September 19, 1963), pp. 33-34.

Industry's marketing leaders have found that product quality and salesmanship are not enough to keep ahead of competition. One marketer after another offers the customer ''something extra'' in service. The role of service in the marketing mix of several major firms is examined in this article.

Murray, Thomas J. ''The Billion Dollar Proposal Industry,'' *Dun's Review and Modern Industry.* (January, 1966), pp. 40-41.

The proposal method of competing for contracts is becoming standard procedure in industrial marketing. The practice has grown in response to the spiralling cost and complexity of commercial contracts, ranging from a sophisticated equipment item to an entire plant. The author sketches the fundamentals of this selling approach along with the opinions and practices of industry leaders.

Simon, Leonard S. "Measuring the Market Impact of Technical Services." *Journal of Marketing Research.* February, 1965, p. 32-39.

This empirical study defines five points of customer sensitivity to the service operation, develops measures of service performance for these points, and delineates a system for ascertaining the impact of technical services.

4. DISTRIBUTION

a. Sales Force

Christian, Richard C. "Have We Forgotten How to Train?" *Journal of Marketing,* Vol. 26, (October, 1962), pp. 81-82.

Product education is just one part of the selling job and should be but one facet of industrial sales training. Important yet widely neglected are customer and market knowledge, and creative selling techniques.

Drucker, Peter. "How to Double Your Sales." *Nation's Business,* Vol. 55 (March, 1963), pp. 80-82, 86.

The author maintains that "the traditional ways of using the salesman, the traditional ways of paying the salesman, and, above all, the traditional reliance on the salesman to sell are, indeed, obsolescent." The center of gravity in selling will increasingly have to shift to promotion; the salesman's function will be to turn the switch.

Easton, Allan. "A Forward Step in Performance Evaluation," *Journal of Marketing,* (July, 1966), pp. 26-32.

Article describes a model and a computational technique for combining multiple criteria used in performance evaluation and decision-making into a single overall figure-of-merit. Exemplified in an evaluation of industrial salesmen, applications are suggested in other marketing and purchasing situations.

Evans, Franklin B. "A Situational Approach to Selling," *AMA Proceedings,* Summer, 1957, pp. 179-84.

The situational approach consists of a study of the interaction between a salesman and his prospective client. It represents a new approach to understanding selling and the complex factors that constitute the selling situation.

Fales, Edward D. "The Complex Job of Selling to Industry's O.E.M.'s" *The American Salesman,* (April, 1959), pp. 49-61.

Salesmen who sell components to O.E.M.'s (original equipment manufacturers) must serve as both technical and business consultants. The complexities of O.E.M. selling are sparking a trend in selling toward more specialization.

Morgan, V. Harley. "Education and Success in Industrial Selling," *University of Washington Business Review,* (October, 1960), pp. 68-75.

The article reports on an empirical study made by the author which explores the relationship between industrial salesmen's education, background and success in selling. Some interesting correlations are revealed.

Morse, Leon. "The Sound of a Different Drummer," *Dun's Review and Modern Industry,* (August, 1963), pp. 26-28.

Emphasizes the expanded role of the industrial salesmen who must now be equipped to generate ideas and help customers solve problems.

Reynolds, William H. "The Fail-Sale Salesman" *Business Horizons,* (Summer, 1966), pp. 19-26.

Many of the concepts used by aerospace engineers can be applied to the selection, training, and supervision of salesmen. Two of these concepts, redundant design and fair-safe reliability, are related to the practical aspects of sales management—the evaluation of salesmen and planning for the certainty of failure in some component of the salesman's job.

"Sales Management Asks Purchasing Agents What They Think of Today's Salesmen." *Sales Management,* (December 3, 1965), pp. 34-35.

Nine purchasing agents tell what type of salesmen they do-and don't—want to buy from.

Shaw, Steven J. "Behavioral Principles in Salesmanship Courses," *Journal of Marketing,* (April, 1961), pp. 47-51.

Stresses the need for greater emphasis of behavioral principles in salesmanship training.

Illustrates how some of these psychological and sociological concepts are applicable to selling situations.

Shaw, Steven J. and Thompson, Joseph W. *Salesmanship: Modern Viewpoints on Personal Communication.* New York: Henry Holt & Co., 1960.

This text provides a collection of readings drawn from a wide range of sources to demonstrate recent developments in the training of salesmen. Its interdisciplinary approach adds depth and insight into the role of salesmanship in our marketing structure.

The volume is organized in three major parts: Part I, The Behavioral Sciences of Selling, Part II, The Nature of Selling, Part III, Techniques of Selling.

"Should Purchasing Limit Sales Calls?" *Purchasing*, (December 2, 1963), pp. 66-68.

Industrial PA's express their opinions on sales calls. Most regard them as invaluable but think salesmen should better use time allowed.

Thayer, Lee O. "Let's Take a New Look at Industrial Sales Psychology," *Industrial Marketing*, (June, 1959), pp. 126-28.

The author claims that industrial sales strategy has neglected some fundamental facts concerning human behavior and discusses some which are particulary apt.

Webster, Frederick E., Jr. "The Industrial Salesman as a Source of Market Information." *Business Horizons*, (Spring, 1965), p. 77-82.

The industrial salesman's knowledge of a specialized market and close contact with customers and competitors make him a good source of market information which can be tapped by his company for product planning, sales forecasting, strategy, and pricing.

b. Channels of Distribution

Christian, Richard C. "Three-Step Method to Better Distribution Channel Analysis." *Journal of Marketing*, (October, 1959), pp. 191-92.

Describes an effective three-step technique for analyzing industrial distributive performance.

Ganzenmuller, George. "How the Sands are Shifting in the Channels of Industrial Distribution" *AMA Proceedings*, Summer, 1960 pp. 229-39.

Reviews changes in industrial channels of distribution related to: functions performed, consumer requirements, products handled, and supplier relationships.

McFarland, Stuart W. "The Marketing Position of Industrial Distributors." *Journal of Marketing*, Vol. XVII, No. 4, (April, 1953), pp. 394.

In defense of the industrial distributor, the author attempts to clarify his relative position in the marketplace and to place him in proper perspective.

Morse, Leon, "The Changing Anatomy of Industrial Distribution," *Dun's Review and Modern Industry* (January, 1963), p. 37.

A new and powerful breed of middleman is emerging on the industrial distribution scene, helping to bring about drastic changes in industrial sales distribution and auguring a major shift in the balance of power in the entire industrial selling process.

c. Physical Distribution (logistics)

Bullen, H. Jay. "New Competitive Selling Weapon—Physical Distribution Management." *Sales Management,* May 7, 1965, pp. 41-44 +

Close control of the distribution system, which can cut costs and improve customer service, emerges as a new competitive selling weapon in industrial marketing.

Magee, John F. "Logistics of Distribution," *Harvard Business Review,* Vol. 38 (July-August, 1960), pp. 89-101.

Examines the pressing need for improved management of companies' distribution systems. Technological changes in transportation, information handling and material handling allow appreciable cost reductions, when introduced in proper balance. A company's choice of distribution system has a long-range impact on production, product design, plant investment, and organization.

Neuschel, R. P. "Physical Distribution—Forgotten Frontier" *Harvard Business Review,* March-April, 1967, pp. 125-34.

Guidelines to profit improvement are revealed through varying company approaches to control information, personnel competence, distribution economics, and the overall distribution problem.

Stewart, Wendell M. "Physical Distribution: Key to Improved Volume and Profits." *Journal of Marketing,* Vol. 29 (January, 1965), pp. 65-70.

Attempts to place the subject of distribution in proper perspective for marketing management, and describes a suggested approach to the development of improved physical distribution operations.

5. PROMOTION POLICY

Bullen, H. Jay. "Industrial Advertising Comes of Age." *Sales Management,* (June 4, 1965), pp. 31-34.

Today's industrial advertisers are sophisticated, knowledgeable managers, equipped with a special brand of expertise which makes them vital members of the industrial marketing management team.

"Can Industrial Advertisers Build a Corporate Image?" *Printers Ink*, (May 8, 1959), pp. 44-45.

Two case histories support the hypothesis that integrated advertising and public relations are successful in the creation of a corporate image in the industrial sphere.

Christian, R. C. "How Important is the Corporate Image?" *Journal of Marketing*, (October, 1959), pp. 79-80.

Discusses the importance of the corporate reputation in the industrial field. Lists specific steps towards a well-coordinated image-building program.

"Do your ads need emotional appeals?" *Industrial Marketing* (July 1960), p. 88.

Experts concur on the necessity of a solid factual foundation for effective industrial advertising.

Evans, J. C. W. "What Buyers Don't Like in Industrial Ads," *Industrial Marketing*, (November, 1962), pp. 94-96.

Reports on research study conducted among IM's readers in the pulp and paper manufacturing industry. Examines in detail what readers of industrial ads do and don't like about such advertising, with illustrative quotations which provide some of the rationale behind the evaluations.

Frank, Goldalie. "Industrial Catalogs: Salesmen in Print." *The Management Record* (condensed from *Management Methods*, February, 1959) April, 1959, pp. 48-50.

Guides to planning and preparing an industrial selling catalogue.

Freeman, Cyril. "Growth Perspective for Industrial Advertising," *Journal of Marketing*, Vol. 28 (July, 1964), pp. 79-82.

Outlines development potential of the industrial advertising manager, the key to coordinated sales promotion that can reflect marketing management's best action at the best time.

——————. ' How to Evaluate Advertising's Contribution." *Harvard Business Review*, (July-August, 1962), pp. 137-48. Describes a method to appraise the value of advertising dollars by comparing their contribution to sales goals with investing the same money on other kinds of selling effort. Two examples, based on applications of the technique to actual decision making situations in industrial firms, are included.

Hall, A. P. "I Predict: Industrial Advertisers Will Turn More to Consumer Advertising," *Printers' Ink*, (January 2, 1959), p. 30.

The author foresees industrial firms putting more emphasis on assisting customers in selling the customers' products.

"Humanized Industrial Ads; How They Combine Rational and Emotional Appeals," *Printers' Ink*, (September 12, 1958), pp. 50-54.

Uses Alexander Cross & Cunningham's definition of the three major industrial ad appeals: rational, emotional, patronage, and describes ways of applying them. Stresses the importance of combining both rational and emotional elements, properly proportioned and designed for a specific audience, in industrial advertising strategy. All other things equal, the purchasing agent must choose the product or supplier he personally feels is most reliable—hence is open to emotional pressure. Standardization, therefore, increases leverage for an emotional appeal.

"Industrial Ads Cover All the Bases," *Sales Management*, (September 20, 1963), pp. 19-20.

A significant accomplishment in industrial advertising is its multilevel approach—focusing on all the buying influences. This article examines reasons for the growing number of influentials, the importance of reaching them all with the promotional message, and complexities involved in developing such an advertising strategy.

Kohlman, C. W. "IPSO in Industrial Advertising." *Journal of Marketing*, (January, 1960), p. 55.

The author suggests four elements for effective industrial advertising: *identity, preference* for doing business with the advertiser, *service* to the salesman, and help toward the end objective of deliverying the *order*.

Lyon, David G. "Let's Humanize Industrial Advertising" *Industrial Marketing* (February, 1960), pp. 61-62.

The author explains why the engineer should be approached as any other human being, particularly in the current corporate climate. He offers nine "basic principles" to improve industrial advertising.

Messner, Frederick R. *Industrial Advertising,* New York: McGraw-Hill Book Company, Inc., 1963.

A concise well organized reference work on modern practices and methods in advertising industrial products or services.

The material is divided into five sections. Section One, "Planning phases of industrial advertising," discusses differences between industrial and consumer purchasing, industrial marketing research, buying-influence patterns, key factors in buying decisions., etc.

——————————. "A Systems Approach to Industrial Marketing Communications." *Journal of Marketing,* Vol. 28, No. 4, October, 1964, pp. 64-67.

Discusses management's increasing concern with the effectiveness of advertising and other forms of marketing communications in the overall marketing process. Outlines a systems approach to marketing communications that is comprised of 12 stages.

Morse, Leon. "Industrial Marketing's New Voice,"*Dun's Review and Modern Industry,* (March, 1963), p. 31.

Every facet of the industrial selling process in U. S. corporations is undergoing thorough reappraisal. The pace of technological change demands continuing redefinition of corporate sales strategies for reaching the ultimate customer: the buying decision-maker(s). Industrial advertising is being tailored to specific marketing objectives and acquiring new importance and sophistication.

Raley, George H. "What Engineers Want in Industrial Ads" *Industrial Marketing,*(Oct., 1961), pp. 108-11.

Presents the engineer's viewpoint on industrial advertising, and the benefits they expect to derive from reading them.

Robinson, Patrick J. and Bent Stidsen, *Personal Selling in a Modern Perspective,* (Boston: Allyn and Bacon, 1967)

Drawing upon theories and research findings, mainly from the behavioral sciences, the authors evolve an interesting concept of communication in marketing and apply it specifically, in the form of a three-dimensional model, to the personal selling function.

Rubel, Nathan W. "A Guide to Researching Industrial Catalogs" *Industrial Marketing* (May, 1962), pp. 110-15.

Outlines the construction of industrial catalogues, designed to serve the needs of customers and salesmen.

Thompson, Donald L. "Industrial Advertising and the Purchasing Agent," *Journal of Purchasing,* Vol. 2 (August, 1966), pp. 5-16. The results of a study of industrial advertisements are presented and analyzed as to appeals, approaches, and techniques used in the copy. Two major conclusions are: 1. there is no identifiable, reasonably homogeneous commodity that may be termed "industrial advertising" and 2. attempting to classify ads as being either "rational" or "irrational" as an extremely difficult, if not impossible, task.

"Total Systems Selling: How Ads Help Sell Complete Operating Systems," *Printers' Ink,* (December 5, 1958), p. 33.

The success of many systems marketing organizations can be attributed to the images they have built of their capacity to appraise the needs of customers and fill them completely. This can best be accomplished through management-oriented advertising and promotion, which supplement and integrate single product advertising.

6. INDUSTRIAL MARKETING RESEARCH

Christian, Richard C. "Is Marketing Research Finally Maturing." *Journal of Marketing,* (April 1960), pp. 82-85.

Discusses the future of IMR and opinions of leading market consultants, practitioners and educators.

——————. "Are You Committing These Research Sins?" *Journal of Marketing,* (April 1959), pp. 432-33.

Discusses some rather prominent areas in which industrial marketing research can be improved.

Cuplin, Robert A. "The Case for Industrial 'Test Marketing.'" *Sales Management,* September 18, 1964, p. 61.

Particularly when design costs are high and plot runs exorbitant or impossible, industrial test marketing—or "concept testing" as it is called—can help eliminate costly errors in judgment, refine product features and specifications, and insure a greater measure of success in introducing new industrial products.

de Koning, Co. "Effective Techniques in Industrial Marketing Research," *Journal of Marketing,* Vol. 28 (April, 1964) pp. 57-61.

There is both need and opportunity for the development and diffusion of objective, reproducible research methods that can lift industrial marketing research above its present level. Some statistical problems of industrial marketing research are considered, and some effective sampling techniques.

Lazer, William. "Interdisciplinary Contributions to Marketing Measurement," *AMA Proceedings,* Winter, 1959, pp. 85-93.

Quantitative methods in marketing are enriched by contributions from five disciplines: sociology, psychology, social psychology, statistics, and operations research. They assist in planning and control of advertising, product and price analysis, sales forecasting, location, competitive strategy, and estimation of market potentials.

Wolf, Harold P. "Industrial Marketing Research" *AMA Proceedings,* Winter, 1961, pp. 185-92.

Identifies four important problem areas of industrial marketing research and notes contributions which industrial marketing research can make. Also discusses differences between consumer and industrial marketing research.

Index